A Journey through Scotland
(1723)

A Journey through Scotland
(1723)

John Macky

Edited and with
an Introduction by
Anne M. McKim

The Grimsay Press

Published by:

The Grimsay Press
An imprint of Zeticula Ltd
The Roan
Kilkerran
KA19 8LS
Scotland
http://www.thegrimsaypress.co.uk

This edition first published in 2014

Cover image: *Vue de Ille de Bas* from James Beeverell's *Les delices de la Grande Bretagne* (1707), with permission of the National Library of Scotland.

ISBN 978-1-84530-146-0

Contents

Acknowledgements

The editor gratefully acknowledges the Faculty of Arts and Social Sciences, University of Waikato, for a research grant for this project, and the research assistance of Rowena McCoy.

Introduction

A Journey through Scotland was first published in London in 1723, three years before Daniel Defoe's *Tour thro' Scotland* appeared as part of the third volume of his *A Tour thro' the Whole Island of Great Britain* (1724-26). The English author, well aware of John Macky's publication, sought to promote his own travel book by pouring scorn on his rival's work. A number of Defoe's modern editors have followed suit. The fact remains that Macky's *A Journey through Scotland* was popular and successful. Running to several editions in the first half of the eighteenth century, it was read by Scots and English tourists alike. It was also plagiarised by contemporaries, including Defoe, and by later writers, well into the nineteenth century. It continues to be excerpted today on Scottish interest websites. In a number of ways it has therefore been an influential work.

While Defoe makes snide passing remarks and references to Macky throughout his three volumes, his most sustained attack on the Scots author is reserved for his 'Introduction to the Account and Description of Scotland'. Here he first denigrates 'the most scandalous Partiality' of 'all the Descriptions of *Scotland*, which have been published in Our Day ... written by Natives of that Country' before going on to accuse Macky (whom he doesn't deign to name) of producing a laughably far-fetched narrative instead of a real description of his country, typical, in his Anglo-centric view, of 'Northern Vanity'.[1] It is unlikely, however, that Macky was aware of Defoe's derision: he spent the last three years of his life abroad, pursuing his other career, as a secret agent, and died in Rotterdam in 1726.

The *Oxford Dictionary of National Biography* identifies John Macky as a 'writer and spy' and 'a Scot of obscure birth, parentage and education'.[2] While little is known of Macky's early years, quite a lot can be learned of his life from the details of his long career as a spy in records kept by government departments, including the Treasury and Post Office, and in correspondence preserved among the papers of Britain's first prime minister, Sir Robert Walpole, and those of other government officials. His espionage activities only became public knowledge with the posthumous publication, by his son, of the *Memoirs of the Secret Services of John Macky, Esq.* (1733), in which he revealed that he had been sent to Paris in 1688, the year of the 'Glorious Revolution', by William III to spy on the court of the recently deposed James II. After uncovering plans to invade England in 1692 and restore James to the throne, Macky fled from France to London.[3] In spring of the following year he was employed by the English Customs Commissioners as a riding surveyor with responsibility for intercepting smugglers operating between Harwich and Dover; in fact, his paymaster was Henry Guy, the Treasury secretary responsible for secret service payments, and Macky saw it as his primary job 'to prevent the treasonable correspondence between England and France, carried on by passengers and letters' (*Memoirs*, v-vi). In his memoirs he recalls how he apprehended a Mrs. Aldbridge returning to England from James II's exiled court at St Germain-en-Laye, and discovered seventy letters, concealed beneath dirty linen in the false bottom of her travelling chest, 'which letters gave the first insight into the second invasion intended from Calais' and a plot to assassinate King William.

By 1697 Macky was director of the packet boats at Dover, in charge of the postal service to Ostend and Nieuport in Flanders, and to Calais and Dunkirk in France. His surveillance role involved intercepting mail between Jacobites in England and the continent to secure intelligence, as well as searching suspect passengers. The costs of supplying and maintaining the service fell to him. By his own admission, he could not have managed if he had not married well – to Sarah, only daughter of Sir William Spring, Baronet, of Pakenham, Suffolk, in May 1697. His new wife's 'portion went entirely in building and fitting out five new packet boats for that service' (*Memoirs*, vi). His wife died the following year, having given birth to their son, Spring Macky.

For the next few years Macky communicated directly with the English ambassadors to Paris, the Earl of Portland and his successor the Earl of Jersey, as well as with the poet and diplomat

Matthew Prior, who was an envoy at the Paris embassy until August 1699. He developed his own intelligence network of secret agents and kept the English administration informed of the movements of Jacobites abroad, including Scottish nobles, William Maxwell, Earl of Nithsdale and John Drummond, Duke of Melfort. His evident usefulness to the English government led to a new contract in 1701 for managing the packet boats to Flanders and France for the next five years, with an annual salary of £1400. Less than a year later England declared war on France (15 May 1702), joining her allies in the War of the Spanish Succession. The packet boat service was suspended after one of Macky's boats was detained in France, and by Christmas four of his packets boats had been decommissioned. Finding himself without an income, yet still with the expense of keeping the discharged boats, he petitioned his immediate employers, the Postmasters General, and was granted an allowance of £75 a year in consideration of his losses.[4]

Mounting debts forced Macky abroad for the next two years. There he acquired a new source of income as part owner of a property in Zante, dominion of Venice, which he inherited from his deceased wife's estate. Some of the time he spent travelling in the company of Edward Wortley-Montagu, visiting the courts of Hanover and Vienna, and touring in Italy where he cultivated the friendship of the Duke of Shrewsbury at Rome. The Duke of Marlborough, then in charge of the allied armies in Flanders, was sufficiently impressed with Macky to intercede on his behalf when Macky wrote to Robert Harley, Secretary of State for the Northern Department, seeking employment (1 May, 1705).[5] Shortly after the allied victory at Ramillies in May 1706, Macky was able to resume the Flanders packet boat service, build 4 new lighter, more versatile vessels, and re-establish his surveillance network at Dunkirk, developing 'the largest and most successful British spy ring of the war'.[6] Amongst his notable services, he discovered the preparations at Dunkirk for the Old Pretender's 1708 invasion plan. Basing himself at Ostend throughout the Flanders campaign, Macky continued the packet boat service for the duration of the war – running grave risks, and incurring some loss of life as well as boats. At least one of the packet boat commanders in Macky's fleet, Captain Richard Laycock, was killed when his vessel was attacked by the enemy.[7] His vigilance also led him to expose a covert peace mission by Matthew Prior in July 1711, and he found himself out of favour with his political masters.[8]

During 1712-13 he was in exile in the Netherlands, largely to escape creditors who, he claimed, were 'hounded out upon him' (*Memoirs*, p. xviii). After he lost his contract for the packet boat service to Flanders and France in May 1713, he wrote to Harley, begging not to be ruined after twenty years of service. Although he secured another contract in 1715, this time to manage packet boats between England and Ireland, it was with the much reduced annual salary of £600. His financial problems grew to such an extent that he ended up in debtors' prison. Released in 1722, through the intervention of the Earl of Sunderland, he proceeded to remind leading members of the government of his thirty year-long faithful service, in the form of a 'memorial', or memoir, recapping his many secret services. This had the desired effect. The Prime Minister, Sir Robert Walpole, commissioned Macky to return to Europe in 1723 to gather counter-intelligence about Jacobite activities in France and Flanders, particularly those involving the recently banished Bishop of Rochester, Francis Atterbury. Macky's knowledge of the territory, and his well-honed abilities for intercepting communications and creating effective networks of spies, were evidently valued by Walpole, as he kept him on the secret service payroll even after this last mission was completed. Given his past experience of financial insecurity, Macky also set out to augment his income through an intensive burst of travel writing between 1722 and 1725.

Macky's Travel Writing

At intervals throughout his life, Macky turned to writing whenever circumstances provided the opportunity, or created the necessity. He gained early success as a writer in 1696 with his anti-Jacobite treatise, *A View of the Court at St. Germains* which, he claimed, sold thirty thousand copies. In 1703-4 he compiled an account of the *Characters of the Court of Great Britain*, including 'Characters of the Nobility of Scotland' for Princess Sophia, the Electress of Hanover, although this was not published until 1733, along with his memoirs.

His *Journey through Scotland* was first projected in 1713/14 as the third part of a three volume account of journeys through

England, Wales and Scotland. While the need to earn an income was the likely inducement, his packet boat contract having expired in May 1713, Macky claimed that he was fulfilling a promise to a friend to undertake these journeys once peace was restored, which it was in 1712-13, and to give a written report of his travels. He stressed that his account is up to date, and based on his own firsthand observations, not derived from other books which, he says, are too often outdated or written by people who have never actually visited Britain. He goes further, and suggests that his is the first such an eyewitness account and it will match the best travel narratives of Italy and France. It is noteworthy that he dedicates his books 'To the Young Nobility and Gentry of Great Britain' and presents them as guidebooks for young noblemen going abroad on the grand tour of Europe. Reading his volumes, he argues, will equip these youths 'to make suitable parallels when [they] go to travel into other nations' and to converse knowledgeably about their native land with foreigners they meet in Paris, Rome, and Vienna. He anticipates that since not all young gentlemen will have 'leisure to visit their own country before they travel abroad [they] ought to carry these books along with them to be able to say something of their own country while they are visiting the curiosities of other countries'.[9] Given the growing popularity of the grand tour in the early eighteenth century, this seems an astute move by Macky. It is important, too, to appreciate that he did not design his travel books as tour guides or itineraries – a mistaken assumption that has led critics to judge them to be defective. Rather, he presented their usefulness in quite different terms – as a portable ready reference resource, particularly for British travellers abroad. His ideal readers are British grand tourists who may, or may not, become domestic tourists. He does express the hope that they will return home with a greater appreciation of their native land.

Given his own travels in Europe over many years, Macky was well qualified to write with some authority of 'suitable parallels'. Throughout his books he invokes comparisons between places in Britain and European sites. Moreover, he was familiar with the very same tour books about Italy and France that his ideal readers were most likely to use, and that supplied him with models for his project: Richard Lassels' *An Italian Voyage*, Maximilien

Misson's *A New Voyage to Italy* and Bishop Gilbert Burnet's *Travels through Switzerland, Italy, some parts of Germany, &c.*, all late seventeenth-century works which continued to appear in new editions during the eighteenth century. He even adapts the convention he found in these tour books which purport to be letters from a traveller abroad to a friend at home: his books are presented as a series of 'letters from a gentleman here to his friend abroad'. Just as Misson defended the aptness of the letter form for his travel account and distinguished it from mere 'descriptions', Macky says his writing responds to his patron's desire for more than 'bare description' and his particular request for information about 'families'.[10] An approach focused on prominent families and 'noble piles' was calculated to appeal to his ideal readers' tastes. Like his models, Macky's *Journeys* cover 'the character of the people, towns, tombs, libraries, villas, pictures, statues and antiquities'.[11]

In the event, the promised second volume (on England and Wales) and third volume (on Scotland), were not published until 1722 (along with a second edition of the first volume of *A Journey through England*) and 1723 respectively when, once again, Macky found himself in dire financial straits. He may even have written these long delayed volumes in debtors' prison. As it was, Macky chose to cite major national events as the reason for the lengthy interval in publication. First there was the death of Queen Anne and the accession of George I in 1714. Then the Jacobite threat had manifested the following year in a rebellion that 'in most parts of the kingdom, made travelling both suspicious and dangerous',[12] and again in 1719 when another Jacobite attempt was mounted with Spain's support. His explanation, credible enough, also contributes to the impression that this is indeed a modern and up to date work. Indeed, he reinforces this by inserting a date, 6 February 1722, at the end of the last letter of *A Journey through England*, sent from Douglas in the Isle of Man, which concludes: 'I have now hired a boat for Kirkcudright in the stewarty of Galloway in Scotland, where I hope to arrive in three hours'. *A Journey through Scotland* begins with his arrival at Kirkcudbright, after a voyage that took five hours.

A Journey through Scotland

Perhaps one of the most intriguing aspects of Macky's travel books, especially of his *Journey through Scotland*, is that he does not reveal that he is Scot. Like the volumes on England and Wales, his account of his travels in Scotland was published in London, anonymously as so many books were at the time. Other writers, including Defoe, knew the author was a Scot. In the record of Macky's marriage to Sarah Spring in the Pakenham Church Parish Register he is identified as 'of the kingdom of Scotland', although no more specific detail is supplied.[13] We can deduce that he was not from the western or northern isles; nor did he visit these in his travels over Scotland, as he acknowledges that his account of these islands is drawn completely from the 'accurate account' published several decades before by Martin Martin, 'a native of those islands' (Letter XIV). It appears that he was not a highlander either. For his generic description of highlanders he quotes at length Sir James Dalrymple's unsympathetic depiction of them as 'rude, warlike, quarrelsome and mischievous people', given to revenge and robbery (Letter VIII).

If Macky was indeed a lowlander, then features of his *Journey through Scotland* may suggest that he came from the south-west of Scotland, where he begins and ends his travel narrative. In Letter I he declares 'I know six gentlemen each called John Maxwell in this stewartry [of Dumfries]' (Letter I), which may be because he was a native of the region. 'Macky', like 'Maxwell, was a common name in Galloway. His knowledge of the clan Macky is detailed in comparison with his coverage of other clans, so although, for example, he refers to Stuart of Galloway, his account of the Stewarts and their origins takes the form of another long quotation from Dalrymple (Letter XIII). It is also notable that the one other lengthy quotation Macky includes in his narrative, from the fifteenth-century Scottish verse chronicler, Andrew of Wyntoun, recounts the memorable deeds of Devorgilla of Galloway (Letter I).

His affinity with Scotland is conveyed implicitly in his many comparisons of Scotland and England. When he describes royal castles and noble residences in Scotland he often compares them favourably to famous English edifices. He writes that Stirling Castle surpasses Windsor Castle, and Hopetoun House not only rivals, but exceeds, Cannons:

> The parterre fronting the saloon is longer than that at Cannons, and like it hath a large basin of water at bottom. It's also adorned with a multitude of statues on pedestals, as at Cannons; but the views here are prodigiously more extensive. (Letter XI)

Melrose Abbey boasts 'a great window over the great gate, which is ... larger than the great window of the minster at York', (Letter II) while the grounds of Yester Palace are 'larger, as well walled, and more regularly planted than Richmond' (Letter III). He acknowledges that 'the nobility have of late run into parking, planting, and gardening, which are great improvements of their estates', and singles out a number of estates for special tribute. For instance:

> The plantation round the house of Alloway is the largest and the finest (laid out by the unhappy earl that commanded in the Rebellion) of any in Britain; it far exceeds either Hampton Court or Kensington, the gardens consisting of two and forty acres; and the wood with vistas cut through it, of one hundred and fifty acres.

Macky's evident pride in such favourable comparisons attracted the criticism of English writers, including Daniel Defoe, as I noted earlier, and led the latter to make specific rejoinders to these superlative praises. Whereas Macky pronounces Glasgow 'the beautifullest little city ... in Britain', Defoe granted his qualified assent and wrote: 'Glasgow is, indeed, a very fine City ... 'tis the cleanest and beautifullest and best built City in *Britain*, *London* excepted'.[14] Macky claims that Edinburgh's High Street is 'the stateliest street in the world' but it is the beauty and impressive deportment of that city's ladies that most captivate him:

> I have been at several concerts of music, and must say that I never saw in any nation an assembly of greater beauties, than those I have seen at Edinburgh. The ladies are particular in a stately firm way of walking, with their joints extended and their toes out. (Letter XI)

His readers are assured that these are the observations of a well-travelled and cultured gentleman, addressing other gentlemen. Travel abroad was considered an integral part of a young gentleman's education. Scots gentlemen, however, venture overseas more than those of other nations because of the education they have received at home:

> The Scots have made a greater figure abroad than any other nation in Europe. This hath been generally ascribed to the barrenness of their country as not being able to maintain its inhabitants; but this is a vulgar error, for it's entirely owing to the fineness of their education. A gentleman in Scotland that hath four or five sons gives them equal education. The eldest son, though often not the finest gentleman, succeeds to the estate and the others, being bred above trades, go to seek their fortune in foreign countries and are thereby lost to their own. (Preface, p. vi)

Macky first dismisses an all too prevalent misconception of the time – that Scotland is a barren country – before asserting his belief about the relationship between a Scottish gentleman's education and travel abroad. After all, he, too, found he had to seek his 'fortune in foreign countries'. From Hanover he wrote to James Ellis in London in 1705 about how he managed to maintain himself as a gentleman in Europe: 'a fair chance offered of going abroad and I made use of it; and in my conduct since I have done nothing directly or indirectly misbecoming a gentleman. I have maintained myself w^{t}out running in any bodys debt and have saved some mony to help to sett me right again'.[15] Once he returned to England he found himself nearly ruined by debts on a number of occasions and, as Defoe had done, may have sought refuge from his creditors in Scotland. This might explain why he extols Holyrood Park as 'the best sanctuary for debtors in the world' and is well aware that in Edinburgh 'no gentleman's person can be seized even for debt' except by an officer from the Herald's Office (Letter XI).

In *A Journey through Scotland* Macky set out to demonstrate that 'that kingdom will not appear so despicable as some parts of the world imagine' (*A Journey through England*, 1714, p.xix). He is therefore at some pains to refute erroneous impressions about Scotland, many of them perpetuated by English writers. His accentuation of the positive, which leads him into exaggeration at times, is motivated by this desire to refute the negative portrayals of Scotland in circulation.[16] Joseph Taylor, a young London barrister, had travelled to Edinburgh with two English friends in 1705, despite what they had heard about Scotland's 'bad character' which, he wrote, 'discourages most Gentlemen from travelling thither'. In his travel journal Taylor complains about 'the nastiness of the Inhabitants' who without exception are condemned as lazy, unwashed and lice-ridden.[17] Macky admits that 'I cannot say that the common people are near so clean or handsome as the English', but he counters accusations of innate idleness by asserting that 'the women are all kept employ'd, from the highest to the lowest of them' (Letter XI). He concedes that Scottish men 'are not so usefully employ'd as in England' but this he attributes to more advanced industries in England – 'iron-works, lead-works, manufactories'– whereas Scotland fails to exploit her natural resources and the opportunities for exporting her plentiful supply of salmon, white fish and herring. He blames this negligence on 'the gentry, or landed men, [who] never concern themselves about it as a thing below them' and is prepared to acknowledge that 'a finer education than what is necessary for trade hath been, in imitation of the French, the misfortune of this kingdom' (Letter XI).

He maintains that sobriety and piety are national characteristics, citing strict observance of the Sabbath to illustrate this, but Macky does not portray Scotland as a 'paradise', as Defoe alleges. Stranraer, for example, is dismissed as 'a most miserable place' (Letter XIV) and Lanark is passed over as 'an inland town of no great signification' (Letter XII). Inns for travellers are sometimes dirty, roads 'very stony bad', and poor weather makes his progress very difficult at times. The voyage from the Isle of Man to Galloway may have taken two hours longer than he expected, but the pleasures of boating down the Clyde from Glasgow to Dumbarton and from Dumbarton to Greenock are nonetheless conveyed in his account. Such details are conducive to the sense of a real journey undertaken, even if, as seems likely, not one but several journeys over time are drawn together in *A Journey through Scotland.*

By and large Macky achieves the impression he set out to create of a contemporary account, based on his own travels and observations. There are many references to the current holders of a noble title, as well as to their ancestors' noteworthy deeds. The fate of estates forfeited by Jacobites following 'the late Rebellion' is a recurrent note. He records recent and ongoing building work in the places he visits, as well as remarking on the interiors of numerous 'noble piles'. He has an ear as well as an eye to the kinds of details most likely to appeal to the tourists who are his target readers. For example, he relates that while Prince James Francis Edward Stewart awaited what he hoped would be his coronation at Scone Palace in 1715, the 'Old Pretender' enjoyed a cup of coffee in the afternoons. Macky adds that the prince drank wine only at meals (Letter IX). Dunfermline Castle is so dilapidated that jackdaws nest in the room where Charles I was once born (Letter IX).

Macky also takes the opportunity to correct mistakes about Scottish history found in other accounts. He provides lists of successive kings of Scotland from earliest times to the present, and devotes considerable attention to Scottish noble families, to the irritation of some contemporary English readers. He informs his readers about the country's customs, traditions, and some aspects of the Scots language, offering contrasts throughout with English usage and practice, relating to houses, manners, and dress. He explains particular Scottish words and concepts, such as *crag*, *links*, *mearns* and *lairdship*, and the suffix *dale* in place-names.

For all his various approaches to enlightening his readers, Macky is not above perpetuating stereotypes. In his account of a visit to Crieff highland fair he provides a largely sympathetic description of the 'highland gentlemen' he sees there. He finds them 'mighty civil', but the drovers among their attendants, hired to move cattle to England for a shilling a day, are portrayed as habitual thieves. The people of Inverness, a gateway to the northern Highlands, are 'more polite than in most towns in Scotland', attributable in part to their excellent command of the English language:

> They speak as good English here as at London, and with an English accent; and ever since Oliver Cromwell was here, they are in their manners and dress entirely English.

Inverness itself is described as a 'pretty town', complete with 'coffee-houses and taverns, as in England' (Letter VIII). When the Englishman Edmund Burt was posted there in 1725, as a collector of rents from forfeited estates, he acquired a copy of Macky's *A Journey through Scotland*, which he said was very popular in Inverness.[18]

Macky's intended readership, as I have indicated, comprised grand tourists. With them in mind, he makes numerous comparisons between Scotland and Italy, specifically alluding to grand tour destinations like Rome and Bologna. He exclaims of Hopetoun House:

> From the terrace to the north of this parterre is the finest view I ever saw anywhere; far beyond Frascati near Rome, or St. Michael del Bosco, near Bologna, for variety.

As well as conveying an astute awareness of his audience, such remarks confirm his authority – he too has been a gentleman traveller to these places and is therefore a reliable guide and commentator.

Macky published one other travel book during his lifetime, but it was not the volume on Ireland he promised his readers. Presumably he planned to capitalize on his knowledge of that country, acquired through his packet boat service from Dublin. Once again, events overtook him. From 1723 he was based in the Netherlands, conducting counter-espionage activities and surveillance of Jacobites on behalf of the British Government. Whether as a cover for his secret service work, as has been suggested, or simply making the most of the opportunity, Macky wrote and published what was to be his last travel book, *A Journey through the Austrian Netherlands* (1725). He died in Rotterdam the following year.

Anne M. McKim

1 *A Tour thro' the Whole Island of Great Britain in Writings on Travel, Discovery and History by Daniel Defoe*, volume 3 ed. John McVeagh (London: Pickering & Chatto, 2001), p. 147. All references to Defoe are to this edition.
2 'Macky, John'. *Oxford Dictionary of National Biography* (2004).
3 Ibid.
4 'Warrant Book: August 28, 1703', *Calendar of Treasury Books, Volume 18: 1703* ed. William Shaw (London, 1936), p. 385.
5 Letter to James Ellis, from Hanover, 1 May 1705. British Library, Add. 28895, fol. 131.
6 *Oxford Dictionary of National Biography* (2004)
7 'Warrant Book: July 1711, 23-31', *Calendar of Treasury Books*, Volume 25: 1711 (1952), p. 380
8 J.D. Alsop, 'The Detection of Matthew Prior's Peace Mission of 1711', *The British Journal for Eighteenth-Century Studies*, 7(1), 1984: 61-67.
9 Preface to *A Journey through England* (London, 1714), p. ii.

10 Preface to *A Journey through England,* second edition (London, 1722), p. ii.
11 Title page of *An Italian Voyage, or, A Compleat Journey through Italy* by Richard Lassels (London, 1698).
12 Preface to *A Journey through England,* second edition (London, 1722), p. i.
13 *Visitation of the county of Suffolk*, p. 196.
14 Defoe, *A Tour*, p. 199.
15 Letter to J. Ellis, British Library Add. 28894 f. 131.
16 See Anne McKim, '"Wild men" and "Wild Notions": Challenging prejudices about Scotland in early 18th Century Travel Writing' in *What Countrey's This?* ed. D. McClure, K. Szatek and R. Penna. (Cambridge Scholars Publishing, 2010), pp. 118-134.
17 *A Journey To Edenborough in Scotland* (1705), first printed by William Cowan (Edinburgh: W. Brown, 1903), p, 134.
18 Edmund Burt, *Letters from a Gentleman in the North of Scotland to his Friend in London*, 2 vols. (London, 1754), I, p. 5.

Editorial Note

For this edition capitalisation and italicisation follow modern practice. I have adjusted the paragraphing in places, and punctuation where this seemed desirable. Generally, eighteenth century spelling has been retained with corrections, most likely to printer's errors, noted in the Textual Notes at the end. For ease of identification, place-names and other proper names are given their modern form. While Macky variously uses the spelling Stuart and Stewart, in my explanatory notes I have adopted the spelling Stuart, except when the reference is to a Scottish monarch before the Union of the Crowns, when the spelling Stewart is used.

A Journey through Scotland

John Macky

Letter I

DUMFRIES

Sir,

In five hours from the Isle of Man, I arrived at Kirkcudbright,[a] in the stewartry of Galloway in Scotland.[1]

Kirkcudbright is an ancient town, with the prettiest navigable river I have seen in Britain.[2] It runs as smooth as Medway at Chatham;[3] and there is depth of water and room enough to hold all the fleet of England, so that the *Britannia* may throw her anchor into the churchyard.[4] It's also land-lock'd from all winds; and there is an island which shuts its mouth with good fresh water springs in it, which, if fortified, would secure the fleet from all attempts of an enemy;[5] but as this harbour lies open only to England and Ireland, it was never worth a government's while to make use of it. The situation of the town is a perfect amphitheatre, like the town of Trent on the confines of Italy,[6] and like it not surrounded with high mountains, but a rocky stony crust, which in this country they call crags; for they make a distinction here between mountains, hills, and crags. The mountains are very high, rocky, and cover'd with heath, or heather.[b] The hills are high, not rocky, and cover'd with grass, which makes the finest pasture for sheep and small black cattle. The crags are hard stony rocks, not high, and thinly cover'd with grass, through which the rocks appear like a scab.

In the middle of this craggy country lies this little town, which consists of a tolerable street, the houses all built with stone, but not at all after the manner of England; even the manners, dress and countenance of the people differ very much from the English. The common people wear all bonnets instead of hats; and though some of the townsmen have hats, they wear them only on Sundays, and extraordinary occasions. There is nothing of the gaiety of the English, but a sedate gravity in every face, without the stiffness of the Spaniards; and I take this to be owing to their praying and frequent long graces, which gives their looks a religious cast. Taciturnity and dulness gain[c] the character of a discreet man, and a gentleman of wit is call'd a sharp man. I arriv'd here on Saturday night, at a good inn; but the room where I lay, I believe, had not been washed in a hundred years.[7] Next day I expected, as in England, a piece of good beef or a pudding to dinner; but my landlord told me, that they never dress dinner on a Sunday, so that I must either take up with bread and butter, a fresh egg, or fast till after the evening sermon, when they never fail of a hot supper. Certainly no nation on earth observes the Sabbath with that strictness of devotion and resignation to the will of God. They all pray in their families before they go to church, and between sermons they fast; after sermon every body retires to his own home, and reads some book of devotion till supper (which is generally very good on Sundays) after which they sing psalms till they go to bed.

This, with the adjacent shire of Galloway, is reckon'd one of the coarsest parts of Scotland, yet is no part of what's called the Highlands, although a high country, and are in clans or tribes as there. The Macdowells, Mackys, McKies, McClurgs,[d] Maclellans and Maxwells, are the common names here; but gentlemen are never called by their names here but, as in France, by their estates. And indeed where so many gentlemen of the same name and surname live in the same county, it would make confusion in business if they were not distingnish'd by their designations. As for example, I know six gentlemen each called John Maxwell in this stewartry. When you ask for any, you never name him, but his lairdship, as they call it. A lairdship is a tract of land with a mansion house upon it, where a gentleman hath his residence, and the name of that house he is distinguish'd by. If you meet a man in the streets, and ask for Maxwell of Gribton, you ask for the laird of Gribton; but if it is a knight, you mention both name and designation: Did you see Sir George Maxwell of Orchardton?

I am the more particular in this because as this is general through the whole kingdom, I may not be putting you after to the trouble of explanations. There are lairds here of 500 pounds a year, and of 15 only; a Galloway laird of 20 or 30 pounds a year is a frequent thing, and all gentlemen, as in Wales.

King Charles I erected this ancient borough into a barony for Mr. Maclellan, a Gentleman of his Bedchamber, by the title of Lord Kirkcudbright; but his estate was so exhausted in the service of his royal master during the civil wars, that at the Restoration none of the family would take the title, till this last parliament of King George, in 1722, there was such a struggle for the electing the sixteen peers,[8] that a poor man, who kept an alehouse in the neighbourhood, and was lineal heir to the title, was persuaded to put in his claim, and accordingly voted, and is now upon the Parliament rolls as Lord Kirkcudbright. There is in the town a good old castle in tolerable good repair, with large gardens, which belonged to the family, but belongs now to the Maxwells.

There is a monument of freestone with a statue as big as the life in the Abbey Church of Dundrannon, near this town, with this inscription in great Roman capitals:

HIC JACET VIR HONORA-
BILIS DOMINUS PATRICIUS
MACLOLANUS DOMINUS DE
WIGTON ET VICECOMES
GALLAVIDIAE QUI OBIJT
ANNO DOMINI MILLESIMO
QUADRAGENTESIMO QUIN-
QUAGESIMO SECUNDO CU-
JUS ANIMA REQUESCAT
IN PACE M'CLELLAN.

There is fine salmon-fishing in this river, and no place can be finer situate for a white-fish fishing on the Bank of Solway and the north coast of Ireland; but the inhabitants neglect both, there being never a ship and scarcely any boat belonging to the whole town.[9] But the Union having encouraged both English and Scots to improve the fishing on the coasts and in the rivers of Scotland, it's to be hoped that this well situated town for that trade may in time come to flourish.

From Kirkcudbright in 24 miles, on the best road I ever knew, being spacious and hard under foot, through this stewartry of Galloway I arriv'd at Dumfries. There is neither hedge nor ditch by the road's side, as in England, but wherever you see a body of trees, there is certainly a laird's house, most of them old towers of stone, built strong, to prevent a surprize from inroads, which were frequent between the two nations before the kings of Scotland came to the crown of England.[10] And three miles off Dumfries I saw Terragles, the paternal seat of the unhappy Maxwell, Earl of Nithsdale, who was taken prisoner at Preston, and made his escape out of the tower.[11] It consists of a large oval court, in which are very stately apartments and large gardens, suitable to the grandeur of so noble a family. Also within a mile I visited New-Abbey, founded by the famous Devorgilla,[e] whose picture we saw in Balliol[f] College in Oxford, for the burying-place of her husband John Balliol, king of Scotland, whose heart is intomb'd here;[12] and she called the monastry *Dulce Cor*; on which Winton, an old Scots poet, made the following inscription:

When Balliol, that was her Lord
Spousit, as you heard record,
His saul send to his Creator,
Or he was laid in sepulture,
She gart apyne his body tyte,
And gart take his heart out quite;
With spicery right well savourand,
And of kind wele floworand,
That ilk heart, as men said,
She balmyt, and gart be laid
In a coffore of ebore,
That she gart be made therefore
Enamylit and perfectly dight,
Locket and bunden with silver bright.
She foundit into Galloway
Of Cestertians order an abby;
Dulce Cor she gart thame all,
That is Sweet Heart that abby call,
But now the men of Galloway
Call that steid New-Abby.[13]

This Devorgilla was daughter to David, Earl of Huntington, brother to King William the Lion, and married to John Balliol of Barnard-Castle[g] in Yorkshire; and by her right her son disputed the crown with Robert Bruce, Earl of Huntington.

I passed the River Nith from Galloway to Dumfries over a fair stone bridge of thirteen large arches, the finest I saw in Britain next to London and Rochester.[14] There is a street that leads from the bridge by an easy ascent to the castle, which is on the east of the town, and hath a commanding prospect of the town and adjacent country. This castle belong'd also to the Earl of Nithsdale; and from it the high street runs by an easy descent to the church at half a mile's distance. This high street is spacious, with good stone buildings on each side; those on the north side having their hanging gardens to the river side.[15] The Exchange and Town-House are about the middle of the street towards the south;[16] and besides this great street, Lockmaben-Street, hath very good houses. This is a very thriving town, yet their shipping don't come up within two miles of the town.

This town hath been famous for being firmly zealous to the Protestant interest ever since the Reformation; and that firmness contributed very much to the Lords Nithsdale, Carnwath and Kenmure's throwing away themselves at Preston in England. If they could have been masters of Dumfries, they had play'd a securer game.[17]

The country round this town is very pleasant, and strewed with gentlemen's seats, all finely planted with trees, the great ornament of seats here. Caerlaverock Castle[h], all of freestone, and a fine piece of architecture, on the banks of Solway, in full view of England, and the capital of the Earls of Nithsdale, hath been a noble seat by its vestiges, which are not so decay'd, but they give a full Idea of what it was in its glory.[18]

This family is very ancient, and for many ages considerable. For it stands recorded that King Robert Bruce, contemporary with the English King Edward the First, gave to Sir Eustace Maxwell of Caerlaverock twenty two pounds sterling, for having of his own accord demolish'd to the ground his castle of Caerlaverock, that it might not be made a garrison by the English, whence they might have annoy'd the country. We find also a Robert, Lord Maxwell sent to France in King James the Fifth's days, and married by proxy for the king, Mary of Lorraine,[i] daughter to the Duke of Guise.[19] He was Lord of the Bedchamber, Colonel of the King's Guards, and warden of the marches. And if we may believe Sir Ralph Sadler, ambassador from Henry the Eighth, this Lord Maxwell was the chief person Henry the Eighth depended upon, for bringing of Scotland under the subjection of England after James the Fifth's death. It is remarkable, that this very Lord Maxwell, to convince King Henry of the power he had in the kingdom, brought in a bill, and carried it in Parliament, for printing and publishing the Bible in the English tongue, notwithstanding the opposition of the Queen Dowager and clergy; and yet the family was then and hath ever since been Roman Catholics.[20]

In King Charles the First's reign we find Robert, Earl of Nithsdale a great negotiator in foreign courts; and the earl who made his escape from the Tower, was allied to all the great families of the two kingdoms.[21]

Letter II

BERWICK

Dumfries stands in the province of Nithsdale, or the valley of the River Nith: for it's the custom over all the south of Scotland to call the country of each side of a river *dale*; as that on the Tweed, Tweeddale; that on the Annan, Annandale; that on Clyde, Clydesdale;[a] that on the Teviot, Teviotsdale; although these are not the proper names of the shires on the rolls of parliament. Annandale is within the shire of Dumfries, adjoining to Nithsdale. It's but a coarse, moorish country, chiefly inhabited by the name of Johnstone, of which the Marquiss of Annandale is chief. His chief seat in this country is Lockhead, near the famous wells of Moffat, that purge like those of Scarborough, and are much frequented; but here is no raffling, walking and dancing, as at Bath and Tunbridge: an universal quietness reigns in the place.[1]

After I had made this little excursion into Annandale, I proceeded up the banks of the Nith, through a most beautiful country of about four miles broad on each side of the river, and in twelve miles riding arriv'd at the palace of Drumlanrig,[2] the ancient paternal seat of the Dukes of Queensberry.[b]

The *Gusto Grande* is what is often mention'd by the Italian architects.[3] They tell you that Lewis, the fourteenth King of France, had it; since, having so many good natural situations in his kingdom to build a palace, he neglected them all; and by building the finest palace in the world, in the barrennest part of his dominions, Versailles, and bringing rivers over mountains to supply it with water, show'd the greatness of his taste. The great Duke of Devonshire, in the situation of his seat at Chatsworth, the same.[4] And the first Duke of Queensberry, who built this noble palace in the reign of Charles the Second, may seem to have had the oddest taste in the world in the situation of it; for it stands on a rock, environ'd with high mountains on every side. The palace is a square building of fine freestone, with a spacious court in the middle, and a turret, and great stone stairs in each corner. The gallery and chief apartments are adorn'd with family pictures, and most richly furnished. The offices below are very noble; and the hanging gardens, cut out of the rock down to the river side with water-works and grottos[c], do every way answer the great genius of William, Duke of Queensberry, its first founder. At the Church of Durisdeer,[d] hard by, is a noble monument of James the late duke in marble, as big as the life, in his garter-robes, with his duchess by him, a sister of the Earl of Burlington.[5] There is a vast plantation of trees round the palace, and the surprize of seeing so fine a building in so coarse a country adds to its beauty.

The first of this noble branch of the Douglases was William Douglas, son to James, Earl of Douglas, who by a deed which I have seen, gave to him in portion the Barony of Drumlanrig in the shire of Dumfries, about the year 1400.[6] The witnesses to this donation are Archibald Douglas, Lord of Galloway, James Douglas, Lord of Dalkeith, James Lindsay, Lord Crawford, William, Lord Lindsay, Robert, Lord Colvil, and William, Lord Borthwick, *cum multis aliis*. After this donation he was sent ambassador of England to release King James the First, then prisoner in London, from whom he obtain'd a charter, all writ by that king's own hand on vellum, curiously done, confirming the Earl Douglas's donation of the lands of Drumlanrig, Hawick,[e] and Selkirk, signed and sealed at Croydon in Surrey, the last day of November, 1412.[7] We find this Sir William a great sharer in all public[f] transactions during the king's absence, and was kill'd at the Battle of Agincourt in France in 1427.[8] We find this family eminent through the whole race of the Stewarts down to Charles the First, who created the Lord Drumlanrig Earl of Queensberry, and Charles the Second created the grandson, first marquis, and then duke. He was esteemed in this kingdom as a very great man, possessed of a vast estate, loved grandeur, and liv'd up to the great posts he enjoyed in the kingdom, and hath a fine monument erected over him at Durisdeer, the burial-place of the family. His son James (the late duke) was one of the politest, well-bred noblemen of the courts of King James, King William and Queen Anne. He join'd early at the Revolution, was one of the Lords of the Bedchamber to King William, commanded the Scots troop of horse guards, and was Lord High Commissioner to several Scots Parliaments, both in the reign of King William and Queen Anne, and presided in that which concluded the Union of the two kingdoms. The present duke is Lord High Admiral of Scotland, but resides mostly at London.[9]

From Drumlanrig I ascended a famous pass cut out on the side of a rock, call'd Enterkin[g] Path. This path or pass is near a mile to the top, and is very steep. There cannot above two go a-breast; and the precipice is much more dreadful than Penmaenmawr[h] in Wales. This path brought me into the wildest, poorest country I ever saw, worse by far than the Peak at Derby, and yet there is a tolerable good house in it belonging to the Earl of Hopetoun,[i] call'd the Leadhills, where he hath very large mines of lead, which bring him in a good revenue.[10] I made haste out of this desart, and in three hours riding I got to Neidpath[j] in the county of Tweeddale, the seat of Douglas, Earl of March.[11] The first earl was second son to the first Duke of Queensberry, and created by King William. The house is a large convenient seat, situated on a precipice, and hath a commanding prospect over the hills of Tweeddale, which very much resemble the downs of Sussex.[12] They are all green, and it's hardly credible the number of sheep one sees upon them. In the bottom, below Neidpath, one sees the foundation of a prodigious house, laid by the Earl of Morton,[k] Regent of Scotland; but it was never finished.[13] Murray of Stanhope hath a handsome seat opposite to this path or precipice; for I must tell you, that all steep roads here are call'd paths. Murray of Stanhope's house makes me observe to you, that in every country I have yet passed thro', I have met with a Murray of above 500 pounds sterling a year rent, *viz.* Murray of Broughton near Kirkcudbright, and Member of Parliament for that stewartry; Murray of Stormont[l] in Nithsdale, and Murray of Stanhope here. And so I am told it will continue through most countries of the kingdom.

From Neidpath in a few miles I arriv'd at Peebles, the capital of the shire, a small town, pleasantly seated on the banks of the River Tweed, over which it hath a fair stone bridge. There is one good street, and some by-lanes, with tolerable stone buildings; and continuing the course of the river, I arriv'd in a few miles at the palace of Traquair. This palace, built by the great Earl of Traquair, who was Lord High Treasurer and Vice-Roy of Scotland in the reign of Charles the First, a great favourite of Archbishop Laud, and promoter of his schemes, is a very large, noble pile of building of freestone, situated in a valley on the banks of the Tweed in the middle of a wood, through which are cut fine avenues.[14] The gardens are also very spacious, and indeed the whole is a fine plantation. The present earl is a Roman-Catholic; [15] but 'tis very remarkable, that in King James's reign he never would accept of any public employment, and in King William and Queen Anne's was never concerned in any of the plots or insurrections of those times, nor in the late Rebellion.[16] He hath always contented himself with being a good country gentleman and admirable neighbour, reconciling all differences in his county, of which he is the general referree. The first of this family was James Stewart, Earl of Buchan, uterine brother to King James the Second, and Lord High Chamberlain of Scotland in the reign of James the Third, who gave to his son by a second marriage the Barony of Traquair, which was confirm'd to him under the great seal of James the Fourth, May 18, 1492.

The great Earl of Traquair before-mention'd liv'd, like his contemporary the great Sir Francis Bacon, to want bread before he died; for, being look'd upon to be promoter of all King Charles's arbitrary schemes, he was generally hated, and even his own party did not pity him. His estate being sequester'd, he linger'd out a miserable life in the greatest penury, till the very year before the Restoration that he died. He became so mean that he would take an alms, though not publicly ask for it; and there are some still alive at Peebles, that have seen him dine upon a salt herring and an onion.[17]

From Traquair, continuing still the course of the Tweed, in a few miles I got to the celebrated ancient monastery of Melrose, whose monks are so famous for handing down from generation to generation the history of their times.[18] The monastery hath been a glorious place, consisting of two spacious courts; and the building is by the vestiges very elegant. The great window over the great gate, which is still entire, gives one an idea of what this hath been. It's larger than the great window of the minster at York; and round the top are the statues of Our Saviour and the Twelve Apostles. There are also a great many statues still left in the niches, where the mob could not reach; for all they could lay their hands on went to pot at the Reformation, according to the maxim of Knox: If you pull down the nest, the birds will not build again. The choir of their church hath been very large; for there are seven large windows still left, with a statue a-top between every window. And the pillars of the cloisters[m] that are left show that it hath been one of the most magnificent buildings in the world. It's also noted for the sepulchral monuments of many of the great family of Douglas, and particularly James, called the Black Douglas, who died of his wounds at the Battle of Otterburne.[19] But the furious zeal of the first reformers has[n] left us only the ruins to guess by. The revenues of this monastery were very great, and their sheep-walk, on the prettiest green downs in the world, extended four miles. This monastery was granted by James the Sixth to Hamilton, Lord Binny, afterwards Earl of Haddington,[o] and is now sold to the Duchess of Buccleuch.[20][p]

When I left Peebles, I left to the south of me a sad piece of a country call'd Minchmoor and the Forest, and from Melrose enter'd the pleasant country of Teviotdale or shire of Roxburgh, which is very much strewed with gentlemen's seats, and well planted with trees. This country belongs chiefly to the Duke of Roxburghe,[q] who hath several good seats here. The chief are the Floors and the Friars[r] on the Tweed.[21] His grace is making great improvements at the Floors: wings, and other additions to the house, and a side of a country planting with trees, laid out in vistas[s] and walks, which, when finished, will be very noble, as its great master, who is the honour of his country abroad, and the ornament of the Court at home; a prince of great learning as well as a fine gentleman; was Secretary of State, when very young, to Queen Anne, and continues the same to King George. The first of this ancient and noble family was Sir Robert Kerr of Cesford, Gentleman of the Bedchamber to King James the Sixth, by the title of Lord Kerr of Cesford; and next year after King James went into England, got a grant of the dissolv'd monastery of Kelso, and on the 19th of Sept. 1616, was created Earl of Roxburghe, and Duke by Queen Anne.[22] His brother Colonel William is one of the finest gentlemen of the Court, and first groom or Gentleman of the Bedchamber to King George.[23]

This village of Kelso hath a fine market-place, with some good streets, and is equal to some of the royal boroughs I have seen. Here are the ruins of an ancient monastery, founded by King David for the Cistertian monks, an order instituted about the year 1000 in Burgundy. It hath been very large, and part of it now serves for the parish church.[24]

This village is just by England; and on the opposite bank of the river are several very fine plantations, besides those of the Duke of Roxburghe; and the River Teviot[t],which gives name to Teviotdale, falls into the Tweed at this place. What adds to the trade of this place, is its being a great thorough-fare from Edinburgh to London. And in a few hours more I arriv'd here, and hope my next letter will be near Edinburgh.

Letter III

INVERESK, near to Edinburgh

Berwick is the gate of Scotland, of which England hath for many ages kept the key. It stands on the Scots side of the River Tweed, over which you come to it from England by a fine stone bridge of 15 arches.[1] It hath been for many ages strongly fortify'd as the barrier between the two nations; but now, since the Union, it's become the center of the dominions. King George since his accession to the throne, to ease the inhabitants of this town from quartering of soldiers, hath built a fine barrack here, consisting of a square spacious court of freestone.[2] At the upper end is the magazine, on each side the soldiers' apartments, in the angles of officers' apartments, and at the entry the *court de guard*.[3] These are the first barracks erected in Great Britain; and it would be a vast ease to the inhabitants in most great towns if they had them everywhere; but English liberty will never consent to what will seem a nest for a standing army. There is also a very fine house, with good gardens, built here for the governor, who is always a considerable person in the army.

The town is also a seaport for small ships, and hath a good trade in exporting of corn. From Berwick I passed by Eyemouth,[a] a little seaport town, famous for giving the first title of peerage to the great Duke of Marlborough, when he was with the Duke of York in Scotland; and in two hours arriv'd at the ancient borough of Dunbar, a famous seaport at the mouth of the Firth of Forth.[4] It hath formerly held out many a siege from the English, and its castle reckoned of that consequence that the French demanded it as a pledge for the troops they sent to Scotland in Queen Mary's time; but it's now entirely demolish'd.[5] The upper part of this town and the church stand very pleasantly; and by the sea-side are several good houses and a pier; but their trade consists chiefly in the herring-fishing. I must say, that Dunbar stands in as delicious a spot of country as you can imagine; and joining to Dunbar is another delicious seat of the Duke of Roxburghe call'd Broxmouth. It consists of a body and two wings, and a fine pav'd court between the wings, with a good avenue coming up to it, and a spacious parterre adorn'd with statues behind it; the whole in the middle of a fine park, prodigiously planted with trees in great thickets between it and the sea.[6] And a little farther is the castle of Tinningham, a noble old seat of the Earls of Haddington, with great additions and improvements made by this present earl. Many millions of trees hath he planted in a sandy down or links, as they call them here, between his house and the sea, and they thrive mightily. He hath also laid out several avenues through his park which, when full grown, will be as noble as any in Britain.[7] The apartments of the house are nobly furnish'd, and the offices, and every thing, answer the grandeur of the great master.

The Earls of Haddington are an ancient branch of the family of Hamilton. The first earl had been Lord Advocate, Lord Register, President of the Session, Secretary of State, Lord Privy Seal, and a great favourite of James the Sixth and First of England. The family have always been great asserters of the Protestant interest; and the present earl is a fine gentleman, one of the sixteen peers to the Parliament of Great Britain, and Knight of the Most Noble Order of the Thistle, or S. Andrew.[8]

Near Dunbar is the famous island of Bass; being but a few miles into the sea, I took a boat and went up to it; and as exactly as I can, with the help of my guides, I give you the description, and on my return I will proceed to Yester.[9]

The Bass is a little island, about a mile distant from the south shore; the prospects of it sufficiently tell you how difficult the access to it is. Upon the top there is a spring, which sufficiently furnishes the garrison with water; and there is a pastorage for twenty or thirty sheep. 'Tis also famous for the great flocks of fowls which resort thither in the months of May and June, the surface of it being almost cover'd with nests, eggs, and young birds. The most delicious amongst these different sorts of wild fowl is the solan goose, and the kittie waicke. There is only one more island in the West of Scotland, call'd Ailsa,[b] where these geese do breed; and from these two places the country is furnish'd with them during the months of July and August. This island, the Bass, was an old possession of the family of Lauder, and in King Charles the Second's reign it was bought and annex'd to the Crown.[10] It was fortify'd when bought by the Crown, and had a garison, with a governor. Though the place be of it self impregnable, it was surpriz'd by some of the late King James's party after the Revolution, and was the last place of the three nations that held out for him, but surrender'd at last.[11] 'Tis on every side a steep, inaccessible rock, except on the south-west, and there only for one at a time,[c] and that not without the access or help of a cable or crane.

At the top of that passage there was a fort mounted with cannon; but it has been neglected since the Revolution, it being no use except for a prison of state, as it was made for the Presbyterians in the reign of King Charles and King James the Second. It might be of use in securing the best effects of the neighbouring country, in case of an invasion. When the solan geese are coming hither, they send some before to fix their mansions, which for that reason are called scouts. The inhabitants are careful not to disturb them till they have built their nests, and then they are not to be disturb'd by what noise soever. They lay but one egg in a year, and fix it so dexterously to the rock by one end, that if it be remov'd 'tis impossible to fix it again. They hatch it with their foot, and scarce leave it till it be hatch'd. They are fatter than any other fowl, and taste much like herring, upon which they feed. The fish catch'd by the old ones does many times serve the inhabitants with food, and the sticks they bring to make their nests serve them for fuel. They make great profit of the young ones, which are taken from their nests by one let down the rock by a cable. When they come to be as big as ordinary geese, they are very good meat, and yield great profit by their flesh and feathers.

They are of an ash colour, but the old ones are all white. They stuff beds with their feathers. They leave this island in September, and where they retire in winter is not known. 'Tis said they cannot fly if they be out of the sight of the sea. They have a crane's neck, and a strong sharp bill, about the length of one's middle finger, with which they strike through their prey with such violence, that it often sticks in a board baited with a herring, so as they cannot pull it out again, and are catch'd by the inhabitants. The island is a mile round. 'Tis reckon'd to belong to Fife, though it lies nearer the coast of Lothian.[d] Though the family of Lauder had ample possessions elsewhere, they chose the Bass for title. There's a small warren for rabbits in it. It rises a great height above the sea in form of a cone; the force of the tide has worn a hole in the bottom almost from one side to the other.[12]

The palace of Yester, the capital seat of Hay, Marquis of Tweeddale, stands in the middle of the best planted park I ever saw.The park walls are about eight miles in circumference; and I dare venture to say, there is a million of full grown trees in it. In short, it's larger, as well walled, and more regularly planted than Richmond in Surrey. The palace stands about half a mile from the park gate, to which you go by a pav'd coach-way, through a thicket. It is of freestone, curiously wrought, of 120 foot front, and 60 foot deep; and on each side of the fore-front are two pavilions, by the way of wings, where the lady marchioness and her son the marquis reside, till the body of the house is finished. The offices under ground are very noble, and vaulted with pav'd galleries of communication. You enter the body of the house up six or eight steps into a large hall thirty-six foot high, and behind it a salon fronting the garden of the same height, and at top is a gallery for music, which opens into both, exactly as at Blenheim House[e] in Woodstock. The rooms of state, that run on each side of this salon fronting the garden, are very stately, and of an exact symmetry; and those from the hall have a communication with the apartments in the two pavilions. There is a mathematical stone stair, ballustraded with iron, which leads you up to the apartments above; but they are not yet so much as floored, although the house is entirely covered at top. No doubt but these apartments will answer those below.[13]

The parterre and garden behind the house is very spacious and fine, rising up by an easy ascent into the park, as those of my Lord Rochester's does near Richmond. There is a handsome basin, with a *jett d'eau* in the middle of the parterre, with four good statues upon pedestals at each corner. There are abundance of evergreens, and green slopes, regularly disposed; and to the west of the garden, on an artificial mount, is a pleasant summer-house. At the upper end of the garden, fronting the salon, are a pair of iron gates, which open into the park. The green-house joins the pavilion to the west, as does a laundry to the east. The great area before the gate is not laid out yet; but according to the disposition design'd, it will be very noble, with vistas from it cut through the wood, and statues at the end of every vista[f] to terminate the view.

There is a pretty rapid stream runs by the house, and by its rustling through the trees as it runs through the park, makes the whole very rural. There is a pretty bowling green by this river side; and the stables, hen-house, and coach-houses are at a distance in the park, as is the custom in all the great houses I have yet seen in Scotland. Every nobleman's house hath what they call the mains, where their land-labourers, grooms, and everybody belonging to the stable and poultry, reside.

This noble family of Yester is very ancient; for in the reign of William the Lion there is mention made of John de Haye, *miles*, brother to William de Haye, *Dominus de Arrol.* We find also Sir Gilbert de Haye of this family in the train of King Robert Bruce; and Sir William de Haye of Yester we find one of the commissioners appointed to treat about the ransom of King David taken at the Battle of Durham; and his son was one of the hostages given for the ransom, *anno* 1357. Sir Thomas Haye of Yester was one of the barons hostages for the ransom of King James I of Scotland; and William, Lord Yester was one of those peers who joined with the utmost zeal for the Reformation in the reign of Queen Mary; and John, who oppos'd all the innovations of religion in King Charles I's time, was, however, created Earl of Tweeddale in 1646. His son John was much in favour with King Charles, King James, and King William, being employ'd in great trusts by all of them, and was Lord-Chancellor of the kingdom, and created a marquis in 1694. John his son was also Lord High Chancellor to Queen Anne, and Lord High Commissioner to that Parliament that pass'd the Act of Security. His son Charles was elected one of the sixteen Scots peers to the first Parliament of King George; and his son, the present marquis, is also elected, and is a youth of very promising parts.[14]

About two little miles from Yester I arriv'd at Lethington, the ancient seat of the Maitlands, Earls of Lauderdale.[15] It's an old tower, full of very good conveniences, and one good apartment made by the Duke of Lauderdale in the reign of King Charles II, who also inclosed the park with a stone wall.[16] There are some beautiful avenues in this park, and a great deal of old planting round the house; but the duke having no sons of his own, and being a little wife-ridden, left this fine seat to Talmash, his lady's son by a former marriage, leaving the castle of Lauder in Lauderdale to his brother, to support the title of earl, the dukedom falling without heirs male.[17] I find this family Lord of Lethington by a charter from King David II in 1346, designed then Sir Robert Maitland of Thirlestane.[g] His grandson's estate was forfeited for holding out the castle of Dunbar for his uncle the Earl of March against the king, for marrying the prince to the Earl Douglas's daughter, after he was contracted and affianced to Elizabeth Dunbar, daughter to the Earl of March; but Sir George Mackenzie, in his *Baronage of Scotland*, says, he was in his life-time restored. But what is worth observing of this family, and a thing very rare, that four of the family succeeding one another, were as great men as ever the kingdom produced, and succeeded to one another's learning, wit and good sense, as well as to the honours and estate.

The first was Senator of the College of Justice in 1561, and Lord Privy Seal till 1567, that he had leave to surrender it to his second son. The second was the famous Maitland of Lethington, Secretary of State to Queen Mary, and had a most difficult course to steer during those troublesome times. When the civil wars broke out in 1567, Lethington's wisdom and reputation were[h] such, that both parties courted him; but he fell in with none, but as they tended in his judgment for the good of the country, and was for that reason often in England, where he was much esteemed by the Lord Burleigh, and stood always upon his own bottom, without the prop of parties. For which reason George Buchanan calls him the cameleon, because they never knew where to have him; and George was a violent party-man. The third was Lord Lethington, Lord High Chancellor in 1586; and lastly, the Duke of Lauderdale, who was sole Secretary of State, Lord High Commissioner, Lord of the Bedchamber, and Knight of the Garter under Charles II.[18]

From Lethington in a mile's riding I arriv'd at Haddington, a pretty market-town, the capital of the shire. There are some very good houses here, and the streets well paved. The post-house is the best inn I have seen in Scotland, and inferior to none on the London road. The church hath been a fine old church but, according to their wonted zeal, they have pulled down the choir, roof and all. There is a vault in the choir, where are some fine monuments of the Maitlands.[19] That of the Chancellor hath an epitaph on it made by King James VI himself too tedious to trouble you with. He expresseth the great loss it is to him and his kingdom, the death of so wise a man. On another there is a long epitaph, which begins thus:

Of those rare worthies who adorn'd our North,
And shin'd like constellations, thou alone
Remainedst last, great Maitland, charg'd with worth,
Second in virtue's theatre to none.

From Haddington I went a little out of my road to Clerkington and Ormiston,[i] two seats belonging to the name of Cockburn, an ancient and good family in this country, though never noble.[20] Ormiston is a perfect English plantation, curiously hedged and ditched, with a fine old seat, where they have for many centuries made a very considerable figure,[j] being always chosen Members of Parliament for their county. This family hath also been very remarkable for their zeal in the Reformation, and their supporting the purity of it ever since. Adam Cockburn of Ormiston came zealously into the measures of the Revolution, was much trusted and employ'd by that discerning prince, King William, being made an officer of state, and one of the senators of the College of Justice. He was most zealous for the Protestant Succession at all times, and in time of danger went over to Hanover to assist his Majesty with his advice. He is now Lord-Chief-Justice for life, called there Lord-Justice Clerk, and is indeed governor of the kingdom, there being no other minister of state residing in it. His eldest son, who is Knight of the Shire for this country, is also one of the Lords of the Admiralty at London.[21] There are few noble families but they are allied to, and they deserve very well to be ranked amongst them for their antiquity, their firmness and zeal. I came into the road again in a few miles riding, and arriv'd at Seton,[k] the ancient seat of the Setons, Earls of Winton.

The palace of Seton stands in the middle of a large plantation of trees, of at least 12 acres, with a large garden to the south, and another to the north. The house consists of three large fronts of freestone, and in the middle is a triangular court. The front to the south-east hath a very noble apartment of a hall, a drawing-room, a handsome parlour, bedchamber, dressing-room and closet. This apartment seems to have been built in the reign of Mary, Queen of Scots, for on the ceiling[l] of the great hall are plaistered the arms of Scotland, with the arms of France on one hand, and those of Francis the Second, then Dauphin, with his consort Queen Mary, in one escutcheon on the other; the arms of Hamilton, Duke of Chatelherault, with several other noblemen's arms and supporters, with the French order of St. Michael round them.[22]

The front to the north seems to be a much older building than this. The apartments of state are on the second storey,[m] and very spacious; three great rooms, at least forty foot high, which they say were finely furnish'd ever since Mary, Queen of Scots on her return from France kept her court there; also two large galleries, that were fill'd with pictures; but on my Lord Winton's forfeiture,[23] all these were sold by the commissioners of enquiry, or stolen by the servants; and now there is not a whole window on that side of the house. The third front is full of good lodging rooms, but all out of order. At every angle of the house, and on each side of the gate, are handsome towers.

There are a great many offices in the outer courts, and a handsome church or chapel, where are some old marble monuments. The situation of this palace is very fine, in the middle of an estate of 5000 pounds sterling a year, and the three towns of Cockenzie,[n] Tranent, and Longniddry,[o] where the tenants live, each within half a mile of his seat; and the whole estate he could see from his windows; yet this earl would throw himself into the Rebellion, and forfeit all.

About two miles from Seton Palace is another palace called Winton Palace, a more modern and fashionable building, yet entirely out of repair; though the gardens, which are very spacious, are very well kept, the York Buildings Company, who purchased the forfeited estates, having lett them to a gardener;[p] but the house is too big for any family, and must fall down.[24]

This family of the Setons is one of the noblest families in the kingdom; there being few families of any antiquity but are either come of them, or are allied to them. They were great opposers of the Reformation, and all revolutions since. They always lean on the popish side, although most of them profess'd themselves Protestant. They are also very ancient.

Shakespear in his tragedy of Macbeth brings in the Lord Seton, but that I take to be no authority. But upon the records there is a charter granted by King William the First, *Alexandro Filio Philippi de Seaton terras que suere patris sui, viz. Seaton Winto & Wisburgh.* The famous Sir Christopher Seaton, who married King Robert Bruce's sister, and was killed near Dumfries, had by his wife, Sir Alexander, the first Lord Seaton, King Robert his uncle having erected his lands of Seaton into a barony. There is one thing very memorable recorded of this Sir Alexander, which I cannot omit telling you. In 1332 King Edward came before Berwick when this Sir Alexander was governor, and summoning him to surrender, threatened to hang his two sons, whom he had amongst his hostages, if he delay'd. The gallows was erected, and the young men led forth under the town wall. His tenderness for his children began to move him when his lady came up and told him, they were young enough to have more children; but if he surrender'd, they could never recover their honour. On which he refus'd, and stood and saw his two sons hanged. She, who was of the name of Cheyns, was as good as her word; for she brought him forth two sons afterwards.[25]

We find George, Lord Seton Governor of Edinburgh during the regency of Mary of Lorraine, and in 1558 was one of the commissioners appointed to treat of a marriage between Mary and the Dauphin of France.[26] We find the same lord sent ambassador to France from King James the Sixth in 1583. His son Robert was created the first Earl of Winton, in 1600; and his son treated King Charles the First, and all his court, when he made a progress to Scotland in 1633, at his palace of Seton. The fine furniture, of crimson velvet lac'd with gold in the great apartments, was sold by the commissioners of enquiry but the other day. The great grandson to the earl was try'd and condemn'd at London for the rebellion at Preston, and forfeited honours and estate.[27]

From Seton to Musselburgh along the coast side are little towns for full two miles, as Port Seton, Cockenzie, Prestonpans, and Preston, all well built and full of pans for making salt. This coast is also full of good coal. Musselburgh is famous for the battle[q] fought by Seymour, Duke of Somerset, when he came to force the Scots into the projected marriage of their Queen Mary with his grandson Edward the Sixth: a very coarse[r] way of wooing, for there was a great slaughter of the Scots, and yet it would not do.[28]

Musselburgh, Inveresk and Fisherrow, three towns that join together, with the River Esk[s] running through them, are a good mile in circumference, and have some handsome streets and good houses, especially at that corner call'd Inveresk, which the famous Doctor Pitcairn call'd the Montpelier of Scotland, for its good air.[29] There is a fine tavern there, with a bowling green and two fine prospects: the one of the shire of Fife, cross the Firth, at nine miles distance; the other to Dalkeith, and southward.

Letter IV

EDINBURGH

My last letter from Inveresk was so long that I had not room to put in the palace of Pinkie[a] joining to Musselburgh, built by Chancellor Seton, Earl of Dunfermline, in the reign of King James the Sixth, and now belonging to the Marquis of Tweeddale, a most noble seat.[1]

In the court before the house is a large stone well, cover'd with an imperial crown of stone, supported by pillars of the Ionick order. The great hall on the right, as you enter, is adorn'd with views of the great cities of Italy; and in a drawing-room off of it is a billiard table, both pav'd with stone. The great stair-case on the left, as you enter, is ballustraded with iron, and crowded with pictures. The first apartment consists of a dining-room, drawing-room and bed-chamber, very spacious, and curiously wainscoted with oak, and all three hung with the seasons in tapestry of the small figures and finest sort. The bed is of crimson velvet in an alcove neatly supported with pillars. The chimneys are of marble, and above that of the dining-room is a picture, the finest inside of a church I ever saw.

The great gallery is very long and spacious, the ceiling full of Latin inscriptions, suitable to the several paintings. This gallery is crowded with pictures, some of them pretty good. There is a family picture of a Lord Seton, with his four sons and daughters, curiously done by Hans Holbein; Mr. Henderson, the famous preacher, by van Dyck;[b] and the whole length of King Charles the First, and the Earl of Dunfermline in his robes, by the same.[2]

The first Marquis of Tweeddale, with his eight sons and seven daughters, all in one picture, as big as the life, takes up almost one end of the room.[3] There are also several church pieces very good, that have been sav'd out of monasteries at the Reformation; a king and queen of Denmark at full length; a good picture of the famous Earl of Strafford and Duke Lauderdale; with a crowd of family pictures of the Hayes and Setons. There is also in this gallery, well preserv'd, the tree of the family of Tweeddales, from 970 to this day, the Giffords[c] and Frasers.[4]

The parterre behind the palace is very large, and nobly adorn'd with evergreens, and on each side of it spacious gardens; the whole in a well-planted park of the circumference of three miles, walled round, and within four miles of Edinburgh. I must own, if I were owner of Pinkie, I should hardly have built Yester. Pinkie stands nobly, and hath a commanding prospect, not only of the adjacent country, but also the whole coast of Fife, over the sea, at nine miles distance; whereas Yester lies in a bottom, and all its views bounded within itself. Besides, Musselburgh, a fine market-town and seaport, almost joins to Pinkie. I am now near Edinburgh, but design to ride two miles out of my way to take in Dalkeith, the famous seat of the Douglases, Earls of Morton, and now belonging to the Duchess[d] of Buccleuch, and in a mile arrived at Smeaton, a seat lately built by the duchess as a jointure-house to her other palace.[5]

Smeaton House is situated on the River Esk, as Ham House is on the River Thames. The house is new built by the Duchess of Buccleuch, and is as large as Ham, and stands in as large a plantation of trees. The front consists of a body of freestone and two wings; and the front of the garden about 120 foot broad. You enter the house by a noble hanging stairs on the outside, as at the Lord Castlemain's.[6] There is a suite of seven rooms, finely furnish'd; as they are also on the storeys[e] above the parterre. Behind the house is as spacious as that at Ham, and adorn'd with evergreens, and rows of trees sent from London; and at the end of the middle gravel-walk are a pair of iron gates, which gives you a view of the country, bounded by Pentlant Hills, some miles west of Edinburgh; and to the west of this parterre is a very spacious garden. The park wall reaches for a mile together, till it joins that of her palace of Dalkeith, and with this junction the park all inclosed with a stone wall, well wooded and well stock'd with deer, makes the circumference of four miles. There's an avenue to be cut through an oak wood, in a direct line east and west, between her grace's palace of Dalkeith, and her seat of Smeaton, which will front both; and what adds to the beauty of this park is that the River North Esk running by the north side of it, and the South Esk by the south, join together at the east, and make the park a peninsula.

The castle of Dalkeith is a noble palace, built by the present Duchess upon the foundation of the old one, belonging then to the great Earl of Morton, Regent of Scotland, in the minority of James VI of Scotland, who was afterwards beheaded by that prince. He was the first inventor of the engine call'd the Maiden, for beheading, which he brought from Halifax[f] in England, and was the first that suffer'd by it.[7] This palace is the very model of King Williams's palace at Loo in Guelderland; only that is of brick, and this of stone.[8] It consists of a front adorn'd with columns of the Corinthian order, and a double wing on each end, as the palace of Winchester. The great court between the palace and the park is very spacious, environ'd with ballustrades of iron, between pillars of freestone; and from the gate of this court is to be an avenue through the park, directly south, of a mile long, and round the palace a terrace, which on the north, where the front of the palace is 120 foot wide, over-looks a precipice to the river, as at Windsor. On the east side there's a natural amphitheatre; in the bottom of which are to be water-works, and a flower-garden, and round the sides green slopes and evergreens. You enter the palace by a great hall, paved with stone. The Duchess's own apartment is in the wings from this hall to the east, from whence she hath a balcony that over-looks the amphitheatre before-mentioned. I am told her Grace's apartments are finely furnish'd; but she being at London had given strict orders to show them to nobody. To the left of the hall is the great stair-case, supported by pillars of marble, and every step curiously inlaid with walnut-tree. At the top of this stair-case is a noble room 40 foot long, 30 foot high and broad; in which are the pictures of all the beauties of the age in whole lengths in panels. King William's Queen Mary is at one end, and Queen Anne at the other; the Duke of Marlborough's four daughters, the Rochester family, and other ladies of court. There are also two fine full lengths of King James VI and his Queen Anne, to be set up in another room. There is also a great room to the north of the hall, in which is the Duke of Monmouth on horseback, by Sir Peter Lely, and the other lords of the court. But this room was also lock'd up, that I could not see it.[9]

The offices join the town of Dalkeith, which is larger and better built than many royal boroughs I have seen. They have a good market here, and kill generally two thousand sheep a week.

This noble family of the name of Scott[g] is very ancient, and were great on the borders, tho' the first nobleman was created only by James VI to countenance his signal merit under the great Prince Maurice of Orange in 1606. His son Walter, who also commanded a regiment under the states of Holland, was created Earl of Buccleuch in 1619; and in 1672 the present Duchess of Buccleuch, by marrying James, Duke of Monmouth, son to King Charles II, was by letters patent created duchess. We find this family often wardens of the borders towards England in the reigns of Alexander III and Robert I. And Mr Rymer, in his *Foedera*, tells you that Sir Walter Scott of Buccleuch was frequently employ'd in the negotiations of peace between the two nations, in the reign of James II of Scotland; as was also his son, David, under King James III and his grandson, Sir Walter was warden of the west-marches at the famous Battle of Solway.[10] About a mile higher on the east lies the pleasant village of Newbattle, belonging[h] to Ker, Marquis of Lothian.[11] This noble seat lies in a bottom, in the middle of a wood, in a park encompass'd with a stone wall of about three miles circumference.

The entry to the palace is as magnificent as can be imagin'd. In the area between the avenue and the outer gate is the statue of a gladiator; and on each side of the gate there is a large stone pavilion; and through four square green courts you come to the palace, each of the three first courts having rows of statues on each side, as big as the life; and in the fourth court the biggest holly[i] trees I ever saw. You ascend to the apartments by a great double stair on the outside of the house. The great hall is fill'd with the greatest collection of whole lengths and heads I ever saw. There's a Charles the First on horseback by van Dyck at one end of the room, and the same sitting, with his son leaning on his knee.[12] One side of the room hath a row of whole lengths of the family of Argyll, with the busts[j] of all the kings of Scotland; above and below them are also the heads of all the dukes of Burgundy and Brabant, with their consorts, emperors of the Turks, popes, cardinals and first reformers, at least five hundred pictures. And the upper end of this spacious room being looking-glass, shows the whole double.

Joining to this hall is a lobby, in which are some very fine antique statues; and from this lobby you enter a salon full of pictures of the beauties and courtiers of the court of France in the reign of the Queen-Mother.[13] Underneath the great stairs you enter a paved court, which makes the centre of the house, and carries you into the gardens.

The first of this noble family was Mark Ker, a younger son of the house of Cesford, now Dukes of Roxburghe. He was Abbot of Newbattle at the Reformation; and turning Protestant, kept his abbacy, and took to wife a daughter of the Earl of Rothes, by whom he had Mark, the first Earl of Lothian, created by James VI in 1606. This branch of the Kers being nobilitated before the elder branch, disputed precedency with them in several parliaments; but the elder branch being now Dukes of Roxburghe, and the other but Marquises of Lothian, ends the dispute.[14]

From Newbattle I pass'd by the old castle of Dalhousie, belonging to the Ramsays, Earls of Dalhousie, a soldierly family and very ancient,[15] and went to see that curious piece of architecture the chapel of Roslin, that would pass for a beauty at Rome, and is the only thing of its kind that escaped the fury of the first reformers. It's a gothick building, on the outside each buttress being adorned with statues as big as the life in the niches; and on[k] each side of the windows, which are very spacious. This chapel lies in Midlothian, four miles from Edinburgh, and is one of the most curious pieces of workmanship in Europe. The foundation of this rare building was laid *anno* 1440 by William St. Clair, Prince of Orkney, Duke of Holdenbourg &c., a man as considerable for the public works which he erected, and for the lands which he possessed, as the honours which were conferred on him by several of the greatest princes of Europe. It is remarkable in all this work that there are not two cuts of one sort. The most curious part of this building is the vault of the choir, and that which is called the Princess's Pillar, so much talk'd of.[16] This chapel was possessed by a provost, and seven canons regular, who were endowed with several considerable revenues through the liberality of the lords of Roslin.

Here lies buried George, Earl of Caithness, who lived about the beginning of the Reformation; Alexander, Earl of Sutherland, great grandchild to King Robert de Bruce; the Earls of Orkney, and nine barons of Roslin. The last lay in a vault so dry that their bodies have been found entire after fourscore years, and as fresh as when they were first buried. There goes a tradition that before any of the family of Roslin dies, this chapel appears to be all on fire.[17]

This place is remarkable according to Buchanan, Lesley, and other Scots historians, for three victories obtain'd over the English in one day in the neighbourhood by John Cuming, Governor of the Kingdom, and John, as others say, Simon, Fraser, with 8000 men, over three desperate bodies of the English, consisting of ten thousand each, the latter end of February, 1302.[18]

Letter V

EDINBURGH

For giving you the description of Edinburgh, I will begin at the east end, where stands the royal palace, and go up the hill to the west, where stands the castle.

The palace of Holyrood was formerly a monastery of canons regular; but being all burnt down, except the church, it was afterwards, by reason of its nearness to Edinburgh, converted into a royal palace.[1] You enter into the outer court of the palace under a large arch (or pend in Scots) a-top of which is the apartment of the porter or housekeeper, consisting of eight good rooms, and where the Dukes of Hamilton, hereditary keepers of this palace, used to reside before the Union of the Crowns; but now they have an apartment in the palace.[2]

The outer court is as large as the mews[a] at London, and coach-houses[b] and stables dispos'd round it as there. On the north side of this bass court is a fine garden, still well kept, and since the kings went to live in London, converted into a physick-garden, with an allowance of fifty pounds a year to the keeper. I am no botanist, so will not pretend to give you an account of the herbs in this garden; but there is a fine dial erected by Mary, Queen of Scots, and repair'd by King Charles the First when he was here. On the south side of the court is another larger garden, which Duke Hamilton as housekeeper lets[c] out to gardeners in several branches.[3]

King Charles the Second pull'd down the old palace, except two double towers which were built by King James the Fifth on the south and north side of the entry into the palace; and by that great architect Sir William Bruce built this new one all of freestone in the form of a square, supported by pillars, as the Royal Exchange at London, and adorn'd with the several orders of architecture. It consists of two noble storeys, besides garrets a-top and offices below.

You enter this palace from the outer court between the four towers I formerly mention'd, under a cupola in the form of an imperial crown, ballustraded on each side of the cupola a-top, and supported with pillars below. You turn to the right to mount to the royal apartments, as at St. James's at London, and the stair-case and rooms of state run exactly as there, only the guard room here is near twice as big as that at St. James's; the drawing-room, the presence,[4] anti-chamber, and other rooms of state both higher and larger; and in a suite from the west through the south and east side of the palace you go to the gallery, which taketh up entirely the north side of the palace, and is adorn'd with all the pictures of the kings of Scotland, from Fergus their first king, 320 years before the birth of Christ, down to the Revolution.[5] Those kings that were eminent, and all the race of the Stewarts, are whole lengths, the others are but bustos. You must not imagine, my friend, that these are all original pictures. Buchanan, I believe, drew the originals in his history, and the painter gives the likeness according to their passions and inclinations; but those of the family of Stewarts, whom I have seen, are extreme like, especially James the Seventh.

Duke Hamilton's apartment is in the double tower to the north, and the Great Council-Chamber in the tower to the south. The Earl of Perth, when Chancellor of Scotland in King James the Seventh's reign, converted this noble room into a popish chapel, and gave the Chancellor's apartment behind it to the Jesuits to keep school; which being demolish'd at the Revolution, this noble room hath lain neglected ever since.[6] It would make a fine theatre for plays or concerts[d], and would be fitter for the election of the sixteen peers than the Presence Chamber, where they now choose.[e] The chimneys of this royal palace are all of marble, and the apartments' two pair of stairs for the officers of state are very well kept, being lent to many of the nobility, who now live in them.

Behind this palace, the church or chapel makes a wing to the north, and the laundry another wing to the south, and between them is a bowling green wall'd in. St. Anne's Yard to the east of the palace was design'd to be branch'd out into gravel walks, adorn'd with statues, but the Revolution coming on, attended with a long and expensive war, and since that an Union with England, hath put an end to these things. The church or chapel is very neat, with the highest roof I have seen, and the pillars as exquisite as St. George's Chapel at Windsor, with two rows of stone galleries above.

King James the Seventh erected a magnificent throne here for the sovereign, and twelve stalls for the twelve Knights Companion[f] of the Order of the Thistle of St. Andrew, all of oak, and the finest masters in carv'd work all over employ'd in it. The floor was finely pav'd with marble, a fine organ was also erected; but the mob at the Revolution pull'd it all to pieces, thinking that it smelt too rank of popery, not leaving so much as a stone of the pavement, but what they pull'd up and carried away.[7]

The park belonging to this palace is about four miles in circumference; but what is very comical, there is neither deer nor tree in it. It is wall'd round with a stone wall, and yet there is nothing in it but high mountains cover'd with grass. King Arthur's Seat is the highest, and is near half a mile to the top. They tell you that Arthur the British king was here, and used to view the country from thence, and ever since it's called his seat.

This palace and park is the best sanctuary for debtors in the world; and nothing but the king's express order can take a man out there. You know that within the verge of the court in England, the Board of Green Cloth will give leave to arrest a man; but here there's no such thing, except I should carry off another man's goods and take sanctuary with them. Here the Lords of the Session may exert their authority as they say; but there is no example.[8]

The suburb, which leads from hence in a direct line to the city gate is called the Canongate,[g] or the street of the cannons regular, who first founded the abbey; but since the abbey was converted into a royal palace, the prime nobility built their palaces in this street, and those that were obliged to attend the court, took their lodgings here;[9] so that nothing can be supposed to have suffer'd so much by the Union as this street.

On the south side, just without the pend, George Heriot,[h] founder of Heriot's Hospital, built a square of freestone, with a good garden behind it, for the nobility of the court to live in, which is still in good repair, and was often inhabited by the Earl of Findlater.[10][i] A little higher, on the south side, is the palace of the Duke of Queensberry, still in good repair; consisting of a front and two wings, with good offices and a handsome garden behind. Over-against that, on the north side, is the palace of the Earls of Winton, torn to pieces by the mob, and now purchased by York Buildings.[11]

A little higher, on the south, is the palace of the Duke of Roxburghe, on a large spot of ground, with a large garden behind it, but much neglected; and on the north, the palace of the Earl of Panmure , in excellent good order, and very fine gardens.[12] A little higher to the north is the Tolbooth, or prison, where a *court de guard* was always kept of regular troops, when the court was at the palace; and on the south, a little higher, is the fine palace of the Earls of Moray of freestone, with a paved court in the middle. The apartment fronting the street consists of three noble rooms of state, and a large iron balcony, the only one I have seen in Scotland.[13] There is a very large parterre or flower-garden behind, with four hanging walks or terraces to the bottom, where there is a bowling green, and a handsome pavilion or pleasure-house; and above the back-entry a stone balcony, which gives a full view of the park.[14] A little higher you enter the city by a gate, called the Netherbow, and this suburb from the palace hither makes half an English mile.

The Netherbow is a gate finer than Ludgate in London, having towers on each side of the gate, and a spire a-top. It is called Netherbow, because there is an Upper Bow or descent that goeth from the Castle Hill to the Grassmarket. There are but six gates by which you can enter this city; this and the Cowgate port or gate to the east, two to the south, one to the west, and one to the north. At the east end of the lake there runs an old Roman wall, kept in good repair, quite round the city, except on the north, which is guarded by a lake or loch.[15]

The High Street of Edinburgh, running by an easy ascent from the Netherbow to the castle, a good half mile, is doubtless the stateliest street in the world, being broad enough for five coaches to drive up a-breast; and the houses on each side are proportionably high to the broadness of the street; all of them six or seven storeys high, and those mostly of free stone, makes this street very august. Half way up this street stands St. Giles's[j] Church,the ancient cathedral of this city, in the form of a cross; but since the Reformation it is turned into four convenient churches, by partitions, called the High Kirk, the Old Kirk, the Tolbooth Kirk, and Haddock's Hole. A-top of this church is erected a large open cupola, in the shape of an imperial crown, that is a great ornament to the city, and seen at a great distance. King David erected a copy after this over St. Nicholas's Church in Newcastle, but it does not near come up to it.[16] Besides these four churches of St. Giles's, there is in the same street a little lower the Tron Church,[k] built after the model of Inigo Jones's St. Paul's, Covent Garden; a very handsome church at the east end of the lake, called the Collegiate Church, built by Mary of Gueldres,[l] Queen to James the Second; a church built by a Lady Yester; a handsome new church in the middle of the Canongate, and two good churches under the same roof at the Greyfriars. There are also some chapels; but they are converted into halls for trades.[18]

To the south of St. Giles's Church is a fine square, with an equestrian statue of King Charles the Second in the middle. In this square stands the Parliament House, where their parliaments were kept; also the Council and Treasury, and all the other public offices. It's a fine modern building of freestone, finished by Charles the First in 1636.[19] Underneath this building is kept the lawyers' library, where there is a fine collection of books, of medals, and of ancient coins, the largest of English and Scots coins I ever saw. I could not perceive that the Scots bore the lion rampant in a tressor of flower-de-luces on the coins, till the Stewarts.[20] Joining to this library is the Register, where are kept all the deeds and securities of the nation, as a common bank. Here is also a very good bank for money, whose notes go current all over the nation. There is also a fine room in this square for the meeting of the royal boroughs, adorn'd with pictures.[21]

In this great street are several stone fountains of water, brought in pipes at three miles distance, disposed at convenient distances to supply the whole city with water; and on each side of this street are lanes, or wynds as they are called here, that run down to the bottom. This made an English gentleman, that was here with the Duke of York, merrily compare it to a double wooden comb, the great street the wood in the middle, and the teeth of each side of lanes. These lanes lead you to a street below, called the Cowgate, which runs the whole length east and west of the other, but is neither half so broad nor well built. The High Street is also the best pav'd street I ever saw. I will not except Florence. One would think the stones inlaid; they are not half a foot square and, notwithstanding the coaches and carts, there is not the least crack in it.

South from the Cowgate lies the High School for Latin, and in its yard is kept a fine bagnio, in a handsome neat house, built for the Company of Surgeons; and in their hall is the picture of the late Duke Hamilton, Earl Findlater in his Chancellor's robes, and of all the eminent surgeons of the town, to the number of about forty, all originals, by Sir John Medina.[22] There is also a pretty garden before and behind the house. Directly north from this, on the other side of the Cowgate, is the Physicians' Hall and garden, where they have a noble museum, founded by Sir Andrew Balfour, physician. The learned and industrious Sir Robert Sibbald[m] has very much augmented it. It contains a treasure of curiosities of art and nature, foreign and domestick, as appears by Sir Robert's account printed in four books 1697.[23]

A little further to the south of the Cowgate is the University, which consists only of one college. The Magistrates of Edinburgh are governors of it; it hath a Principal or Warden, and four Philosophy Regents or Professors. There is also a Professor of Divinity, of Civil Law, of History, Mathematicks and Hebrew. In studying four years at this college you commence Master of Arts. The scholars are not in commons, and kept to strict rules as in the colleges in England, nor wear gowns; they lodge and diet in the town, as at the colleges in Holland, and are required to attend at their several classes from eight in the morning till twelve, and from two to four. I wonder how a college in a town used to so much business and diversion to take off from the study of youth, should ever produce a good scholar.

This college consists of two lower courts, and one upper one, tolerably well built; the upper court, to which you ascend by steps of stairs, is larger than the other two. On the left of that court is the library, a long spacious room, and the books neatly kept, and cloister'd with doors of wire that none can open but the keeper, more commodious than the multitude of chains used in the English libraries. The several benefactions are kept in distinct apartments, with the donor's name over them in gold letters; and over these cases of books are pictures of most of the kings of Scotland, and of all the reformers both at home and abroad. Here is kept Buchanan's skull, and the original Bohemian Protest against the Council of Constance for burning John Huss and Jerome of Prague, 1417, with 105 seals of the great men of Bohemia and Moravia appended to it.[24] From this library there's a pair of stairs, which leads you to a great room above the common hall, where there are some natural curiosities, and in that hall are made the public exercises and orations. This college was founded only in the year 1580.[25]

Joining to the college is a neat hospital for girls, with a pretty garden, and bowling green;[26] and a little further is the churchyard of the Greyfriars, the burial-place of all the eminent burghers of the city; for they don't affect so much as the English to be buried in churches; that they think smells too much of the popish stamp. Round this churchyard, which may contain six acres, are abundance of fine monuments of freestone, but some of them defaced by Oliver Cromwell's soldiers. Sir George Mackenzie built a fine mausoleum for his family, still entire; as is a fine monument of the family descendants of Fowlis of Collington, from whom the Fowlis of Ingoldsby in Yorkshire are descended, the Trotters, and abundance of others.[27]

To the westward of this churchyard stands the most celebrated hospital of George Heriot, jeweller to James the Sixth, for the bringing up of 130 poor boys, children of decay'd merchants and tradesmen of this city. The building exceeds any thing of the kind in Europe. Sutton's hospital, called the Charter House at London, is a noble foundation; but the house neither of that, Christ Church, nor any thing of the kind at Rome or Venice, comes up to the magnificence of this building; which I suppose is owing to Dr. Balcanqual, his executor, who was a great architect, was Dean of Rochester, and helped King James the Sixth to write his *Basilicon Doron*, and was left in full power by Mr. Heriot to build this hospital, which he hath done more like a princely palace than a habitation for necessitous children.[28]

The house is an exact square, piazza'd within like the Exchange at London, all built of freestone, but too much embellish'd with carved work over the windows and doors for an hospital. Over the gate is a high tower, with a clock and bells; and on each corner of the building a square tower, floored with lead, and little turrets of stone covered with lead at each corner of every tower, which give you so many different views of the city and adjacent country. There is a fine well in the middle of the inner court, and George Heriot's effigy[n] is in a niche[o] over the inside of the gate, as big as the life, in his cloak, cut in stone, with a jewel in his hand. There is a handsome chapel and hall for the boys to eat in. The towers on each corner are four storeys high, and the body of the house three; and in each of the four corners, in the inside, is a fine turnpike, or winding stairs, which leads up to the apartments above. There is a fine parlour, floored with marble, where the Magistrates of Edinburgh meet, who are for ever guardians of the hospital. Such of the scholars as take to learning are sent to the college at the expence of the hospital; and those that choose trades are put apprentice, and the masters receive 13l.10s. in money with them. The gardens are very well kept, consisting of a flower garden, an orchard, and kitchen garden. As Dr. Balconqual was an elegant man, and contemporary with Sir Inigo Jones, I know not but he erected this building to show his skill in architecture; for its entry, by an easy ascent through three spacious courts, looks more like an avenue to a royal palace than an hospital. The house and gardens contain between nine and ten acres of ground, on a rising ground, a much finer situation than the palace of Holyrood House.

To the north of Heriot's work,[29] from whence its fine avenue ascends, and to the west of the Cowgate, is the Grassmarket, like Smithfield at London, where they sell their horses, corn and hay, and is as spacious as Smithfield is; and from it is the west port or gate, out of which is a large suburb, as is at most of the others. The city of Edinburgh is a good English mile from the palace to the castle in a direct line; and taking in the suburbs call'd the West-Port, Bristo, Potterrow,[p] Pleasants, Canongate, and Calton, may be four miles in circumference.

This Grassmarket, or Smithfield, lies directly under the castle, which is built on a high rock at the west end of the city, and overlooks and commands it. The rock on which this castle is built is inaccessible on all sides, except just the front from the town, which rises by an easy ascent on the ridge of the hill all the way from the palace. However, this front is secur'd by a half-moon, at least 200 foot perpendicularly high, well stored with artillery, besides other lower works towards the gate, that make it impregnable. There is also a royal palace in this castle, finely built of freestone, with very noble apartments; in one of which, King James the Sixth of Scotland, and First of England, was born. You may imagine the prospect very delicious and unbounded from such a height as this;

for you not only see all Edinburgh under you, but the whole course of the Firth from the Bass to Stirling, the coasts of Fife on the side of the sea, and many score miles into the country. This castle was called the Maiden-Castle; and the king's and noblemen's daughters were kept here till they were married; but this I take to be a common mistake of the Scots authors; for Maiden signifies in the Highland language a castle on a rock. Other historians call it a winged castle, as if it had fortifications as wings to it, but when ones sees it, they will find that impossible. The wings mentioned by the ancients, I suppose, are meant to [signify] the rock or situation, and not to the castle; for there are two mountains on each side of the Canongate below it; that to the south called Salisbury Crags, and that to the north called Neil's,[q] or the Calton[r], Crags, which from the top of the castle look like wings, but never had house or fortification upon them; so that *Castrum Allatum* seems to be without foundation.[30]

In a mile from Edinburgh is its seaport, call'd Leith, which is also under its jurisdiction. This town is divided into two, by a river running through its middle, which composes the harbour, which will in a little time be one of the finest in the world; they having carried out their pier heads, all of substantial freestone, to low-water-mark, and composed a mole bigger than either that of Genoa or Leghorn, with dry and wet docks for the conveniency of all ships, either men of war, or merchant-men, that shall come in there.[31]

This city of Edinburgh, with its dependancies, is govern'd by a Lord Provost (whose office is much the same with that of the Lord Mayor at London) and four bailiffs who, besides the power common to aldermen, have that of sheriffs. They have also a Common Council, which consists of twenty-five persons. All these are chosen annually, and the Provost, Dean of Guild, and Treasurer are to be merchants. Or, if any tradesman is to be chosen to any of those offices for his qualifications, he is to leave off trade, and not return to it without leave of the Magistrates and Town Council; and no man is to be chosen Provost, Bailiff, Dean of Guild, or Treasurer, without having been a year or two a member of the Common Council. No person is to continue in that council above two years at a time, except he be a member of it by virtue of a superior office. The bailiffs are to be chosen indifferently out of twelve candidates propos'd, and none to be elected deacon of the fourteen incorporated trades, unless he has been master of his trade two years; and none is to continue deacon above two years at a time. The said fourteen incorporated trades are surgeons, goldsmiths, skinners, furriers, hammermen, wrights or carpenters, masons, taylors, bakers, butchers, cordwainers, weavers, fullers, and bonnet or cap-makers.

The Magistrates are chosen annually on Tuesday after Michaelmas, by thirty-eight citizens, whereof twenty are to be merchants, and eighteen tradesmen. They are to choose such as in their conscience they think to be best qualified; and the said Magistrates, with the town council, are to have the administration of the government, except in such reserv'd cases as the election of Magistrates, Dean of Guild, and Treasurer, and letting of feus[s] or leases, giving bounties or places, and other public matters; in which cases they are to take the counsel of the fourteen deacons of trades. None of the merchants or trades are to have any particular conventions, or to make any by-laws amongst themselves, without the consent of the Magistrates and town council, except it be to choose their own deacons at the time appointed, to make persons free of their trade, or to try their work; and one of the commissioners for parliament was always to be chosen out of the tradesmen, and another out of the merchants. The auditors of the accounts are to be chosen by equal number of merchants and tradesmen. The Lord Provost, Dean of Guild, and Treasurer, are not to continue above two years at a time, and the Bailiff is to be but one year Bailiff, one year old Bailiff, and one year free of office. The Lord Provost, for the time being, was always one of the Privy Council. The train'd-bands of the city consist of sixteen companies; besides which they have a standing company of town guards. There are many other good regulations about public contributions, watching and warding, apprentices, journeymen &c., and may be seen by that called the set or *Decret Arbitral*[t] of King James the Sixth, for deciding differences between the merchants and tradesmen, and about the government of the city, which was ratified by parliament. This was printed in 1683, together, with several acts of the town council relating to these affairs.[32]

Letter VI

ST. ANDREWS

From Leith I cross'd the Firth of Forth to Fife. This Firth is a bay of the sea, which runs from east to west into the country near forty miles, that the River Forth falls into: its mouth at the Island of Bass, which reaches from East Lothian[a] to Fife, is about 18 English miles over; and from Leith, which I cross'd, about seven; and it diminishes in its breadth proportionably to its bottom. There are four islands in this Firth within the view of Edinburgh, which have good fountains of water, and grazing for sheep, but have no inhabitants. They are called here inches, as Inchcolm,[b] Inchkeith,[c] &c.[1]

Burntisland, the first of the towns upon the coast of Fife, hath a very good harbour, with 20 foot water at high water, and room enough for a hundred sail of ships land-lock'd.[2] The town hath a good appearance at a distance, like an old lady in decay; but when you come into it, those large stone white houses, which seem like palaces afar off, prove to be heaps of decay when you approach them, as indeed are all the royal boroughs, which are very numerous from this town to the mouth of the Firth.

Kinghorn, the next royal borough, is well built, but decay'd like this.

Kirkcaldy[d] is a town of a better air than the other two. From the east bridge to the west is a good English mile long, and hath one very handsome street, with very good houses, and consists of two parishes, and seems to be a place of good trade.[3]

Dysart,[e] the next royal borough, each about a mile's distance from one another, hath been by its buildings a celebrated town, but now like Pisa in Italy the structures remain, but hardly a glass window, or any furniture in any of the houses, and so on to all the royal boroughs on that coast to the mouth of the Firth.[4] A ship that comes up the Firth, and never goes a-shore, must have a fine idea of these towns at a distance, by reason of the stately appearance on each side of the Firth; but when he comes a-shore, there is nothing but poverty in palaces; however, their streets are all pav'd with stone.

About a mile from Dysart, still on the sea coast, is the Castle of Weems, the seat of that ancient family, that is built upon an eminence, and with awful look hath a commanding prospect over the Firth, into East Lothian, to the south; to the Bass, to the east; and to Edinburgh, West Lothian, and the bottom of the Firth, to the west. Its gardens and spacious park run to the north. This palace is above 200 foot front to the south, with a terrace on the top of the rock, as at Windsor; and, like it, being of freestone and white, is seen at a very great distance. It hath two wings to the north, and a great area between the castle and the gardens, which is the entry into the house. This noble lord hath four considerable seaports, about half a mile distance from one another, on the coast under this castle, where he makes his salt, and exports his coal, which doth bring him in a great revenue.[5]

This family was nobilitated only by Charles the First in 1633; but they were an ancient family of gentlemen long before; for the first John, Baron of Weems was a younger branch of Macduff, Thane of Fife. And we find by the records, Sir David de Weems of Weems was sent to Norway in the year 1290 by the Regency of Scotland, to bring over their young Queen Margaret, who dying at the Orkneys, occasion'd the fatal competition between the Bruce and Balliol. And we find a lineal succession of the family in great trust in most reigns ever since.[6]

Passing by the old royal boroughs of Pittenweem and Crail,[f] decay'd as the rest, I arriv'd at the metropolitan city of St. Andrews. St. Andrews at three miles distance makes a very august appearance, being situated on an easy eminence on the coast of the German Ocean.[7] It appears much like Bruges in Flanders at a distance, its colleges and five steeples making a goodly appearance. You enter the city by a gate, which, through a spacious street of a quarter of a mile long, leads in a direct line to the cathedral. This street is broad and well pav'd; but the buildings on each side, which have been pretty magnificent, are much in decay.

The cathedral by its vestiges hath been longer than St. Paul's at London, and built like that of the cathedral at Canterbury, in the form of a cross, with a spire on each side of the entry to the west, a high tower in the middle of the cross, and a spire to the east of each side as at the west. This church was built over a limb of the apostle St. Andrew, which, according to those superstitious times, was made a present to them by a pope, which brought such shoals of pilgrims from all the corners of Europe, as made it a rich and populous place. But this brought down the fury of the first reformers so much upon them, that at the Reformation they not only tore up the shrine which occasion'd the superstition, but pull'd down the church.[8]

This city was also erected into a university in the reign of James the First; for in the year 1411, the schools were erected by that prince here. The university consists of three colleges: St. Salvator,[g] or the Old College; St. Leonard's College; and St. Mary's, or the New College.[9]

St. Salvator was founded by James Kennedy, grandson to Robert the Third, King of Scotland, by his daughter Mary, married to the Lord Kennedy. He was Chancellor of Scotland, and Archbishop of St. Andrews, in the reign of King James the Second; it was founded in the year 1456. This college consists of two spacious courts. Over the gate is a very fine stone spire; and to the right, as in the colleges at Oxford, is a handsome church or chapel, in which is an ancient noble monument of the founder; and behind it, which makes one side of the court, a neat cloister well paved and supported with pillars; but neither it, nor the church, so well preserv'd as in the colleges of England, but seem rather entirely neglected.[10] On the ground floor of the other side of the other court are the common schools, very spacious; and over these schools a hall, full 50 foot long, and 30 foot wide and high. There are in this court very good apartments for the masters and scholars, all built of freestone, but unaccountably out of repair, they being hardly at the pains of keeping out the rain, or mending the windows.

This second court is more spacious than the first, but not quite finished, and worse kept. In short, if ever a college wanted a visitation, this does; a happiness which the colleges in England enjoy; for upon a representation from the visitors, that the revenues of a college do not support it, there are always funds to supply that want, and a severe enquiry in case of mismanagement.[11]

There are three silver maces in this college, as old as its foundation; one of them gilt, and of the finest workmanship I ever saw, which weighs seventeen pound weight. It hath, under a carved spire, or canopy, the figures of Our Saviour and his Twelve Apostles, about the length of one's finger; and below, the figures of several saints, excellently done at Paris, as by a pendal chain'd to this mace, by order of Archbishop Kennedy, the founder. These maces, to the number of nine, were found in the archbishop's tomb, in the reign of King Charles the Second. It's not to be imagin'd they were buried with him; but, I suppose, at the violence of the Reformation, when they pull'd down every thing of silver, gold, or stone that had images upon it, the masters of the college, fearing the fate of the maces, hid them in this tomb; and they being also driven from their colleges, they lay conceal'd. But this, my dear friend, being all of my own conjecture, I hope you'll think a reasonable one. The other six maces they sent to the other colleges in Scotland.[12]

St. Leonard's College hath a better revenue, and is more frequented than that of St. Salvator. It was anciently a monastery of Benedictine monks, and was converted into a college by the Earl of Lennox,[h] whose arms are fresh over the gate, and Scott of Scots-Tarbet endow'd it with an additional revenue.[13] It consists of one spacious square: on the south side are still the old cells of the monks, consisting of two storeys, just as the monasteries are abroad; on the north is the chapel, and to the west is a goodly pile of building, but all out of repair. From the chapel to these buildings they are now erecting some new good apartments. The gardens behind the south apartments are very spacious and well kept. Here is a library consisting of several donations, and a cupboard containing a very fine one from Francis, Earl of Buccleuch, of ancient folio books, finely bound in leather, and gilt with the arms of the family. Here is also kept a silver arrow, which was shot for by bows and arrows by the students every year, to keep up that noble ancient exercise of archery, and he that wins it appends to it his coat of arms on a silver plate. This was brought to such a height by the emulation of the scholars, that some plates are as large as salvers; which discouraging the poorer sort, who, althou' good archers, durst not shoot their best for fear of winning, and so exposing their poverty, the University suppress'd this ponderous arrow, and set up another, with a rule that no plate appended to it should exceed an ounce.[14]

St. Mary's College, commonly call'd the New College, hath on the left as you go in a spacious room where King Charles the First held a parliament. There are three rows of seats above one another round the room, which will contain four hundred persons, besides the area in which is a table for clerks and other officers. There is also a pulpit for prayers. This room is now sometimes made use of for public exercises. Above this parliament room is the publick library, a very spacious room, full of old books, but no curious manuscripts. Mr. Hutcheson hath sent down his book of computations to all these libraries.[15]

This college is the best kept of the three; but here are no scholars; only those who have pass'd their course at the other colleges of Philosophy may study Divinity, Hebrew, or Mathematics here. There is a fine observatory built of freestone at the bottom of the garden; but it is neither finish'd, nor ever made use of, which is a pity, considering the expence the building cost.[16]

The Archbishops of St. Andrews were always Chancellors of this University; but on the establishment of Presbytery at the Revolution, King William sent them his *Conge d'Eslire*, to choose the Duke of Atholl[j] their Chancellor, who continues so.[17] The Vice-Chancellor or Rector of the University is chose from amongst themselves, and each college is govern'd by a Provost or Principal. They have the same professors in all faculties as at Edinburgh; and the great Duke of Chandos,[k] out of his inimitable generosity, hath given a thousand pounds sterling to be laid out at interest for a Professor in Medicine for ever.[18]

The city of St. Andrews consists of three spacious streets, all of an equal length, from east to west, with some little lanes of communication between each. In the middle of those streets stands the Church of St. Michael, now parochial. It's a very spacious, handsome church, with a good steeple at top; and in it is a good marble monument of Archbishop Sharp, who was murder'd coming from Edinburgh in his coach and six in the latter end of King Charles the Second's reign; the manner of which is finely engraved in bass-relief on the tomb, with his statue at top, kneeling, as big as the life.[19] This murder occasion'd the rebellion at Bothwell Bridge, which the unfortunate Duke of Monmouth was sent by his father, King Charles the Second, to suppress.[20] I am sure you will not think it any digression to give you an account of the occasion of this murder.

Dr. Sharp was one of the four commissioners appointed by the Kirk of Scotland to go to London, on King Charles the Second's Restoration, to obtain the continuation and establishment of their church on the foot it was then; but King Charles being resolv'd to establish episcopacy, and finding Mr. Sharp an ingenious man, tempted him with the Archbishopric[l] of St. Andrews, which he not only accepted of, but brought in his other brother-commissioners to accept of bishoprics[m] also, and came down to Scotland with a spirit of persecuting them that employ'd him. Several of the ministers were hang'd for not complying with the episcopal ordination and their preaching on the mountains in defence of the parliamentary establishment. This brought some of the sufferers to perpetrate this murder; and yet the murderers all escap'd, except one Hackston of Rathellet, who held the horses while the others kill'd him, who was hang'd at Edinburgh.[21]

On the north side stands the ancient castle, which was demolish'd by Oliver Cromwell.[n] By the front apartment, which still remains, one can see it hath been a noble palace, much embellish'd by Cardinal Beaton, in the reign of King James the Fifth of Scotland. The apartment where he was murder'd by Norman Leslie, brother to the Earl of Rothes, for his great persecution of the Protestants at the Reformation, and the window he threw his body out at, is still remaining, as a monument of that action.[22]

This cardinal was another Wolsey[o] of England. He was *legate a latere* from the pope, and had a bishopric in France; one that Henry the Eighth dreaded more than all the rest of Scotland. For at the head of a numerous clergy he prevented that interview, which was so much desired by King Henry with his nephew James the Fifth, and would, in all probability have brought on the Reformation sooner; and continu'd violently opposing it in Queen Mary's reign, till he was cut off; and then it spread itself all over the nation, his murder animating them to pull down churches, monasteries, and every thing that favour'd of popery.[23]

Patrick Hepburn,[p] prior of the Benedictine monastery, now St. Leonard's College, began[q] a great work at his own expence, of walling in this city with watch-towers at proper distances, which he carry'd on round two parts of the three of this city, but the Reformation hinder'd his finishing it. The wall and towers are still in good repair, with his arms in many places upon it. I must say, it's the best wall I have seen in Britain.[24]

There's a harbour, but no great trade in this city. It's the best situation I have seen for a university, being out of all common roads; and fine downs, or links as they call them here, for exercising the scholars.[25]

This town, before the limb of St. Andrew was brought to it, was called *Fanum Regulae* or the temple of St. Rule, which is the neatest and completest[r] piece of building, still standing, with a beautiful square tower. They tell you that it's fourteen hundred years old; but as I have no authority but hearsay, I won't vouch for it, for it looks as fresh as churches built but yesterday.[26]

From St. Andrews I pass'd by the palace of Leuchers, formerly belonging to the Earls of Southesk, but forfeited in the late Rebellion, and purchas'd by the York Buildings Company. There is one apartment of six rooms, with marble chimney pieces, and wainscoted with oak, curiously done, may serve any nobleman. The gardens are also large, and the whole moted round, and would make a very good barracks[s] for soldiers.[27] From hence, in two miles riding, I came to the ferry of the River Tay, which is two miles broad, to Dundee.[28]

Letter VII

ABERDEEN

Dundee stands in the shire of Angus, on the banks of the River Tay, about two miles from its mouth; and the river is here two miles broad, where they have boats that cross constantly between the shire of Fife and it, as the boats do between Leith and the south part of Fife over the Firth. The harbour of Dundee is rather a mole than a harbour, having no backwater to clean it, which it wants very much; for the freshes of the River Tay choke[a] it with soft clay, or slike, and their revenue will not afford the carrying it off by flat-bottom'd boats as in Holland. There are three entrances into this harbour, which may contain a hundred sail of ships, but not of any great burthen; and from this harbour up to the town is a pleasant walk, pav'd with flagstones, and rows of trees on each side, which serves for an Exchange to the merchants and masters of ships; and on one side of it are large store-houses for goods, and granaries for corn.[1]

The town is the best built of any I have yet seen, except Edinburgh, and hath a great face of trade. It is [a] good two miles in circumference; its market-place is almost as spacious as that of Nottingham, and the Town-House, a stately venerable pile of freestone, is a great ornament of the market. The city runs in four large streets, each from this market-place.

The Collegiate Church here, which is an exact cross, is larger than that of St. Giles at Edinburgh. The west end next the steeple was beat down by Oliver Cromwell's army; the other three parts are now divided into three separate churches. The steeple has a fine town like Wrexham in Wales, and higher than that of the Brill in Holland. The churchyard is out of town, and fill'd with fine monuments round the walls, as at the Greyfriars at Edinburgh.[2] On the west of this town is a handsome hospital for decay'd burghers, where they have a good maintenance, and gardens running down to the river side.[3] In the hall there are lists of good benefactions, amongst whom, Sir William Davison, consul in the Low-Countries, was a very considerable one, and one Alexander Johnson from London sent them a thousand pounds sterling.[4] They have also a chaplain who says prayers to them morning and evening. Joining to this hospital is a good house and gardening, where the Chevalier St. George kept his court when he was here.[5]

Joining to Dundee is the palace of Dudhope,[b] a noble ancient pile, consisting of a square court with a tower at each corner, in the middle of the park, extremely well planted with old trees. This was the ancient seat of the Scrimgeors, earls and constables of Dundee, and hereditary standard bearers of Scotland; who, after a long succession, extinguished at the Restoration for want of heirs male, and the king succeeded as *ultimus haeres.* King James the Seventh of Scotland, and Second of England, gave this estate, constabulary[c] and title of Dundee, to a branch of the Grahams, who, commanding an army for the Prince at the Revolution, was kill'd at the famous Battle of Killiecrankie,[d] when he obtain'd the victory, but lost his life.[6] He was a fine gentleman. Doctor Pitcairn made an elegant epitaph on him in Latin, which Mr. Dryden the poet englisheth thus:

O last and best of Scots! who didst maintain
Thy country's freedom from a foreign reign.
New people fill the land now thou art gone,
New gods the temples, and new kings the throne.
Scotland and thou did each in th'other live,
Thou could'st not her, nor could she thee survive.
Farewel thou, living, that didst support the state
And could'st not fall but by thy country's fate.[7]

On this lord's death, the constabulary and estate were given to the Duke of Douglas, who as Earl of Angus hath very great superiorities in this shire. Few of the nobility but are his vassals: but I shall say more of this most ancient and most noble family when I come to his castle of Douglas.[8]

From Dundee in six miles I arriv'd at the palace of Panmure,[e] in the middle of a great wood. You go up to the house thro' an avenue, cut thro' the wood, of half a mile in length, and 150 foot broad, which gives you a view of the house at once; and on each side of this avenue is a fine hedge which reaches the branches of the trees of the wood. At the end of this avenue is a large circular outer court for coaches to turn in, and the inner court is ballustraded with iron on each side, which gives you a view of the delicious gardens, which go quite round the house, and are very well kept, with a great variety of evergreens and grass-plats, cover'd walks and labyrinths. From these gardens there are eight or nine vistas cut thro' the wood, with ballustrades of iron at every vista, and all the doors of iron. The house is a square building, of 150 foot front, with a pavilion at each end, as at Yester. The apartments are very good, but all unfurnish'd at the Rebellion. The offices without doors are very neat, and as well dispos'd as any I saw in England. The multitude of trees in the park, the deer, and the fine views even cross the sea, from whence it's not above a mile distance, make it a delightful habitation.

This place belonged to the Maules, Earls of Panmure,[g] a very ancient family in this county: for we find them in the annals one of those barons who did homage to Edward the First of England in 1292 for the lands of Panmure. The last earl was unfortunately drawn into the late Rebellion by his nephew, the Earl of Mar,[g] commanded a regiment at the Battle of Sheriffmuir,[h] and was wounded there; for which he forfeited this fine seat, and a great estate to the public, which hath been since sold by Act of Parliament to the York Buildings Company, whose agent receives the rents. But the present countess, sister to the late Duke Hamilton, is allow'd the use of the house and gardens, paying a hundred pounds sterling a year for rent.[9]

From Panmure in six miles more I arriv'd at the ancient town of Arbroath,[i] in which are the ruins of a very large monastery, even larger than that of Melrose,[j] but more ruinous; and in eight miles more to the town of Montrose.[k] This is a pretty seaport town, and one street very good, the houses well built, and the street well pav'd. The inhabitants here, as at Dundee, are very genteel, and have more the air of gentlemen than merchants; and indeed by North Tay the inhabitants[l] are more courteous, familiar and affable, than in the southern parts of Scotland, and seem to be another people.[10] This town gives title of duke to the ancient and noble family of Graham, of whom I shall give you a more distinct account when I come to his grace's palace at Glasgow.[m] Near this town are two considerable families of the name of Carnegie,[n] Earls of Southesk, and Northesk. The former had an ancient paternal seat at Kinnaird,[o] with fine gardens and parks, and a great estate; but the present earl running into the Rebellion forfeited all, and is purchased by the York Buildings. The Earl of Northesk was wiser, staid at home, and joined with neither party.[11] I saw abundance of gentlemen's seats in this road, with plantations of trees round their houses; for the gentry of Angus are very numerous, and universal enemies to the Union with England, and not so much Presbyterian as in the southern parts.

This shire of Angus is a good country all along the coast; but it's narrow; for in some places it's not five miles broad, till you come to the hills, which run in a row to the west and north, and are inhabited with highlanders. From Montrose, in a few miles, I enter'd the shire of Kincardine, commonly called the Mearns,[p] and came to Dunnottar Castle,[q] a peninsula on the German Ocean. It's inaccessible, for from a streight passage which is well fortified, and would be a pass of great importance if it lay on any road, but as it is, is only a good prison, and hath been often made use of as such in several reigns. It belongs to Keith, Earl Marischal[r] of Scotland, whose capital seat of Fetteresso[s] is near it; as is a borough town, call'd Stonehaven,[t] belonging also to that noble family, who have been hereditary marischals of Scotland since Malcolm the Second's reign, before the year 1000. And in the contests between the Bruces and Balliols for the throne, in the reign of Edward the First of England, we find this family one of the most conspicuous of the kingdom. And in the reigns of the Stewarts the earl marischal was one of the hostages for the ransom of King James the First of Scotland. The family was also very zealous for the Reformation; and if we may believe Sir Ralph Sadler, ambassador for Henry the Eighth, was one of the lords the most courted by the English at that time. They had also a vast estate, which induced George, Earl Marischal at his own charge to go to Denmark, to espouse Anne, the daughter of the king of Denmark, for King James the First of England, and Sixth of Scotland. This noble lord also founded the College of Aberdeen, and did other great acts of munificence. He never would accept any employment while the king liv'd in Scotland; but when his sovereign came to be king of England, he represented his person in the parliament called in 1609. The family were firm adherers to King Charles the First in his adversity, and very much exhausted their estate by it; and the last earl going into the Rebellion with the Earl of Mar, his estate was forfeited, and his honours extinguish'd. He is now in the service of King Philip of Spain, and is reckon'd a very fine gentleman.[12]

From Stonehaven, in eight miles of a very stony bad road, I arriv'd at the fine city of Aberdeen. This city hath not only a great air of trade, but the people are very polite.[13] The ladies are more conversable, dress better, and of easier access, than in most of the other towns; they have their concerts of music, where strangers are always well receiv'd. The market-place here is much larger than at Dundee, and may be as large as that at Nottingham in England; but the streets are up hill and down, as at Newcastle.

This city gives title of earl to an ancient branch of the family of Gordon, who were old barons of Haddo. This earl's grandfather was beheaded at Edinburgh in 1644, for holding out the castle of Haddo for the king against the parliament's army; and his father was created by King Charles the Second, Earl of Aberdeen, and constituted Lord High Chancellor of Scotland; and he himself is one of the sixteen peers to the Parliament of Great Britain.[14]

Old Aberdeen is situated a mile to the north of the new town, commonly call'd *Bonaccord;*[15] it has its name from its situation, being placed on the mouth of the Water Don.[u] The name of the river sufficiently shows that the Picts, who inhabited this part of the country, were of a Scythian descent; for the river, which is called by the Latins *Danubius*, by the Germans is called Dunave, by the Polonians Danaum, by the Turks Tuna, being of the very same name with our Don. The river is remarkable for the multitude of salmon and perches which are taken up in it. About half a mile from Old Aberdeen it hath a bridge of one single arch, which is both large and stately; it is made up for the most part of hewn stone, both the ends of it being fix'd on rocks. The river by its crooked winding breaks the force of the stream so that nature itself seems to have made way for its situation. A little below it Don enters the sea.

Two miles above the bridge is a heap of stone, artificially cast in the mouth of the channel, for the easier catching of the salmon. It was the bishop's seat, and hath a cathedral church commonly call'd

St. Machars, of a large and stately structure, being built of hewn stone by the several bishops of that see. It anciently consisted of two rows of stone pillars, another cross the church, and three turrets, the greatest of which was the steeple, which was set upon four pillars of vaulted works. In the church likewise was a library; but about the year 1560 it was almost wholly destroy'd, so that the ruins do now only remain.[16]

But the chief ornament of this town is the King's College, placed on the south side of the town, conspicuous beyond the rest of the houses for the neatness and stateliness of its structure. 'Tis inferior to no college in Scotland. One side of it is cover'd with slate, the rest with lead. The church and turret, or steeple, are of hewn stone. The windows were of old remarkable for painted glass; and some relicks of their old splendor do yet remain. Here is a fine monument of Bishop Elphinstone.[v]

The steeple, besides others, has two bells of an extraordinary bigness. The top of it is vaulted[w] with a double cross arch, above which is a king's crown, having eight corners, upheld by as many pillars of stone, a round globe of stone, with two gilded crosses closing the crown. In the year 1641 it was over-turn'd by a storm, but shortly after was built in a more stately manner. It was begun by Bishop Forbes, continued by William Gordon, Doctor of Physic, and helped on by several nobility and gentlemen of that country. Close to the church there is a library provided with books, much enrich'd by those of which Dr. Henry Scougall, Professor of Divinity there, and the Rt. Revd. Dr. Patrick Scougall, Bishop of Aberdeen, his father, did lately bequeath to it. This college was founded by Bishop Elphinstone, *an. dom.* 1500, and the greatest part of the work was likewise built by him; but King James the Fourth assumed the patronage of it himself, from whence it was call'd the King's College.[17] In it there is a *primar* or Principal, a Professor of Theology, three of the Laws, thirteen of Philosophy, an organist, and five singing boys, who were students of Humanity. There are since added three more Professors of Philosophy, a Professor of the Oriental tongues, and one for the Mathematics. While episcopacy lasted, the Bishop of Aberdeen was always Chancellor, and had the power of conferring Doctor of Divinity; the official or commissary was Vice-Chancellor, and they chose a Rector yearly, who, with four assessors, was to enquire into abuses, and make a return of them to the Chancellor for a reformation. King James the Sixth bestow'd upon this college the rents of the Carmelite friars of Banff,[x] and two chaplinaries. King Charles the First gave it out of the vacant revenues of the bishopric an endowment for eight bursars, from whence it is call'd the Caroline University. And King Charles the Second, by advice in parliament in 1672, gave the benefices of vacant churches in several dioceses for seven years. There are many other benefactors, whom we have not room to mention. The election of the Rector, Dean of Faculty, Professor of the Oriental Languages, Professors of Philosophy, janitors, &c., is by the major part of the masters; but the Principal, and the rest of the prebendaries, are chosen not only by the major part, but also by four *procuratores nationum*; but the Principal in all elections has a sort of negative voice. The *procuratores nationum* are four, and derive their power of voting in elections from the scholars of the four provinces, which are: 1. *Provincia Aberdonensis*, containing the shires of Aberdeen and Banff;[x] 2. *Provincia Moravinensis*, including all the counties to the north of Spey; 3. *Provincia Angusiensis*, containing Angus and Mearns; and 4. *Provincia Laudoniensis*, comprehending, besides Lothian,[y] all the rest of Scotland.[18] A Professor of the Civil Law, a Professor of Physic, a Sub-Principal, who is also a Professor of Philosophy, three other Philosophy Professors, and a Professor of the Languages. This college, and that in the new town, make up one university, call'd the University of King Charles.[19]

In the reign of King Alexander the Second, there was a *studium generale in collegio canonicorum* here, where there were Professors, and Doctors of Divinity, and of the Canon and Civil Laws; so that many learned men were bred in this place before it was an university, which was A.D. 1494, when King James the Fourth and William Elphinstone, Bishop of Aberdeen, procur'd from Pope Alexander the Sixth a bull for erecting an university in this place, with as ample privileges as any in Christendom, and particularly as those of Paris and Bononia.[20] These privileges were afterwards confirm'd by succeeding popes and kings. And because King James the Fourth did assume the patronage of it to himself and his successors, it was call'd the King's College. He bestow'd upon it the rents of the hospital of St. Germains in Lothian.[21] Bishop Elphinstone, who built most of the fabrick, furnish'd the great steeple with ten bells, and gave many costly ornaments, hangings, books, &c. to the college. The first endowments were for a Doctor of Divinity, who was Principal; a Doctor of the Canon Law, a Doctor of the Civil Law, and a Doctor of Physic. The other endowments were for a Professor of Humanity, to teach Latin and Greek; a sub-Principal, to teach Philosophy; a cantor, a sacrist, six students of Divinity.

Aberdeen, as I have said, is twofold, the new town and the old; they are distant the one from the other about a mile.[22] Aberdeen seems to be the same which Ptolemy calls the city Devena, placed in the province call'd Texale, upon the mouth of the River Dee; for *aber* in the old British tongue signifies or denotes the mouth of a river, and Deva or Dee is the name of the river upon whose mouth the town is situated; but New Aberdeen is the capital of the sheriffdom of Aberdeen, and the seat of the sheriff for trial of causes; it is placed at the eastern corner of the shire, where it is wash'd with the German Sea . This city very much exceeds the rest of the cities of the north of Scotland in bigness, greatness of traffick, and beauty. It enjoys a wholesome air, and abounds with well-bred inhabitants, and has a great revenue for the salmon-fishery. The old city seems to have been placed upon a bank of the sea, because it is the common opinion that the monastery of the Holy Trinity, which is thought to have been formerly the palace of King William, is situate in the very creek of the sea; and not far from it are the ruins of an old pretorium.[23] In tract of time the inhabitants seem'd to have fill'd several neighbouring little hills with houses; and now the city is chiefly built upon three of those little hills, and the greatest part upon the highest. It hath ascent every way, and the exterior parts thereof are spread out upon the place, as suburbs, in many places.

That there was a mint formerly in the city, appears by silver coins stampt with this inscription, *Urbs Aberdoneae*, which are yet preserv'd in the closets of the curious.[24]

The streets are pav'd with flint, or a very hard stone resembling flint; the houses beautiful both within and without. They are four storeys high, or more, and have for the most part gardens or orchards belonging to them, so that the whole city, to those that approach it, seems the resemblance of a wood.

At the west end of the city, a little round hill adjoining offers itself to sight, from the foot of which hill breaks forth a fountain of clear water; and in the middle of the same, another spring, flowing down to the foot of the hill, bubbles out and sends forth a stream as rapid as a torrent; but the spring itself is easily distinguish'd both in colour and taste from the torrent. It is call'd the Aberdonian Spaw, because both in taste and quality it comes near the spaw water in the bishopric of Liege. This water is cold to the touch. Doctor William Barclay, a physician, has written a treatise concerning it.[25]

In the high street there is a church of the Franciscans, worthy to be taken notice of, built of freestone; a work begun by Doctor William Elphinstone, then Bishop; and finished at the charge of Gavinus Dunbar, Bishop of Aberdeen, about the year of Christ 1500. The said Bishop Gavinus Dunbar hath also got himself immortal honour by a famous bridge of seven arches laid over the River Dee, about a mile from the city, built very firm and durable of freestone which, in more places than one, by inscription testifies its author or builder.[26]

But the great ornament of this city is its college, called the Marshallian Academy, as founded by Earl Marischal, George Keith, in the year 1593, which the city of Aberdeen hath adorn'd with several additional buildings. It has besides a primary Professor, who is call'd Principal, four Professors of Philosophy, a Professor of Theology, and a Professor of the Mathematics. There is also a famous library, founded by the city of Aberdeen, supplied by the gift of learned men, and furnished with divers mathematical instruments.[27] Add to these the school-house, founded by Dr. Dun,[y] which has one headmaster, and three ushers under him.[28] There is also a school for musick.

The cathedral church, nominated from St. Nicholas, its patron, is built of freestone, and covered with lead; has a steeple resembling a pyramid, and cover'd likewise with sheets of lead to a considerable height. It was divided formerly into three churches; the biggest was call'd the Old Church, the other the New Church, and the third, the arched, named the Arch of the Lady of Mercy. This cathedral is propt with pillars of freestone, and has three bells of a vast weight, which by their quick and continual sounds divide the half-hours. The body of this church is adorn'd with a tower and pinnacle steeple. Here is kept the court for the public tryals of the townsmen, and the county courts, where are also a prison and a work-house. Besides these there is an alms-house for the maintenance of the old people of Aberdeen that are come to decay, with hospitals founded by several persons; and adjoining to the custom-house lies the port or wharf.[29]

The Marischal College here was originally a Franciscan monastery, and when turn'd to a college had so small a revenue that it must have sunk, had it not been for the liberality of the benefactors. The first was the said earl, who gave for maintenance of the professors some lands near Aberdeen; and at Bervie[z] in the Mearns. Most of the edifice was built by the city. Sir Alexander Irvine[aa] of Drum gave 1000*l.* sterling toward the maintenance of poor scholars; and in 1641 King Charles the First gave part of the revenues of the vacant bishopric of Aberdeen to this college. A Professor of Physic is lately added to it.[30]

Letter VIII

PERTH

The shire of Aberdeen is divided into two districts: Mar and Buchan, and althou' mountainous and stony, yet there's abundance of gentry in it. Kildrummy,[a] the ancient seat of the Earls of Mar, makes a noble appearance above the River Don; but as that family have chosen their residence at Alloway near Stirling for some generations, I shall say nothing of it till I come thither.[1] The Forbeses[b] are also in many branches in this shire, of which two of them are peers, the Lord Forbes, the first Baron of Scotland, and the Lord Pitsligo. The Lord Forbeses had a grant of the lands of Forbes in the reign of Alexander the Second, and were great men ever since, but not peers till James the 3d was Gentleman of the Bedchamber to James the 5th, and a general under Gustavus Adolphus in the reign of Charles the 1st. William, the last lord, was zealous for the Revolution, and his son the present lord is a very fine gentleman. The Lord Pitsligo was nobilitated only by K. Charles the First.[2] Here is also a good family of the Frasers Lord Fraser, of whom Sir Alexander Fraser, physician to King Charles II was a branch. Keith, Earl of Kintore,[c] hath also a good old seat here. He was brother to an Earl Marischal, Privy-Counsellor and Treasurer Depute to Charles the Second; and the Earl of Aboyne, uncle to the late Duke of Gordon, had his residence here; as hath his grandson the present earl, with several other branches of that ancient and noble family. Here also resides Crichton, Viscount Frendraught,[d] descended from the Lord Crichton, Chancellor to James the Second. In this shire is also the usual residence of Hay, Earl of Erroll,[e] Lord High Constable of Scotland, and who are often sheriffs of the shire.[3]

All historians agree that this family had its rise in the reign of Kenneth the Third, *anno* 980, on a victory obtain'd over the Danes in the reign of King Malcolme IV. William de Hay is witness to that king's charter to the Abbey of Scone, as Baron Erroll; and Sir Gilbert Hay of Erroll was constituted by Robert Bruce Lord High Constable of Scotland, to him and his heirs for ever, by a charter dated Nov. 12, 1315. They were created Earls of Erroll by James II *anno* 1452, and have continued great men in every reign since. The last earl enter'd the following protest on the concluding of the Union between the two kingdoms.

> I, Charles, Earl of Erroll, Lord-High Constable of Scotland, do hereby protest, that the office of High-Constable of Scotland, with all the rights and privileges of the same, belonging to me heritably, and depending upon the monarchy, sovereignty, and ancient constitution of this kingdom, may not be weaken'd nor prejudiced by the conclusion of a Treaty of Union between Scotland and England, nor any article, clause or condition thereof; but that said heritable office, with all the rights and privileges thereof, may continue and remain to me, and my successors, entire and unhurt by any votes or Acts of Parliament, or other proceedings whatsoever relating to the said Union. And I crave this my protestation may be admitted and recorded in the registers and rolls of parliament.[4]

The other division of Aberdeenshire is called Buchan, which gives title of earl to an ancient branch of the name of Erskine, and the present earl is one of the sixteen peers of the British parliament.[5] There is neither fine architecture nor gardening in this large shire, but abundance of good cheer and good neighbourhood, and the city of Aberdeen furnishes them with good wine, and all other foreign commodities. The rivers Dee and Don afford salmon in the greatest plenty that can be imagin'd, to that degree that in some of the summer months the servants won't eat them but twice a week, they are so fat and fulsome; it's almost incredible how they spread. In autumn they engender, and in shallow pools of the river they cast their spawn, and cover it with sand, and then they are so poor and lean that they are only skin and bone; of that spawn in the spring comes a fry of tender little fishes, who make directly to the sea, and growing to their full bigness return to the river where they were spawned. And it's surprizing to see how they will jump over stones, and everything that lies in their way, with a jerk of their tail, till they arrive at the very place they were spawn'd in, and there they stay till they breed; during which time, which is from the Assumption of Our Lady to St. Andrew's Day, they are by law not to be caught.[6]

Buchanan, in his *History of Scotland*, says, that near Stangs Castle, on the banks of the River Ratra in this county, there is a cave, where the water distilling in drops as they fall turn into pyramidical stones; but I did not see it, and therefore will not vouch for it.[7]

From Buchan I enter'd a better country, called the shire of Banff, and pass'd thro'a pleasant little vale call'd Strathbogie, where the Duke of Gordon hath an ancient seat, as hath Ogilvy, Earl of Findlater, the Lord Banff, Lord Saltoun,[f] and several gentlemen of the names of Gordon, Ogilvy and Fraser; and near the River Spey arriv'd at Castle-Gordon, the capital seat of the Duke of Gordon, a very great and powerful family in this country, and all by north it.[8] The palace is one of the largest I have seen in Scotland and very high. The apartments are large, noble and well furnished, [with] fine gardens, and a very spacious deer park. This noble family is also very ancient, for they had the Lordship of Strathbogie from Robert Bruce, were created Earls of Huntly by King James II *anno* 1449, were often Lord High Chancellors, and in 1549 created Marquises of Huntley, and by King Charles II, Dukes of Gordon. But the family continuing always Roman Catholicks, they were not in any place of trust, till King James the Seventh, dispensing with a breach of law, by his absolute power and prerogative royal, gave the command of Edinburgh Castle to the Duke of Gordon, and which he at the Revolution held out, till King William under the great seal pardoned him, and confirmed to him his estate. The present duke joined the Earl of Mar; but before the Rebellion was over made his peace, and submitted to King George.[9]

There are many branches of this noble family: the Earls of Aboyne and Aberdeen, the Viscount Kenmure, and many baronets. The last Earl of Sutherland also carried the surname[g] of Gordon, and quartered their arms; but this earl hath left off both, and keeps the surname of Sutherland.[10]

The Ogilvies, Earls of Findlater, are very ancient gentlemen in this country, though not nobilitated till the reign of King Charles the First. There is another family of the same name, Earls of Airlie, who pretend to be the oldest; but as that is disputed, it's none of my business to decide it. I will only tell you, that the present Earl of Findlater was Secretary of State to King William, and in his father's life-time created Earl of Seafield. He was also Lord High Chancellor, and again Secretary of State to Queen Anne, Knight of the Noble Order of St. Andrew, and Lord High Chancellor at the making of the Union. He is now one of the sixteen peers to the Parliament of Great Britain.[11]

From Banff I crossed the River Spey, and came into one of the beautifullest countries I had seen in Britain, which very much surprized me, called the shire of Moray. The vale of Evesham,[h] on the banks of the Severn, is not comparable to it for fertility nor evenness of ground; for in twenty-four miles, from Elgin to Inverness, it is all a bowling green.

Elgin, the capital of this charming country, is the Richmond of Scotland. Its cathedral has been very august and noble but, like the rest of the fine churches of Scotland, the best part of it in ruins; but there is still left entire a part call'd the Prentices Isle, which surpasses in architecture Westminster Abbey.[12] In Elgin many of the neighbouring gentry have their winter habitations, and make an agreeable society. The Castle of Rothes, of which Leslie is earl, stands on the banks of the Spey; a noble family, of which I shall give you an account when I arrive at his palace of Fife.[13] Here are some commoners of the best estates in Scotland: Duff of Braco[i] reckoned at 5000 pounds sterling a year, Gordon of Gordonstoun at 2000, a family of the Dunbars, hereditary sheriffs who, with their branches, have their handsome seats strewed all over the country.[14]

At the end of this country is the pretty town of Inverness, situated at the mouth of the River Ness, which runs from a lake of that name full twenty-three miles long. There are two very good streets in this town, and the people are more polite than in most towns in Scotland. They speak as good English here as at London, and with an English accent; and ever since Oliver Cromwell was here, they are in their manners and dress entirely English.[15] Here are coffee-houses and taverns, as in England. Here are the ruins of an old castle; and indeed this place deserves to be well fortified, for it is one of the most considerable passes between the Low Country and the Highlands. You cross the Ness over a stone bridge to enter the North Highlands, which consists of the shires of Ross,

Cromarty, Sutherland, Caithness,[j] Strathnaver and Lochaber, of which I shall give you an account as they lie in my way; and of the other parts of the Highlands, when I come to Dumbarton, the other great pass of the west.[16]

The shires of Ross and Cromarty[k] extend themselves from the West Ocean to the East or German Ocean, being a vast tract of a very mountainous country, chiefly inhabited by the clan or tribe of Mackenzie.[l] This tribe derived their origin from Colin Fitzgerald, a son of the Earl of Kildare[m] in Ireland, who with a few volunteers[n] came from that kingdom to the assistance of Alexander the Third, King of Scotland, against the Norwegians and Danes, and who behaved so well at the Battle of Largs[o] in the year 1263, that the king by his charter, dated at Kincardine[p] in January 1266, gave him the Barony of Kintail in the shire of Ross, in which charter he is called *Colino Hibernico*. His son Kenneth having a numerous offspring, they were call'd after the Highland manner MacKenneths, and by the English since Mackenzie. They were successively Barons of Kintail till the year 1623, that they were created by James the Sixth earls of Seaforth. King Charles the Second nobilitated another branch by the title of Viscount Tarbet, who was created Earl of Cromarty by Queen Anne.[17]

This country is very mountainous, cover'd in most places with wood, and abounds with cattle, stags, roebucks, fallow-deer, and wild-fowl. It was on the western shore of this shire where the Spaniards landed with the Lord Seaforth to support the interest of the Pretender, at the time that the Duke of Ormond design'd for England, and were here taken prisoners.[18] On the German Ocean of this shire is a harbour like Porto Specie in the Mediterranean, between Genoa and Leghorn, call'd Cromarty Firth,[q] which will contain all the fleets of Europe land-lock'd, and may be of great advantage to the United Kingdom of Great Britain, if ever they have a war with any of the princes in the Baltick, in victualling and cleansing their ships there.

To the west of Loch Ness, which empties itself into the eastern ocean, there is another loch[r] or lake call'd Lochy,[s] which by a branch of the sea call'd the Aber, emptieth itself into the western ocean; and the mountainous country round it is call'd Lochaber. This being the centre between the north and west Highlands, K. William III of Britain built a regular fort at Inverlochy, the mouth of the Aber, call'd Fort William, which serves as a bridle to keep the inhabitants in awe, who on all revolutions or emergencies of government have been very unruly.[19] They differ as much in their dress, manners and language from the Low Country, as the Indians in Mexico do from the Spaniards. I told you from Wales, that although the Welsh have preserv'd their language, yet they write in a Roman character, and have entirely lost their ancient one; but here they have preserv'd their language in its native purity, and the character, which hath a greater resemblance of the Greek or Hebrew than the Roman. The universal dress here is a striped plaid,[t] which serves them as a covering by night, and a cloak by day. The gentry wear trousings, which are breeches and stockings of one piece of the same striped stuff; and the common people have a short hose, which reaches to the calf of the leg, and all above is bare. They lie very coarsely, and yet worse than we did in Westphalia, where we had clean straw.[20] As for the nature of the people, I will give you the words of that famous antiquary Sir James Dalrymple,[u] uncle to the present Earl of Stair, in his observations on Camden's description of Britain:[21]

> The inhabitants of these regions are a kind of rude, warlike, quarrelsome and mischievous people, who being the unmixed progeny of the ancient Scots, speak Irish, and call themselves Albanick. Their bodies are firmly and compactly made, withal strong and nimble of foot, high-minded, bred in warlike exercises, and inured to robberies on their neighbours, and, upon a hatred, most desperately forward to take revenge. They live by hunting, fishing, fowling and stealing; and like the Spaniards wear their long hair. They are divided into kindreds and families, which they call clans, and are so united to the cause of their clan, that there is an Act of Parliament, that if any of a clan does a mischief, the whole clan is answerable for it; and they must either deliver up the aggressor, or the first man that is apprehended of the clan suffers for it; and the whole clan bears feud for hurt receiv'd by any one member of it, even although they suffer justly. Many gentlemen in the Highlands shun one another's company, lest they should revive a quarrel that happen'd between their forefathers

perhaps 300 years ago. They are also as warm in their friendships; for if they meet with one of the name in amity with their own clan, be it in any country of the world, there is immediately the most intimate friendship. The Macdonalds are by much the most powerful of all the clans. They are divided into four classes, and inhabit distinct countries: upon the Loch Ness, the Macdonalds of Glengary inhabit; in Lochaber and Isle of Skye, the Macdonalds of Slate; towards Argyllshire, the Capt. of Clan Ronald, and Macdonald of Keppoch and those of Kintyre. The other clans, clan Katin, clan Cameron, the Macleans, and almost innumerable other Macs, although independent one of another, yet are entirely guided by the Macdonalds, who have been so powerful as often to assume the name of Kings of the Isles. And one of them enter'd into a league with Edward the Fourth of England as such in 1460, according to Mr. Rymer's *Foedera Angliae*, against the King of Scotland. They have taken a mighty fit of loyalty upon them since the Revolution, and have taken up arms on any invasion for the invaders, which shows that their resentments were not so much against the family of the Stewarts, as against the establish'd government of Scotland, which in all reigns they have endeavour'd to disturb. Robert, the first of the Stewarts, king of Scotland, married his daughter Margaret to MacDonald, Lord of the Isles, to secure him in his interest; but all would not do. They were the common disturbers of the nation, till King James the Fifth privately, with a body of men, took shipping and landed in every clan and island, and brought them in person to his obedience, making them give hostages for their good behaviour. I can compare them to nothing liker than the Arabs, who are divided into tribes as they, and have their chiefs. They are very good subjects to the *Grand Signior*, while the porte sends them their annual allowance; but whenever that is wanting, they make bold with the caravans and the pilgrimages to Mecca, to make reprisals and so make their revenue from the porte absolutely necessary.[22]

There is one clan in this shire of Ross, call'd the Frasers, that never joins with the rest, and are mostly compos'd of gentlemen on horseback. Sir James Dalrymple gives a good reason for their not joining with the other highlanders; for the clan Ronald cut off once the whole clan, so that if eighty gentlemen of them had not left their wives with child, who all brought forth sons, the clan had been extinguished. There are three peers of this clan, the Lords Lovat,[v] Saltoun and Fraser, of which Lovat is the chief. This noble family hath been great ever since Malcolm the Fourth. In Robert Bruce's reign they were Lord High Chamberlains of Scotland, and married Lady Mary Bruce, the king's sister, and widow to Sir Nicholas Campbell of Lochow,[w] predecessor to the Duke of Argyll. And in 1369 King David Bruce created Sir Alexander Fraser, his nephew, Thane of Dores in the shire of Kincardine, and Robert the first Stewart, Lord Lovat. This shire hath mountains so high that they are cover'd with snow all the year round.[23]

From Ross you enter the shire of Sutherland, very hilly, but not so mountainous as Ross. The castle of Dunrobin, the ancient seat of the earls of Sutherland, and built by Robert, earl about the year 1100, is a noble seat, call'd after his own name the Hall of Robin.[24] Its antiquity will tell you that it is not built according to the exactest rules of architecture, but very strong, as the incursions of the Danes required. This family were Thanes of Sutherland, before earls or lords were known, and when King Malcolm Canmore first introduced those titles, were amongst the first created earls.[25] King David Bruce married his sister to the Earl of Sutherland; and on some disgust to the Stewart, who married the other sister, obliged the nobility, after his release from his imprisonment at Durham, to acknowledge his nephew Earl of Sutherland for his successor to the throne; but that earl dying unmarried, the dispute was ended, and the Stewart succeeded.[26] This family was always popish till 1616, that John, Earl of Sutherland joined strenuously in opposing the innovations that King Charles the First was introducing into the Church of Scotland, and was by the party constituted Lord Privy Seal. His son George continued the same zeal for the Protestant interest in the reigns of King Charles the Second, King James, and King William. And his son John, the present earl, hath at all times strongly and loudly maintain'd the Protestant succession in the House of Hanover, for which his Majesty honoured him with the Order of St. Andrew, or the Thistle, and appointed him Lord Lieutenant of all the northern shires of Inverness, Elgin, Nairn,

Cromarty, Ross, Sutherland, Caithness, and the Isles of Orkney and Shetland.[x] [27]

In the northermost part of this shire is a large mountainous country call'd Strathnaver, full of wild deer and cattle, and inhabited by the clan of the Mackeys, anciently barons of Far, but created Lord Rea by King Charles the First. This clan hath produced many gallant officers. Donald Mackey of Far carried over an entire regiment of his clan to the service of Gustavus Adolphus, King of Sweden, into Germany. Hugh Mackey of Scoury behav'd himself gallantly in the service of the Venetians at the Siege of Candia, was afterwards a captain in the French service, a colonel in the Dutch, and came over a major general with King William at the Revolution. He took the town of Athlone in Ireland sword in hand, was made a lieutenant-general, and commander in chief of the forces in Scotland, where he had not so good success at the head of a Lowland army against his countrymen the clans; for they beat him at Killiecrankie; and it was with reluctancy that he took that command. He was afterwards kill'd at Steinkirk in Flanders.[28] This gentleman, when he was in the French service, put an a between the k and the y in his name, to give it the greater sound, calling himself Mackay, which is imitated by all the younger people of the clan, and those in Kintyre. But the branches in Fife, the Carse of Stirling and Galloway, still write it after the old way, Macky, as does the Lord Rea.[29] Colonel Aeneas and Robert Macky[y] had both regiments under King William, and died of their wounds. They were soldiers from their cradles, and sons of the Lord Rea.[30]

This country lieth in 59 degrees and 40 m. so that it's prodigiously cold in winter, and the sun seldom sets in summer. From Dunsby Head in this country to the Mull of Kintyre[z] towards Ireland, which is the length of the Highlands, is above six degrees distance all along the West Ocean; and to the east of Strathnaver[aa] lieth the county of Caithness, more fertile than the other, and inhabited by the name of St. Clair, whose chief is Earl of Caithness.[31]

The Highlands, which make a good third of Scotland, are divided into the following districts, who all speak Irish: Dumbarton,[bb] Lennox, Bute, Argyll, Kintyre, Lorne, Breadalbane,[cc] Lochaber, Atholl, Mar, Buchan, Ross, Sutherland, Strathnaver, Caithness, and the islands.

I return'd back through a very mountainous country for four days, and crossed the famous Cairney[dd] Mount, a mountain which from its bottom on the one side, to the town of Fetteresso, its bottom on the other side, is full seven miles of a very stony country; from whence I got to the ancient town of Brechin. Its castle, which belong'd to the Earl of Panmure, is situated exactly like Warwick Castle in England, and is very well kept, with its terrace-walks cut out of the rock down to the river, where there is a fine salmon-fishing, which you see them catch from the windows of the castle. This palace hath a greater air of grandeur than Panmure, and belongs to the York Buildings.[32]

Here I enter'd the country of Strathmore, a valley that runs from Brechin all the way by Perth to Stirling, full forty miles, with ridges of hills on each side. I told you that in the south of Scotland a valley was call'd a dale; but in the north they are call'd straths, of which there are vast numbers between the mountains, all with their proper denominations, as Strathearn, Strathallen, &c. In entring Strathmore, I arriv'd at the noble palace of Glamis,[ee] belonging to Lyon,[ff] Earl of Strathmore. This palace, as you approach it, strikes you with awe and admiration, by the many turrets and gilded ballustrades at top. It stands in the middle of a well-planted park, with avenues cut through every way to the house. The great avenue, thickly planted on each side, at the entrance of which is a great stone gate, with offices on each side of freestone, like a little town, leads you in half a mile to the outer court, which has a statue on each side of the top of the gate as big as the life. On the great gate of the inner court are ballustrades of stone, finely adorn'd with statues, and in the court are four brazen statues, bigger than the life, on pedestals. The one of James the Sixth and First of England in his stole; the other of Charles the First in his boots, spurs and sword, as he is sometimes painted by Van Dyck; Charles the Second in a Roman dress, as on the Exchange at London; and James the Second in the same dress he is in at Whitehall.

From this court, by ballustrades of iron, you have a full prospect of the gardens on each side, cut out into grass-plats, and adorn'd with ever-greens, which are very well kept. The house is the highest I ever saw, consisting of a high tower in the middle, with two wings and a tower at each end, the whole above 200 foot broad. The stairs from the entry to the top of the house consist of

143 steps, of which the great stairs, where five people can mount a-breast, are 86, each of one stone. In the first floor are 38 fire-rooms. The hall is adorn'd with family-pictures, and behind the hall is a handsome chapel, with an organ for the Church of England service.[33] On the altar is a good picture of the Last Supper, and on the ceiling an Ascension done by one De Wet[gg] a Dutchman, whom Earl Patrick, this earl's grandfather, brought from Holland, and who has painted the ceilings of most of the rooms.[34]

In the drawing-room next to the hall is the best picture I ever saw of Queen Mary of Modena, the Pretender's mother, the Duke of Lauderdale in his robes by Sir Peter Lely,[hh] and the late Lord Dundee, with a crowd of half-lengths of the nobility of Scotland; and over a chimney a curious Italian piece of Our Saviour disputing with the doctors of the temple.[35]

When the Pretender lay here, they made 88 beds within the house for him and his retinue, besides the inferior servants, who lay in the offices out of doors. The present earl's elder brother sav'd the estate from being forfeited, by being kill'd at the head of his regiment on Sheriffmuir.[36]

The family is very noble, for King Robert the Second married him to his own daughter Jane, and created him Lord of this Glamis in 1374, and constituted him Lord High Chamberlain of Scotland; and we find several of the family chancellors in the succeeding reigns. In 1606 they were created earls of Kinghorn,[ii] and afterwards changed that title by the king's consent to Strathmore.[37]

From Glamis I crossed the country towards the River Tay, and in eight miles riding enter'd the Carse of Gowrie[jj] at the castle of Gray. This Carse of Gowrie is the beautifullest spot of ground in Scotland, being fourteen miles long, and from four to two miles broad on the north side of the River Tay, from Dundee to Perth, and all a perfect garden.

The house of Gray is but just building, consisting of a front and two wings, in the middle of three avenues of well-grown trees; and, when finished, will be one of the prettiest seats in Scotland. But altho' the symmetry of the apartments are exactly just, I am afraid the house will be too big for the estate. This family are an ancient branch of the Grays of Chillingham and Werk in Northumberland. Their first coming to Scotland was with King Robert Bruce, who gave a son of that family who followed his fortunes, the lands of

Browfield in Teviotdale;[kk] and a successor of his, Andrew Lord Gray, Justice General in the reign of James the Third, exchanged them for the castle of Broughty, and this house now called Gray, which have continued in the family ever since; and we find them very conspicuous in most reigns.[38]

Three miles further in this carse is Castle-Lyon, another seat of the Earl of Strathmore, in the middle of a vast plantation of trees, with avenues above a mile long on all sides. This is generally the earl's summer-dwelling, and the jointure-house of the ladies. It is a high tower-house like Glamis, but no wings to it, and is compleatly furnish'd like Glamis. The great avenue to this house is very stately, having two pyramids of freestone at the entry, with a gate on each side of each pyramid, like triumphal arches; and one is surprised, when he enters them, to find the house at so great a distance at the other end of the avenue.[39]

About two miles from Castle-Lyon, I passed by Drimmie,[ll] the present seat of the Lord Kinnaird, an ancient gentleman's family in this country, taking their name from the castle of Kinnaird about two miles distance, and now in possession of the York Buildings.[40] They were nobilitated by King Charles II in 1682; and continuing my road to the end of this carse, I ferried over the Tay, and arriv'd at Perth.

Letter IX

DUNFERMLINE[a]

Sir,

Perth is pleasantly situated in a spacious plain, on the west banks of the River Tay, twenty miles from the sea, and navigable to the town. It is a compact little town, consisting of two principal streets from east to west, and several cross-lanes from north to south, the houses so thickly built, that it quarter'd with ease four thousand men when the Earl of Mar made it his headquarters during the Rebellion; at which time it grew so rich, by the expence of the nobility that flock'd hither on that occasion, and the expence of the Dutch troops afterwards, that they have built themselves a very fine guild-hall, a handsome piece of architecture, and several other public and private buildings.[1] The Church of St. John, from whence it is sometimes called St. John's Town, stands in the middle of the town, and is now divided into two neat churches.

Here is a vast trade for linen,[b] and it is the capital of Perthshire, the largest county in Scotland. Here is an old palace, which devolv'd to the Crown by the conspiracy of the Gowries,[c] a story that hath made so great a noise all over Europe, and to this day is so little understood, that I'm sure you'll thank me to give you the particulars impartially, as I could learn them.[2]

Patrick, Lord Ruthven,[d] who was very active in the Reformation, and forward in the murder of David Rizzio, was so powerful, his son was created Earl of Gowrie, and Lord High Treasurer of Scotland; who endeavouring to seize the king's person from another party (for you must know, that during the minority of James the VIth, whatever party had his person, had the power) was attainted of treason, and beheaded; however, the honour and estate were restor'd to his sons the year after.

His two sons were then travelling in France, and on the restoration of the honours, return'd by the way of England, where Queen Elizabeth was particularly civil to them; their mother being daughter to Stuart, Lord Methuen,[e] married to her Aunt Margaret, daughter to Henry the VIIth of England, and dowager to James the IVth of Scotland.[3] On their arrival in Scotland, they retir'd to their seat in this town, where they led a private life for some time; when the king, who kept his court at Falkland, twelve miles off, hunting in that neighbourhood, on the 5th of August, 1600, was either invited by them to dinner, or sent word that he would dine with them. But while the dinner was making ready, the king desiring to see the house, as they passed through the rooms, Mr. Erskine and Mr. Ramsay,[f] two of the Gentlemen of the King's Bedchamber, jump'd in at a window, upon the king's calling out treason, and kill'd the two brothers, which was all of that family. So the greatest estate in Scotland came to the Crown.

The great Mackenzie hath writ some treatises to show the blackness of this conspiracy. I must add, that it was a very foolish one in two boys, without any assistance, to murder their sovereign, whilst he had so numerous a court round him. Yet the town of Perth being alarm'd at the death of their Provost, the Lord Gowrie, arose in a tumult, and had cut the courtiers to pieces if William, Earl of Tullibardine,[g] had not been providentially in the town that day, who, with his followers, carried the king off; for which service he obtain'd a special grant of sheriffship of Perthshire to his heirs for ever. And Mr. Erskine was made Earl of Kellie,[h] and Ramsay, Earl of Holderness, for this service.[4]

Mr. Crawford, the Historiographer of Scotland, in his history of the family of the Stuarts, doubts whether the Earl Gowrie's mother was daughter to Queen Margaret, but by a succeeding wife, to take off the suspicion of their being cut off, because of their being equally related to the crown of England with the king; but this is impossible, for the Earl of Angus, that was also married to her, married the daughter of the Lord Maxwell afterwards, so that both husbands could not survive her.[5]

About a mile above Perth, on the other side of the river, lies the palace of Scone,[i] where the kings of Scotland used to be crown'd, and from whence King Edward the First of England carried the chair in which the kings of England are now crowned in Westminster

Abbey. The Scots were almost as much griev'd at the loss of this stone, as they would be now at the loss of their crown, which is close lock'd up in Edinburgh Castle.[6] This palace consists of two square courts of freestone, besides two spacious outer courts. The front towards the chapel is two hundred foot; there are two very good apartments, the one call'd royal, where the Pretender lodg'd, and the other for my Lord Stormont, housekeeper.[7]

The royal apartment is very magnificent, consisting of a dining-room forty foot long, and thirty wide and high, a bed-chamber, drawing-room, and closet, all neatly wainscotted with oak, the chimney-pieces of marble, finer than those at Milton or Burghley,[i] being raised as chimney-pieces to the ceiling. There are abundance of very good pictures: amongst others, Queen Mary of Modena, by an Italian, when she was affianced by the Earl of Peterborough for the Duke of York. There is also a very good half-length of a Lord Stormont, by Van Dyck;[8] there is a gallery of communication from this apartment one hundred and seventy-five foot long, the ceiling painted by some Flanderkin two hundred years ago, in which is express'd in several panels, all the manners of hunting, hawking, setting, and fishing.[9]

The hereditary keeper of this palace is Murray, Viscount Stormont, a younger branch of the house of Tullibardine; the first was Sir David Murray, bred up with King James the VIth, and was first Cup-bearer, then Master of the Horse, and Captain of the Guards to that prince, and created Lord Scone, and Viscount Stormont; on whom there is a noble marble monument, done at Rome in his life-time, one of the noblest and finest I ever saw.[10] The present viscount was prisoner in Edinburgh Castle when the Pretender was here, and so sav'd his estate, though his second son was Secretary to the Pretender, and is now with him at Rome. The Pretender liv'd three weeks here, in all the grandeur of an English king. He din'd and supp'd alone, being served on the knee by his Lord of the Bedchamber in Waiting, and admitted everybody to come into the room whilst at table. His constant course was eight dishes of meat, a course of milks, and a dessert; he was never known to drink a glass of wine but at meals all the time he was here, but would sometimes drink coffee in the afternoon. He writ all his dispatches with his own hand, and went out every morning to see the guards reliev'd; and the Lord of his Bedchamber in

Waiting always lay in a lobby joining to his bed-chamber. He kept a very sumptuous table for his nobility, and a board of green cloth for all the country gentlemen that came to wait on him, but never would go into the town of Perth, till the very day he was going away from Scone.[11]

Continuing the coast of the River Tay, I went to Dunkeld, a pass on this side towards the Highlands, as Inverness is on the other side. The Duke of Atholl hath here a very noble seat, with large gardens; but his general residence is at the castle of Blair in Atholl, several miles above this, where he lives like a sovereign prince, keeps a great table, whether company or no, and hath his degrees of gentlemen about him, as a Lord Lieutenant of Ireland, or the Dukes of Somerset or Chandos in England. This family of the Murrays are ancient Lords of Tullibardine , as appears by a charter dated in 1282; and was so considerable in the reign of Edward the First of England, that he was summoned by that prince on the part of John Balliol to Berwick. But what made them most considerable was that William, Earl of Tullibardine, married in the reign of James the VIth of Scotland, Dorothy Stewart, heiress to the Earl of Atholl, and his son succeeded to the title, dignity and precedency of that noble family, and became thereby related to the Crown. However, they still retain the surname of Murray, though they quarter the Stuarts' arms with theirs; and give this motto of that family of Atholl, which I defy all the heralds of Europe to explain: *furth fortune, and file the fetters*. King Charles the Second created the late earl Marquis of Atholl in 1676, and he was made Knight of the Order of St. Andrew by King James the Seventh, and his eldest son was created duke by Queen Anne in 1703, and made Knight of the Order of St. Andrew in 1704.[12]

Returning to Strathearn,[k] I pass'd by Huntingtower, another good seat of the Duke of Atholl, in a spacious park, well planted with trees, and in three miles arrived at Dupplin,[l] the seat of the Earls of Kinnoull, situated near the banks of the River Earn, the park finely wall'd round, and is the best wooded I ever saw. The trees are not so full grown as at Yester, but there is more of them, and I think too much crowded. The entry to the house is by two spacious courts, with a pavilion at each corner of them. On the right of the inner court are just built offices, consisting of kitchen, cellars, laundry, buttery &c., with a fine pav'd gallery from one end to the other; and a-top of them and another gallery are lodging-rooms for the servants belonging to these offices. The kitchen, having two rows of windows a-top of one another, is the largest and highest I ever saw; they design the like of the other side, but the foundation is not yet laid. Mr. Smith, the architect, lives there till he finishes it, and by his plan the whole will be very grand. The gardens of each side the courts, and behind the house, are laid out, but hardly begun. They are filling up a deep precipice between two hills, to make them regular; and the great avenue fronting the outer court, through the middle of the park, is very long.[13]

The house is a good double house, of freestone. Behind the hall, on the ground floor, is a very handsome apartment, fill'd with family-pictures; and on the chimney-piece of the bed-chamber of this apartment is a picture of K. Charles the First, delivering a letter to his son the Duke of York, to carry on to France. There is also in the parlour a Rubens by Van Dyck, a Prince Rupert by Sir Peter Lely, and the Regent Morton, finely done by Antonio Moro.[14] On the first-floor there's a handsome apartment of six rooms, extremely well furnish'd, and wainscotted with oak adorn'd with carv'd work. The dining-room is very spacious, and full of good pictures. There is an Italian piece of three figures, in half-lengh, for which the family hath been offer'd eight hundred pounds sterling. There is a whole length of that Earl of Kinnoull, who was Chancellor of Scotland in the reign of James the Sixth; a good half-length of Oliver Cromwell and General Monk, when they were here, with a crowd of other noblemen's pictures.[15] There is also a great deal of rich furniture, as velvet beds, fine tapistry hangings; and what I had almost forgot to tell you, there is at the upper end of the dining-room, an equestrian statue of K. Charles the Second, on a fine pedestal of oak, adorn'd with other brazen figures, and a picture of Van Dyck and his wife, said to be done by himself.[16]

This family of Kinnoull proceeds from a branch of the ancient and noble family of Hay, Earls of Erroll, and Lord High Constables of Scotland. George Hay, after having improv'd himself abroad, came to London to visit his kinsman James Hay, Earl of Carlisle, the great favourite of King James the First of England; who introduc'd him at court, and quickly got him to be one of the Gentlemen of His Majesty's Bedchamber. In which office he gain'd so much of the king's affections that he was sent down in 1616 Lord Register of Scotland, and in 1622 was made Lord High Chancellor; in which post he continued in K. Charles the First's reign, who created him in 1633 Earl of Kinnoull, and continued him Chancellor to his death.[18] On his tomb is the following epitaph:

Gone is the wise Lycurgus of our time,
The great and grave dictator of our clime;
To whose desert the sacred sisters owe
As much as e're of old they did bestow
Of their Pyrean treasure, to give fame
To painful Curius, or great Cato's name.
Hadst thou, brave judge, liv'd in such golden days,
Thy head e're now had long been crown'd with bays:
But wisdom now is richly priz'd by none,
Nor virtue guardian finds, till she be gone.
Six hundred years ago, how happy I
That day, when thy brave ancestor did dye
His face with Danick blood; he did bequeath
Life to his country, at the doors of death:
Yet this brave act was clos'd with one fair day;
But thou didst still for many years display
The ensigns of thy virtues, and fierce jars,
Intestine broils, worse than the worst of wars,
Didst quell combustions; safe did keep from harm
Chaste piety, and raging wrath disarm.

This Chancellor had a fine gentleman to his son, who was captain of the yeomen of the guards to King Charles the First, and one of the Lords of the Privy Council. But his successors turning Roman Catholics, and marrying and living always in England, they made no great figure, till the honour and estate devolv'd on Thomas Hay of Balhousie,[m] great-grandson to the Chancellor's brother, who was one of the sixteen peers of the Parliament of Great Britain in the last of Queen Anne; and his son, the present earl, was created a peer of England, by the title of Lord Hay.[18]

I should have told you, that the seat Balhousie joins to the town of Perth, and has a good stone house, and fine plantation of trees round it. From Dupplin, I continued the course of the River Earn[n] till it falls into the Tay, that I might see the other parts of Fife, that were not in my way to Dundee, before I go to Stirling[o] and the western parts of the kingdom.[19]

Strathearn is a fine valley from the lake of Earn in the Highlands, from whence the river proceeds; which, to its entry into the Tay, is above thirty miles, and the valley about four miles broad, from mountains to mountains. It's extremely fertile, and strow'd with gentlemen's seats, on the declension of the hills, with plantations of trees, which makes the valley the more agreeable. Kincardine, the ancient paternal estate of the Grahams, Dukes of Montrose, is on this strath, and by its vestiges hath been very large and strong, some of its remaining walls being fifteen foot thick. It was ruin'd by the Parliament's army, when the great Marquis of Montrose was in arms for King Charles, and hath never been repair'd since.[20] The castle of Drummond is also on this strath, a most noble ancient seat belonging to the Drummonds, Earls of Perth; but as that family follow'd King James the VIIth's and IId's fortunes into France, it lies much neglected. This family is so ancient, that we find John, Earl of Carrick, afterwards king of Scotland, and the second of the Stuarts, married to Annabella, daughter to the Lord Drummond; by whom all the kings of the race of Stuart are descended of that family, and the houses of Austria and Burgundy, that married the king's daughters, by that marriage ally'd to them.[21] We find the Earl of Perth sent ambassador with Charles, Earl of Nottingham, Lord High-Admiral of England to Philip the Third of Spain, to take that king's oath on the ratification of the articles of peace concluded between Great Britain and Spain in 1603. And the last earl was Lord High Chancellor of Scotland at the Revolution, and follow'd King James, who created him a duke, made him Knight of the Garter, and Governor to the Pretender, in which station he continued to his death. His eldest son, the Lord Drummond, dy'd at St. Germains, Master of the Horse to the Queen-Dowager; and the other sons are in the service of the Pretender.[22]

In crossing the Bridge of Earn to return into Fife, I pass'd by a neat little seat belonging to Sir Thomas Moncrieff,[p] built of freestone, after the manner of the country-seats in the villages about London, with a glass cupola or lantern[q] at top, and very neatly wainscoted and furnished within. It stands on the declension of a hill, in a well wooded park; and, what's rare in this country, in the middle of two thousand pounds sterling a year.[23]

From the Bridge of Earn, through the ancient town of Abernethy, in two hours I arriv'd at the palace of Melville,[r] the seat of a very ancient family of that name. This palace was built by the late earl, and consists of a body and two short wings of each side, like an H. You ascend to it, as at Panmure, by a long avenue, the full breadth of the house, with a spacious wood on[s] each side of the avenue, and more fir-trees than ever I saw anywhere.[24] The wood of Yester very much surpriz'd me, so did Panmure, and Dupplin more than both. But when the trees here come to be full grown, this will very far exceed the others.

In the outer court are very convenient stablings, and other offices, with a handsome pavilion on each side; and from the inner court, of each side, and behind the house, are to be the gardens, as at Panmure; which tho' they are laid out, are not yet finish'd. The great stair-case is very noble; and in each wing there is a good stone stair, which leads up to the apartments above. At the head of the great stairs, as at Dalkeith, is a spacious room, full forty foot long, and thirty broad and high, fill'd with the pictures of the family, all done by Sir John Medina, whom the late earl brought from London on purpose.[25] There are two apartments on each side of this great room, of a drawing-room, bed-chamber, dressing-room and closet each, all wainscotted with oak; the chimney-pieces of different colour'd marble, and adorn'd with carv'd work in wood, and the apartment of state as well furnish'd as in any of the royal palaces. The bed of state is very noble, of crimson velvet, richly lin'd and adorn'd; the chairs of the same, with the finest small-figur'd tapistry I have seen. The tapistry of the dressing-room is also very rich. Up two pair of stairs are abundance of handsome lodging-rooms; and the apartments on the ground floor are pretty good. In the whole, it's a very delightful seat.

This family, by the name, seems to be French, but they say they are Hungarian, and came in with Queen Margaret, wife to King Malcolm Canmore. However, they are pretty ancient in this country; for we find Sir John de Melville, of the county of Fife, one of the barons that swore fealty to King Edward the First of England, in the year 1296. This family were amongst the first reformers, for Sir John Melville was beheaded in 1549, by the implacable malice of Cardinal Beaton and Bishop Hamilton, and his numerous family dispers'd. Sir Robert, his son, who after being some time in the service of Henry the Second of France, returning to his native country, grew in great esteem, and was a faithful servant to the distress'd Queen Mary, and was her minister at the court of Queen Elizabeth; for which, after that unhappy princess was beheaded, her son, King James, made Sir Robert Treasurer-Depute, Vice-Chancellor of Scotland, and a Lord of the Sessions, and at last, in 1516, a peer, by the title of Lord Melville.[26] George, this lord's grandson, being a zealous asserter of the reform'd religion, in opposition to the encroachments of episcopacy, at the Restoration of King Charles the Second was obliged to take shelter in Holland till the Revolution, and then came over with King William, who made him Secretary of State, Lord High Commissioner to the Parliament, and created him Earl of Melville. But his eldest son dying childless before him, this estate fell to his second son, who inheriting the honours of Leven by right of his mother, is obliged to take the name and arms of Leslie. This Earl of Leven hath been often Commander in Chief of the forces, and a Privy-Counsellor, both in the reigns of King William and Queen Anne, and continued so, till by the Union that employment remained no longer fix'd.[27]

From Melville, in four miles I got to the royal palace of Falkland, built by K. James the Fifth. This palace, by its ruins, hath been very large and noble; and two sides that still stand in the inner square show[t] the beautifullest piece of architecture in Britain. It consists of two storeys, with rows of round marble pillars of the Corinthian order, set in sockets of stone between every window; on[u] each side of the window, a busto in bass-relief of the emperors and empresses, and at the top of each pillar a statue as big as the life. There are twenty-two bustos, and twelve pillars still remaining. The other two parts of the quadrangle were burnt down by Oliver Cromwell's army. You enter this palace, as you do that of Holyrood House, by two stately towers, and on the right, a chapel still well preserv'd, with statues as big as the life in the niches on the outside. Here were spacious gardens, with a park well planted with oak, and well stock'd with deer, pal'd round for eight miles; but

Nunc Seges est ubique Troja fuit.

The oaks were all cut down by Oliver, to build his citadel at Perth, and the barracks; the park plough'd up, and only here and there some of the pales left; and the steward made an estate out of what was left, pretending that the English had destroy'd the whole. The hereditary keeping of this palace and park belongs to the Duke of Atholl, who lets out the gardens and park. I went through fifteen of the finest vaults for cellaring, with two large kitchens under ground, and a spacious gallery of communication, and well pav'd with flag-stones.[28]

King James the Fifth, the politest gentleman that ever sat on the Scottish throne, delighted in this place for the conveniency of sport; and I suppose, when he went to France, to marry King Francis the First's daughter, brought the model of the palace from thence with him, as he did that of Linlithgow, where he revived and embellished his Order of St. Andrew after the manner of St. Michael in France.[29] The French historians are full of the praises of this prince; and I have seen some pieces in Italian by eye-witnesses to his gallantry and address at that court. He was a severe justiciary, and generally sat judge in all criminal causes himself; and would go from one extremity of his kingdom to the other to try thieves, especially cow-[v] and horse-stealers; and went round all the Highlands and Islands by sea in person, bringing the highlanders to a stricter subjection than ever they had been before. For they knew little of any other king than MacDonald, Lord of the Isles; and he used to say, he would make the rushbush keep the cow.[30]

He was also a prince of a lively wit, and a poet. He compos'd several merry songs, still extant; and us'd to go disguis'd to the country-weddings, and dance whole nights among them, without ever discovering himself. He would also often go to the country fairs, dress'd like a farmer, and buy and sell cattle, and that way inform himself of the state of the country, or the oppressions of his ministry. Being son-in-law to the French king, and nephew and next heir-male to K. Henry the Eighth at the Reformation, great pains were taken by these courts to have him. King Henry solicited hard for an interview, offering to make him his lieutenant of the kingdom of England, if he would come into his measures; but France and the popish clergy fearing the Reformation, hinder'd him. Yet he was no bigot prince, but did not like the methods by which his uncle brought it about. He died in the prime of his years at this palace, of grief for the loss of the Battle of Solway, and the death of his two sons.[31]

King James the Sixth resided also here sometimes, and was here when Carey brought him the news of Queen Elizabeth's death; for which he created him Viscount Falkland; and on his departure for England, gave away some courts of this palace, with a garden, to the Lord Stormont, keeper of the palace of Scone, which still belongs to the family. King Charles the First was also here, and model'd the chapel according to the form then used in the Church of England.[32]

The town of Falkland is a most clean little town, its market-place well pav'd and not unlike Woodstock in Oxfordshire. It's also a borough corporate, of which the king is always provost; and they choose aldermen out of their own town council.[33] The town is oddly situated on the north-east foot of the Lomond hill, a mountain not rocky, which is a full English mile to the top, all cover'd with the finest pastorage for sheep. On the top of this hill is a most extensive prospect of the country all round: the shire of Fife, of which it's in the middle, you see from end to end; the Firth at seven miles distance looks like an ordinary river; and beyond it Edinburgh and the Lothians. You see very plain, almost to Berwick, northward Perthshire, and Angus, with the Strath of Earn; and to the westward, as far as the hills by Stirling.

From Falkland, in four miles, I went to Balgonie,[w] another seat of the Earl of Leven's, whose gardens and parks are very spacious, all wall'd round, and well stock'd with deer; this being the paternal seat of General Leslie, a general of Gustavus Adolphus, King of Sweden, who commanded sometimes the king's, and sometimes the parliament's, army during the civil wars, was created by King Charles the First Earl of Leven; and the present earl, a son of the Earl Melville, succeeds to it by the right of his mother. He came over with King William at the Revolution, and hath been a firm adherent to the Protestant interest ever since; and, as I told you from Melville, hath been often Commander in Chief of the forces in this kingdom.[34]

From Balgonie, in three miles, I arriv'd at the noble palace of Leslie, the ancient paternal seat of the Leslies, Earls of Rothes. This seat, after the finishing of Holyrood House for the king, was built by that great architect, Sir William Bruce, then Master of the Works for Scotland, for his grace the Duke of Rothes, Governor and Lord High Chancellor of Scotland, during all the reign of Charles the Second. It stands in the middle of a park, surrounded with a stone wall of six miles in circumference, on a point of land where two rivers washeth it on each side, and join in one at the end of the gardens. It is extremely well planted with full grown trees that, at a distance, seem to be a large wood. There's a noble parterre to the east, cut out into green slopes, adorn'd with evergreens, that reacheth to the point where these two rivers meet; and from this parterre on the south of the house is a long terrace[x] walk, and under it five several terraces, to which you descend by stately stairs to another square garden by the river-side, with a water-work in the middle, and round which the present earl designs to carry the river.

You enter the palace by two spacious courts, with a pavilion at each end of the first court; the house is a large square, with a paved court in the middle. You enter it by a vestibule,[y] ballustraded with marble, into a large hall, pav'd with black and white marble, with a spacious parlour to the right and left. My lord's own apartment on the ground floor to the south is very noble, as is the great staircase which leads to the apartments of state above. This apartment, where King James lodged when he was Duke of York, consists of a spacious dining-room, antichamber, drawing-room, bed-chamber, dressing-room and closet, with a gallery, the longest I ever[z] saw, fill'd from one end to the other with family pictures. The offices of this noble palace are also very well disposed, with noble stables, and a kitchen-garden on the north side of the river. Here is also a very good market-town about half a mile from the palace.[35]

This family is of great antiquity in this kingdom; for I saw a charter granted by Robert Bruce, confirming the baronies of Rothes and Banbrich, to Sir Andrew Leslie, son of Sir Norman Leslie, who was also one of the barons who signed that memorable letter to the pope, in 1320, asserting the independency of Scotland. In 1449 they were created Earls of Rothes by James the Second of Scotland. They were zealous at the Reformation, and have constantly made the greatest figure in their country ever since. John, Earl of Rothes, in 1637, was the principal governing person of the nation; and at the Treaty of Rippon, first commissioner. My Lord Clarendon says, in his history, that the king expected, by the help and interest of the Earl of Rothes, such a party in Scotland, as would have been more tender of his honour if the earl had been present in that kingdom; and that his death at London was reckon'd by His Majesty an irreparable loss. His son, John, was Lord High Commissioner to the second session of the first parliament of King Charles the Second, Lord High Treasurer, and Lord High Chancellor during his life, and created a duke. His grandson was zealous at the Revolution, and went through all the great offices of the kingdom, both in the reigns of Queen Anne and King George; and at his death was Lord High Admiral of Scotland, Governor of Stirling Castle, and Lord Lieutenant of the counties of Fife and Aberdeen. His son, the present earl, is endow'd with all the shining good qualities of the family, and is an honour to his country both at court and camp.[36]

From Lashly[37] in six miles, I arriv'd at the famous lake of Lochleven, of about eleven miles in circumference, and in the middle of which is an old castle, which hath often serv'd for a state prison; and particularly to Mary, Queen of Scots, who made her escape from hence, by the means of one of the governor's sons, when she took refuge in England.[38] The Douglases,[aa] Earls of Morton, have been governors and proprietors of this lake and castle, from the year 1353 till the reign of King Charles the Second, that it was purchas'd by that great architect Sir William Bruce, who built a noble palace on the banks of this lake, and joining to the town of Kinross. This is by much the finest seat I have yet seen in Scotland, and Melville is it in miniature. It is built of freestone, adorn'd with columns of the Corinthian order, the offices under ground all vaulted, and galleries of communication paved with stone are the noblest I have seen anywhere. The great stair-case is the same as at Melville, but the great salloon that goes from it is two storeys high, with a lantern at top, as at Montague House at London, and the apartments of state on each side, as at Melville.[39] The great saloon is crowded with pictures, and there are two good whole-lengths of King Charles the First and his Queen.

The great avenue from the town of Kinross is the noblest you can imagine. You enter it by a pair of stately stone gates, and in a quarter of a mile you reach the outer court, with a pavilion, stables and coach-houses on each corner. The inner court is beautiful, adorn'd with green grass-plats; and on each side of this court, and behind the house are the gardens. There are two other[bb] avenues from the outer court, that run to the lake on one side, and through a wood on the other. There are also some curious vistas cut through this wood. This lake is full of fish, particularly the finest trouts in the[cc] world; and the town of Kinross adjoining is a good market-town.

This Sir William Bruce, was a younger brother of the family of Bruces in this kingdom, and a relation of the Earl of Ailsbury in England.[40]

From Kinross, in eight miles more, I arriv'd at the royal palace of Dunfermline. This was the habitation of King James the Sixth, before he came to the crown of England. It was here that Prince Henry, King Charles the First, and the Princess Elizabeth, Queen of Bohemia, were born. It was also the jointure-house of Queen Anne of Denmark, who built an apartment for herself, at top of the entry or pend, with a gallery of communication with the royal apartments. This palace consists of two courts, the upper and lower. The lower was a mews as large as that at London, for stables, hawks and hounds, and the officers belonging to them; the upper court makes the palace, the royal apartments are to the south and west, Queen Anne's jointure-house to the north, and the church and remnants of the ancient monastery to the east.[41]

The church was above three hundred foot long. It was built after the manner of that at Lichfield, with a steeple between two spires on the west, and two spires more on each side of the middle of the church; but this church being entirely demolish'd at the Reformation, King James the Sixth repair'd and buttressed the west end of it, for a Protestant parochial church. The body of the church and choir, where several kings of Scotland lye buried, continuing still a heap of rubbish, their tombs are still preserv'd in the open air; and particularly that of St. Margaret, in black alabaster, the daughter of Edward the Confessor, and Queen to King Malcolm Canmore.[42] This queen is famous, both in the histories of England and Scotland, for many virtuous good actions, and rectifying many barbarous customs amongst the Scots; particularly the taking off that custom of the Lord of the Mannor having the first night of the bride of all his vassals, and procuring a law, that for paying a mark, the bridegroom should have the bride to himself. Another institution of hers was the grace-drink; that every gentleman that staid till grace was said should have a full glass, thereby bringing them to have a sense of religion, for the sake of the liquor.[43]

From this church to the refectory, or frater-hall, as they call it here, was a noble cloister, turn'd into a tennis court after the Reformation. The refectory was a noble room, fifty foot long, forty high, and thirty broad; in it are nine windows to the south, twelve foot high, and three broad, from whence one hath a most delicious prospect of the Firth, at four miles distance, all the shore of West-Lothian on the other side of the Firth, and a full view of Edinburgh and the country adjacent, at twelve miles distance. This hall is erected upon two several vaults, supported by pillars, like the foundation of some of the cathedrals in England. The lowermost vault, as I suppose, was a burying-place there; but what use the second vaulted storey was, I cannot imagine. The roof of this hall, as also of the royal apartments, is all down, and jackdaws build now in the room where King Charles the First was born. I believe this was a royal palace, before the Reformation; for the arms of James the Fifth, with his Queen, of the House of Guise, are still fresh upon the apartments; as are those of the Lord Hamilton, Governor of Scotland in the minority of Queen Mary. The gardens, as appears by the walls still standing, have been very spacious, with a rivulet running through them. The Marquis of Tweeddale is hereditary keeper of this palace, and hath a good revenue from it.[44]

Letter X

STIRLING

Sir,

From Dunfermline I made an excursion of six miles east to Aberdour, the ancient seat of Douglas, Earl of Morton. The house was built by that earl who was Regent of Scotland during the minority of King James the Sixth, and First of England, and was beheaded twenty years after, for being privy to the murder of the Lord Darnley, the king's father, although he had no hand in it. It's a fine old seat, with terrace-walks to the Firth, almost opposite to Edinburgh, at seven miles distance.[1] This is one of the ancientest branches of the family of Douglas, and hath been very considerable in most reigns. The first of them was Sir James Douglas, the great favourite of King Robert Bruce, in 1306,[a] and carried his heart, after his death, to be buried in the sepulchre at Jerusalem in the Holy Land; his servant who kept it being original of the Lockharts, a good family in Clydesdale.

In 1402 James, Lord Dalkeith and Aberdour[b] married a daughter of King Robert the Third, and the second Stuart; and his grandson, James, was created Earl of Morton by his cousin King James the Second in *anno* 1457, and married Jane, daughter to King James the First. The present earl is a very worthy nobleman, and a great assertor of the present interest.[2]

About two miles westward on the Firth lies the fine seat of Donibristle,[c] belonging to the noble family of Stuart, Earl of Moray. Donibristle was built by that Earl of Moray who was Regent of Scotland during the minority of King James the Sixth; both for the fineness of its situation, and its nearness to Edinburgh; but the present earl hath much enlarged it by two wings join'd to the old body, and a long parterre betwixt the two wings, with terrace-walks down to the sea-side. The furniture of this palace is very rich, and one can hardly see better old tapistry at Brussels than here.[3]

The first Earl of Moray of the name of Stuart was a natural son of King James the Fifth, who became a zealous reformer from popery, and was chosen Regent of the kingdom, during the minority of King James the Sixth, and First of England. He had only a daughter, whom he married to the Lord Doune, one of the ancientest branches of the Stuarts, and the title continues to the eldest son of the Earl of Moray to this day. The present Earl of Moray lives up to the splendour of the ancient nobility as much as any peer of the three kingdoms. He was bred at court under his father, who was Secretary of State to King Charles the Second, and Lord High Commissioner to King James the Seventh.[4]

From Donibristle, in two miles, lies the borough of Inverkeithing,[d] a pretty seaport with a good harbour, if it were kept clean; and near it St. Margaret's Bay, so called from her landing there, when she married King Malcolm Canmore. From the point of this bay there is a constant ferry cross the Firth, about two miles broad only, and which serves at all times of tide, and is the surest way from all parts of the north to Edinburgh, being but seven miles distant by land. It's called the Queen's ferry from the aforesaid Queen Margaret; and there is a very large good borough town for the conveniency of passengers.

Continuing my course westwards by Firth banks, I arrived in four miles at Culross, a most noble ancient seat of the Bruces, Earls of Kincairn; it stands on an eminence, as that of Weems does, and hath a noble prospect cross the firth of the country of West-Lothian, up the firth to the mountains above Stirling, and down below Edinburgh. One cannot imagine a nobler palace. It's built all of freestone; the front to the south, is above two hundred foot, with a tower, three storeys high at each corner; and under this front is a terrace, as long and as broad as that at Windsor, with a pavilion at each end; and below the terrace run hanging gardens for half a mile, down to the Firth. The design of these gardens was vast; but as they are, you can only judge of what they were to be, and might be. When my Lord Mar was laying out his fine gardens at Alloway,[e] I am told, that when he saw these, he thanked God that Culross was not his, for the expence of keeping it up would ruin him. The house is well furnished, and in the great stair-case are some very good pictures of Knights of the Golden Fleece, cardinals, bishops, abbots, and other eminent men of the name of Bruce. This branch of the Bruces is sprung from that of Blairhall,[f] as that of Ailesbury in England is; and all of them from Bruce of Clackmannan[g] in this neighbourhood. They are a very ancient clan, and very great in this neighbourhood.[5] Culross is also a good market-town, and there hath been a large old monastery, whose ruins join the outer court of the Lord Kincairn's palace.[6]

From Culross, in six miles, I arrived at the fine village of Alloway, belonging to Erskine,[h] Earls of Mar. The plantation round the house of Alloway is the largest and the finest (laid out by the unhappy earl that commanded in the Rebellion) of any in Britain; it far exceeds either Hampton Court or Kensington, the gardens consisting of two and forty acres; and the wood with vistas cut through it, of one hundred and fifty acres. The entry from the town is from the west, by a pair of fine stone gates, through a spacious avenue, which leads you to an area fronting the house on that side, in the middle of which is a gladiator, after the manner of that at Hampton Court, and on the right hand of this area is a spacious garden, with a fine terrace, and bowling green, adorn'd with the largest evergreens you can see anywhere.[7]

To the south of the house is the parterre, spacious and finely adorn'd with statues and vases; and from this parterre to the River Forth runs a fine terrace, or avenue; from whence, and from the parterre, you have thirty-two different vistas, each ending on some remarkable seat or mountain at some miles distance. One of them shows you Stirling Castle, at four miles distance; another the palace of Elphinstone,[i] on the other side of the river; a third the castle of Clackmannan; and so the rest. In the middle of this long terrace is a basin[j] of water, like that of the Duke of Chandos, at Cannons, in the which is the statue of Cain slaying of Abel; and at the end, to the river, are a pair of pyramidical gates, where a ship of three hundred tuns may unload. The avenue to the east through the wood is prodigiously long and large; and between each vista, from the parterre, are wildernesses of trees for birds, and little grottos. The house was not yet quite finished; but by the great stair-cases from every front, one can guess at its grandeur. It will be an additional honour to the Duke of Argyll, that when he was with his army at Stirling, and the lord of this house at the head of the army against him, he gave strict orders for the preservation of this place, and the government still keeps it in good order.

The town of Alloway is larger and better built, though a village, than most borough-towns. There is one street that runs down to the harbour, the broadest, and best pav'd of any I have seen, next to Edinburgh, with rows of lime-trees down to the river, as at Dundee, and in the towns of Holland.[8] The river is as broad here as at London Bridge, and as navigable for as large ships, tho' thirty miles from the sea, it being here that the River Forth falls into that arm of the sea called the Firth. The town hath a great face of business. There's a rope-walk for making cables and other ropes for ships; a manufactory for sail-cloth, and two mills for sawing of deals.[9]

This noble family of Erskine is very ancient; for we find them eminent in the reign of Alexander the Second, in 1226. One of the family was also a firm adherent to King Robert de Bruce, and to King David; and was one of those commissioners sent to redeem that prince when he was taken at the Battle of Durham, 1346, and which he effected in 1357, for one hundred thousand marks sterling; for which service he was made Lord High Chamberlain of Scotland, and Governor of the castles of Edinburgh, Stirling and Dumbarton, by which means he brought Robert, the first Stuart, peaceably to the throne.[10]

They have always been governors to the king's children, since the Stuarts came to the throne. One of them was slain with King James the Fourth at the Battle of Flodden;[k] and his son had the tuition of James the Fifth in Stirling Castle; and when his prince came at age, went to France and procured a match between Magdalen, the French king's daughter, and his master, and afterwards accompanied the king thither. He had also the keeping of Mary, Queen of Scots in his castle of Stirling; and notwithstanding all the endeavours of Henry the Eighth to get her out of his hands, carried her to France in 1548. It was now that his title to the earldom of Mar was confirm'd by the parliament, though they had been Lords Erskine for many years before. And it is remarkable, that when Queen Mary was brought to bed of James the Sixth, she immediately committed the infant to the care of the Earl of Mar, in the castle of Edinburgh; from whence all the endeavours of the Queen, and the Earl Bothwell, could never get him, till he set the crown upon the young infant's head. He was also Regent of the kingdom during that prince's minority, in the year 1593.[11] When King James the Sixth had Prince Henry, he committed him immediately to the care of the Earl of Mar, by the following letter, writ by his majesty's[l] own hand.

> My Lord of Mar,
> Because in the security of my son consisteth my security, I have concredid[12] to you the charge of his keeping, upon the trust I have in your honesty. This I command you out of my own mouth, being in the company of those I like, otherwise from any charge that can come from me, you shall not deliver him. And in case God call me at any time, see that neither for the Queen or estates, their pleasure, you deliver him, till he be eighteen years of age, and then he commands you himself.

On the king's accession to the throne of England, this noble lord was made Knight of the Garter, and Privy Counsellor of England, and Lord High Treasurer of Scotland. The present unhappy earl was early in the administration in the reign of Queen Anne; but being at the head of the fatal Rebellion to this nation, is now in exile in France.

From Alloway in four miles I arriv'd at Stirling. This is the great pass between the northern and the southern parts in Scotland, the River Forth being only passable here by a bridge of four arches.[13] Stirling is situated much like Edinburgh, with its castle on an eminence to the west, and the town running down the descent of the hill to the east. Besides the natural strength of this castle, on a high iron rock, it is also fortified with batteries and ramparts on every side. King James the Fifth also built a noble palace here, adorn'd without with pillars finely engrav'd, and statues as big as the life at the top and bottom. In this palace is one apartment of six rooms of state, the noblest I ever saw in Europe, both for height,[m] length, and breadth.[14] And for the fineness of the carv'd work, in wainscot and on the ceiling, there's no apartment in Windsor or Hampton Court that comes near it. And at the top of this royal apartment, the late Earl of Mar, when he was governor, made a very convenient apartment of a dozen rooms of a floor, for the governors to lodge in.

Joining to the royal apartments afore-mention'd, is the Great Hall of Audience, roofed at the top with Irish oak, like that of Westminster Hall at London. And in the roof of the Presence Chamber are carv'd the heads of the kings and queens of Scotland. Under the castle, to the south, were very fine gardens, as under the terrace at Windsor, the vestiges of which are still very plain; and round the whole a spacious park wall'd round. There is also in the castle a spacious chapel, its roof being supported without pillars. Architecture must certainly have been in great perfection in King James the Fifth's reign in this kingdom, and that prince must have had a good taste that way.

That Earl of Mar, who was a clergyman in the reign of King James the Fifth, and on the death of his two brothers quitted the church, and married, built a fine palace on the top of the hill, fronting the great market-place of Stirling, which is still a fine old building of hewn stone, adorn'd with pillars, and many statues at top and bottom, after the manner of the palace in the castle. He put several inscriptions on the doors of this palace, still extant. On the gate of the tower, on the right as you enter, is:

The more I stand in open height,
My faults more subject are to sight.

And over the great gate, on the inside of the court:

Speak furth, and spare nocht;
Consider well, I care nocht.

I suppose, alluding to the censures of the times, on his building this palace out of the stones of the dissolv'd Abbey of Cambuskenneth,[n] of which he had been prior when a clergyman. This palace, however, hath been seldom inhabited by any of the succeeding Earls of Mar; they being hereditary governors of the castle, always resided there when in Stirling, their usual residence being at Alloway.[15]

The market-place is spacious, with a handsome Town-House in it; and from the Earl of Mar's house, to the bottom of the town, may be about half an English mile, all upon a descent, with good houses. The Duke of Argyll hath also a fine seat near the castle, which his grandfather purchas'd from the family of Alexander, Earls of Stirling, and added two wings to it.[16] It consists of a pav'd court, between the body of the house and the two wings, with a very noble gate and ballustrades of stone, which forms the square. Although I shall not go to Inverary, his capital seat in Argyllshire, nor to Campbeltown in Kintyre, I know you will expect that I should say something of that noble family somewhere, and therefore I will take the liberty of doing it here.

The origin of the ancient and noble family of Argyll is not be to trac'd from history or tradition. The bards, in their ancient songs, mention them in the reign of Fergus the Second, in the year 404. In the reign of King Malcolm Canmore, was Duncan Campbell Lord of Lochow,[o] and was then called by the Irish, MacCallum[p] More. When King Edward the First of England came to Berwick in 1292, to decide the dispute between the Bruces and the Balliols, Sir Nial[q] Campbell of Lochow was one of the barons summon'd on the part of Robert Bruce; and was one of those that enter'd into an association to defend King Robert's right against all mortals. And in the reign of King James the Second, in 1457, one of his successors was created Earl of Argyll.[17] They were successively Lord High Chancellors of the kingdom, in the reigns of James the Third, Fourth, and Fifth; and by the last, hereditary Master of the Household; and were the first of their quality who embrac'd the Protestant religion at the beginning of the Reformation, and have firmly adher'd to it ever since. Archibald, Earl of Argyll was created a marquis by King Charles the First in the year 1641; but being a zealous asserter of the Presbyterian church government, and joining with Oliver Cromwell, he was found guilty of treason, by the first parliament after the Restoration of King Charles the Second, and beheaded at Edinburgh on the 27th of May, 1661.[18] However, King Charles the Second restor'd his son Archibald to the estate and title of earl; but he firmly adhering to the Protestant interest when the Duke of York was in Scotland, was also beheaded at Edinburgh, on the 30th Day of June, 1685, leaving this epitaph to be put upon his tomb-stone:

Thou, passenger, that shalt have so much time
To view my grave, and ask what was my crime:
No stain of error, no black vice's brand,

Did me compel to leave my native land:
Love to my country, truth condemn'd to dye,
Did force my hands forgotten arms to try.
More from friends' fraud my fall proceeded hath,
Than foes; tho' thrice they did attempt my death.
On my design tho' providence did frown,
Yet God at last will surely raise his own:
Another hand, with more successful speed,
Shall raise the remnant, bruise the serpent's head.

His son came over with King William, and was created a duke. The present duke, his son, was colonel of a regiment of foot when but seventeen years old. You knew him lead on the English at the Battle of Malplaquet. He was Lord High Commissioner to the parliament in Scotland when but twenty-three years of age. He is now Knight of the Garter, Duke of Greenwich in England; reduc'd the Rebellion in Scotland, was lately Lord High Steward to his majesty's household.[19]

From the castle of Stirling is a very beautiful prospect, of much more variety than that from Windsor. The windings of the River Forth from Stirling to Alloway, which is eighteen miles by water, and four by land, makes a beautiful part of the prospect; as doth the Forth to the ocean at thirty miles distance, and the castle of Edinburgh at twenty four. The prospect to the west is also very extensive through the country of Monteith, to the mountains of Argyllshire and Dumbartonshire. The Duke of Montrose is sheriff of this shire, and also hereditary sheriff of Dumbartonshire, and hath a great power and interest all over the neighbouring countries of Monteith and Lennox.[20] About half a mile from Stirling lies the ancient monastery of Cambuskeneth, where I saw the grave of King James the Third, under a hawthorn tree. It's now a heap of ruins, the stones being carried away by that Earl of Mar who turned Protestant at the Reformation, to build his fine palace at Stirling; and the superstitious people give that for the reason why that palace hath never had the luck to be inhabited.[21]

The Highland fair of Crieff[r] happening when I was at Stirling, I had the curiosity to go see it. There were at least thirty thousand cattle sold there, most of them to English drovers, who paid down above thirty thousand guineas in ready money to the highlanders; a sum they had never seen before, and proves one good effect of the Union.[22] The Highland gentlemen were mighty civil, dress'd in their slash'd short waistcoats, a trousing, (which is breeches and stockings of one piece of strip'd stuff) with a plaid for a cloak, and a blue bonnet. They have a poniard[s] knife and fork in one sheath hanging at one side of their belt, their pistol at the other, and their snuff-mill before; with a great broad-sword by their side. Their attendance were very numerous, all in belted plaids, girt like women's petticoats down to the knee, their thighs and half of the leg all bare. They had also each their broad-sword and poniard, and spake all Irish, an unintelligible language to the English. However, these poor creatures hir'd themselves out for a shilling a day, to drive the cattle to England, and to return home at their own charge. There was no leaving anything loose here, but it would have been stolen.[23]

I return'd by Sheriffmuir, where the battle was fought between the Duke of Argyll and the Earl of Mar (a strange piece of ground to draw up an army in), and took the little pleasant town of Dunblane[t] in my way. It's a perfect amphitheatre, in a pleasant bottom surrounded with hills, and was a bishopric in the time of episcopacy.

Mr. Callendar hath built a very neat seat at Crocsforth, on the declension of a mountain, on which he hath made a fine plantation of trees, with a spacious avenue of near half a mile down to the river.[24] From hence one hath a fine prospect to the castle of Doune through a fine valley to the west, and all Stirling Castle and town to the east. But the best prospect of Stirling is from the Abbey of Cambuskenneth, where may be seen every house in Stirling. Joining to the castle is a mountain call'd Bal'lengeich;[u] from whence K. James the Fifth took the title, when he made his nocturnal excursions, being called by his followers among the country people, Goodman of Bal'lengeich, goodman being the same as yeoman in England. And it is by this title that the Jacobites drink the Pretender's health among strangers.[25]

There is a very good church in Stirling, divided now into two, with a large churchyard fill'd with monuments, as in the other great towns of Scotland. Joining to this church, on the top of the hill, is a very neat hospital for decay'd merchants, after the manner of that at Dundee. It was founded by James Cowane,[v] merchant, and very richly endow'd. His statue, as big as the life, is at the top of the gate, with an inscription from the 25th of St. Matthew, the 35th verse. And in the garden of this hospital is a pleasant bowling green, for the use of the gentlemen and merchants.[26]

King Charles the First erected this town into an earldom in favour of a gentleman of the name of Alexander, a great projector for the plantations in America, who obtain'd the order of baronets to be instituted for Nova Scotia, to encourage the Scotch gentry to settle there, as the baronets of England were for the reduction of Ulster in Ireland.[27] This family hath no estate in Scotland, having transplanted themselves during the Civil War to Nova Scotia in America, from whence they were driven by the French. There is still a representative of them in England, who sends his proxy to Scotland at the election of the sixteen peers to sit in the Parliament of Great Britain.

There are several beautiful seats in the neighbourhood, and particularly that of Sir John Erskine of Alva, with fine avenues and vistas cut through his wood. He was in the Rebellion, but sav'd his estate by discovering to the government a silver mine in his lands, which produces a great deal of silver.[28] I must not forget the ancient seat of Elphinstone, a very noble old pile, standing on an eminence in the middle of a flat fine country, by the banks of the River Forth,[w] in full view of Stirling, belonging to the Lord Elphinstone. This family is very ancient as well as noble; for we find Sir William Elphinstone, of Elphinstone, slain in the Battle of Piperdean,[x] in 1436. They were created Lords Elphinstone by King James the Fourth; and one of them was Lord High Treasurer of Scotland in the reign of King James the Sixth, in 1599. The present lord commanded a company in Flanders, and in Ireland; and is a very industrious worthy nobleman, carrying on his coal-works, and other improvements, to great advantage.[29]

There was a concert of music when I was at Stirling, where the ladies from the neighbourhood made a very good appearance. The young gentlemen, in every thing, imitate the French, and have a hauteur, which makes good the French saying, *fier comme une Ecossais*. Their education being in France, and the title of laird (like marquis in France) being their general appellation, gives them these French airs.

Letter XI

EDINBURGH

Sir,

From Stirling, I proceeded down the south side of the Firth, as I had ascended the north side, and in six miles arrived at Falkirk, a clean market town belonging to the Livingstones, Earls of Lithgow. On my road near a village called St. Ringin remains the stone in which King Robert Bruce's standard was fixed, at the famous Battle of Bannockburn,[a] when the English, after many scuffles, were entirely drove out of Scotland, in the beginning of Edward the Second, of England. This parish of St. Ringins is the largest I have heard of, containing above ten thousand inhabitants; and at a sacrament will have seven thousand communicants. A few miles beyond Falkirk is the ancient seat of Callendar, belonging to the Earl of Lithgow, which being forfeited in the late Rebellion, now belongs to the York Buildings Company.[1]

In two miles more I arrived at the ancient town of Lithgow, where the kings of Scotland have a sumptuous and noble palace. This palace consists of two courts: on the gate of the outer court are the arms of Scotland, incircled with the four Orders of the Garter, St. Andrew, St. Michael, and the Golden Fleece, of all which Orders James the Fifth was Companion. On the left of this court were the offices, and on the right the chapel or church of St. Michael. The inner court is a spacious square, larger than the inner court at Hampton Court, with a fine tower at each of the four corners and, in the middle, the beautifulest fountain in the world. It's after the shape of an imperial crown, adorn'd with statues and other fine carved work, each statue pouring forth water into a cistern below them. This seems to have been the work of King James the Fifth, for the arms of Scotland and France, in one escutcheon, are upon the fountain.[2]

The apartment to the south of this square is a large guard-chamber, and Hall of Audience, which joins to the parliament hall, which makes the whole front to the east; and on the north and west were the royal apartments. These were rebuilt by King James the Sixth, and First of England; and there are still a dozen rooms to the north in good repair, where the Earl of Lithgow, as hereditary keeper, used to reside. Behind these apartments are fine green walks which reach down to the lake, which gives a noble beauty to the palace, and runs the whole length of the town.

It was in this palace that King James the Fifth, in imitation of the kings of England and France, called a chapter of the worthiest amongst his nobility, and added a collar of thyme and rue to his Order of St. Andrew, ordering the thistle to be wore on their mantles, in the centre of the cross; and changed the motto from *en defance*, to *nemo me impune lacessit*; and ordered a throne and twelve stalls to be erected in St. Michael's Church for the sovereign and twelve knights of his Order, where their banners were to be hung up, as in France and England. But that king's sudden death, after the Battle of Solway, and the troubles that follow'd after, put an end to his noble views, and indeed to the Order, till James the Seventh revived it in a blue ribbon, and Queen Anne restored it to the green; but the knights have as yet no chapel or hall for their banners.[3]

The town of Lithgow is above half a mile long, consisting of one good street, well built; and in the market-place is a fountain, in imitation of that in the palace, and runs in so many different places, that a dozen may be served at once. The Town-House adjoining is a very beautiful piece of modern architecture; and the whole town hath a good face of business.[4] This town gives the title of earl to the ancient family of Livingstone. We find Thurstanus, Lord of Livingstone, in the reign of David the First; and, in the seventeenth of King David the Second, Sir William Livingstone had a grant of the Barony of Callendar.[b] He was also one of the commissioners appointed to treat with England for the redemption of that King David, taken at the Battle of Durham; which having effected on the 3d of October, 1357 for one hundred thousand marks sterling, he deliver'd his son for one of the hostages for payment. Alexander, his son, was also one of the hostages for the ransom of King James the First, in 1423, and by the three estates of parliament appointed governor of the young King James the Second.

This family hath continued, in all succeeding kings' reigns, in great power, both at court and country. Alexander, Lord Livingstone, had the honour of educating the Princess Elizabeth, grandmother to our present King George; and carried that princess from Linlithgow to London, with a retinue suitable to her birth and dignity, at his own charges; and was created, in 1600, Earl of Linlithgow, and his brother, Sir James, Earl of Callendar.[5] The Earl of Linlithgow was Commander in Chief of the forces, in the reign of King Charles the Second, and Lord Justice General, and his son Captain of the Horse Guards, in the reign of King James the Seventh. The late earl, now abroad with the Pretender, was one of the sixteen peers to the Parliament of Great Britain in Queen Anne's reign, [and] was with my Lord Mar in the Rebellion. His estate was bought by the York Buildings Company, and the keeping of the palace of Linlithgow given to the Duke of Montrose.

From Linlithgow, in two little miles, I came to Kinneil,[c] a seat belonging to the Duke of Hamilton. It's finely wooded, and its gardens pretty well kept; but being the jointure-house of the present duchess, who resides generally about London, it is not quite in so good order as otherwise it might. Joining to it is the town of Boroughstoness,[d] belonging also to the duke. This town consists of one good street and long, like Kirkcaldy in Fife. It was the town of greatest trade with Holland before the Union, of any town in Scotland; but now this kingdom being supplied with all these commodities, without paying any duty, directly from England, this town is much decayed in trade, although they have still a good export in coals and salt.[6]

Two little miles further is the castle of Blackness, a state prison, being a peninsula, and built exactly like a great ship unrigg'd. It's a safe prison, but could not hold out long against cannon.[7] And in two miles further I arrived at Hopetoun, the fine seat of the Earl of Hopetoun. This palace was built some years ago of fine freestone, exactly after the model of the house of Kinross; but my lord is now adding two semicircular wings of four storeys high to the front, adorn'd with pillars and which, when finished, will be by much the finest seat in Britain. You enter it from a vestibule, supported with pillars, into a large hall, floored with marble, from whence runs of each side to the front a drawing-room, dining-room, bed-chamber and closet. And behind this hall, fronting the garden is a spacious saloon, with the same site of rooms. The stair-case is in the middle between the hall and saloon, and is finely adorned with the history of the heathen gods, done at Antwerp, and put into panels from top to bottom. [8] In the great dining-room are a great many family pictures; and over the chimney Noah and his family offering up sacrifice for their deliverance in the ark, a fine picture done at Rome by Giuseppe[e] Chiari.

The court-yard is collonaded,[f] and adorn'd with statues and vases; but since the building the two wings, the court is to be extended to the breadth of them, and proportionably longer. The parterre fronting the saloon is longer than that at Cannons, and like it hath a large basin of water at bottom. It's also adorned with a multitude of statues on pedestals, as at Cannons; but the views here are prodigiously more extensive. From the terrace to the north of this parterre is the finest view I ever saw anywhere; far beyond Frascati[g] near Rome, or St. Michael del Bosco, near Bologna,[h] for variety. Looking to the east you see all the islands of the Firth to its mouth; all the towns on the coast of Fife and Lothian as far as St. Andrews one way, and North-Berwick the other. Looking to the west you see all the rest of the Firth, Stirling and its castle, with the mountains of Perthshire, and Argyllshire; and looking north you have Dunfermline, and all the country round it, full in view, the Firth lying under you like a pond, which is here about two miles broad. There are also several vistas from each of the many walks that run from this parterre; some of them ending in a parish church, some in an old tower. And through the great avenue fronting the palace, your view terminates on North-Berwick Law, near the Bass, at thirty miles distance, appearing like a sugar-loaf.

This fine palace and garden lies in the middle of a spacious park, well stock'd with deer, environ'd with a stone wall. To the south of the great avenue lies the kitchen-garden; and joining to it a house and walk for pheasants, and a plantation for other fowls and beasts; and under his great terrace there is a bed of oysters, from whence his kitchen is supplied all the year round, in the greatest quantities. This family of Hopetoun was very considerable in the law in King James the First and King Charles the First's reigns. The present lord's father was drowned in the *Gloucester* Frigate, accompanying the Duke of York to Scotland, and the son was created earl by Queen Anne.[10]

A mile beyond Hopetoun lies a good town, called the Queen's Ferry, from Queen Margaret and Queen Magdalen's landing there. And in a mile further I got to Craigiehall,[i] a neat seat of Johnstone, Marquis of Annandale. It's Kinross House in miniature and would be a fine seat if it was not so near to Hopetoun, as Heythrop[j] in Oxfordshire, if it were not so near Blenheim. There is a vast deal of regular planting round it, with very good gardens.[11]

This family of Johnstone are very ancient in Annandale, and very powerful in the borders, of which they have been often wardens. They were called to the peerage by King Charles the First on the 20th of June 1633; and in 1643 created Earls of Hatfield, which title they changed for Annandale at the Restoration; and by King William was created a marquis, had the Order of St. Andrew from Queen Anne, and was one of the sixteen peers in the first parliament of King George, and Keeper of the Great Seal. The present marquis is a hopeful nobleman, just returned from his travels.[12]

A mile further lies the fine seat of Barnton, belonging to Hamilton, Earl of Raglan,[k] brother to the late Duke Hamilton, and to the Earls of Orkney and Selkirk; and between Barnton and the sea, and Barnton and Edinburgh, are very many pretty little seats, particularly Barnbougle,[l] surrounded with the sea, as Blackness, and furnished with a fine collection of pictures by Primrose, Earl of Rosebury, who was Gentleman of the Bedchamber to Prince George of Denmark, and one of the sixteen peers in the reign of Queen Anne.[13] He is a *bon vivant*, and a fine gentleman. And now I am returned from the north of Scotland, you will expect, before I proceed westward, that I should give you some account of the government and policy of this kingdom, and wherein it differs from England, being in the metropolis, where the chief courts of justice are kept.

Know then, that in Scotland, besides the two hereditary officers of the crown, the Earl of Erroll, Lord High Constable, and the Earl Marischal, Lord High Marischal, there were eight officers of state, who by their offices were Members of Parliament and Privy Council, whether peers or not. The four principal were:

The Lord High Chancellor,
Lord High Treasurer,
Lord Privy Seal, and the
Lord-Secretary.

The inferior were:

Lord Register, or Keeper of the Records, who was also Clerk of the Crown in Parliament;

Lord Advocate, or Attorney-General;

Lord Treasurer-Depute, or Chancellor of the Exchequer;

and Lord Justice Clerk, or *Justiciarius Clerici*, who judges criminal causes.

Since the Union, the offices of High Treasurer and Treasurer-Depute are suppress'd, and in their room, a Chief Baron, and other Barons of the Exchequer, establish'd after the manner of England, before whom all causes between the Crown and the subject, in relation to the revenue, are tried. The chief court of judicature now in Scotland for all civil matters is the College of Justice, or Lords of the Session. They consist of a President and fourteen judges, first established by King James the Fifth on his return from France, in imitation of the parliament of Paris; and they wear when on the bench, purple and scarlet gowns. They sit on a bench, in a semicircle, with their President in the middle, and seven on each hand of him. The king usually adds three to their number out of the young nobility, to instruct them in the laws of their country, who are called Extraordinary Lords, and who also have votes in the determination of all causes, by an Act of Parliament made in the reign of King James the Fifth, *anno* 1532. This court hath also six clerks, who are also called Clerks of Session. They sit from the first of November to the last of February; and from the first of June to the last of July. These judges are not peers, yet have the appellation of lords. They give judgement according to the Acts of Parliament, municipal laws and, where they are defective, by the civil law. There is also a court for criminal causes, called the Justiciary, where the Lord Justice Clerk presides, to whom is joined five Lords of the Session, named by the king, who are call'd Lords of the Justiciary, and go their circuits round the shires of the country, as in England. In this court the defendants are allowed counsel[m] to plead for them.

In the outer house there is a bench where one of the senators sits a week (and all of them except the President have their turns in it), who hears all causes originally, and where the case is clear, gives sentence. But if it be difficult, or either party desires it, he reports it to the other senators, who either send out their answer by him, or order it to be heard at their bar in the inner house. This is a court of great dispatch; but besides the judge upon the bench, there is a side-bar, where a judge weekly receives and answers all bills and petitions.

In England the sheriffs of shires are appointed by the king, and are only executioners of the law; but here the sheriffs of shires are generally hereditary offices in great families, who by their deputies hold courts and are judges in all causes in their shire, but appealable to the Lords of the Session; as also from that court to the House of Peers of Great Britain, who are now the dernier resort of the dominion of Great Britain. Instead of the English Doctors' Commons, they have here commissary courts for confirmation and proving of wills and testaments, and of divorces, and other ecclesiastical causes, which courts are in all the counties of the kingdom. There are also Courts of Regalty and Barony, within several lords' lands, from whence, however, one may appeal to the House of Peers.

The degrees of nobility are the same with England; only the eldest son of a baron is called Master of the same title with his father; and the baronets are of Nova Scotia, as those of England are of Ulster. In England, every shoemaker or taylor is called Master before his Christian name; but here none are so but such as have been graduated Master of Arts of the University; of which there are so many that Mr. John, or Mr. James, is as contemptible here as a common curate of a cathedral is in Italy.

The names of the hundred and fourteen kings of Scotland:[14]

Fergus.
Feritharis.
Meinus.
Dornadilla.
Nothatus.
Rutherus.
Reutha.
Thereus.
Josma.
Finnanus.
Durstus.
Evenus I.
Gillus Nothus.
Evenus II.
Evenus III.
Metellanus.
Caractacus.
Corbredus I.
Dardanus.
Corbredus Galdus II.
Luctacus.
Moggaldus.
Conarus.
Ethodius I.
Satrael.
Donald I.
Ethodius II.
Athirco.

Ederus.
Findoch.
Donald II.
Donald III.
Crathilinthus.
Fincormach.
Romachus.
Angus, or Aeneas.
Fethelmachus.
Eugene I.
Fergus II.
Eugene II.
Dongardus.
Constantine I.
Congallus I.
Coranus.
Eugene III.
Congallus II.
Kinnatallus.
Lidanus.
Kenneth.
Eugene IV.
Ferchard I.
Donald IV.
Ferchard II.
Malduin.
Eugene V.
Eugene VI.
Amberkelethus.
Eugene VII.
Murdoch.
Etfinus.
William I.
Alexander II.
Alexander III.
John Balliol.
Robert Bruce.
David Bruce.
Edward Balliol.
Robert Stewart.
Robert III. or
John Farneyar.
James I.
James II.

Natholocus.
Eugene VIII.
Fergus III.
Solvathius.
Acajus.
Congallus.
Dongallus.
Alpin
Kenneth II.
Donald V.
Constantine II.
Ethus.
Gregory.
Donald VI.
Constantine III.
Malcolm I.
Indolph.
Duff.
Colin.
Kenneth III.
Constantine IV.
Greme.
Malcolm II.
Duncan I.
Macbeth.
Malcolm III.
Donald Bane.
Duncan II.
Edgar.
Alexander I.
David I.
Malcolm IV.
James III.
James IV.
James V.
Mary.
James VI.
Charles I.
Charles II.
James VII.
William and Mary.
Anne.
George.

The nobility of Scotland, with the titles of their eldest sons.[15]

This peerage is now represented in the British Parliament by the following sixteen:

Duke of Montrose.	Earl of Findlater.
Duke of Roxburgh.	Earl of Orkney.
Marq. of Tweeddale.	Earl of Selkirk.
Earl of Sutherland.	Earl of Delorain.
Earl of Buchan.	Earl of Stair.
Earl of Haddington.	Earl of Bute.
Earl of Loudon.	Earl of Hopetoun.
Earl of Islay.	Earl of Aberdeen.

The Scots have been very zealous asserters of whatever religion they profess'd. In times of popery, besides two archbishops, and twelve suffragan bishops, there were no less than one and thirty abbacies, and thirty-seven priories, whose abbots and priors had seats in parliament. At the Reformation they ran[n] into the same zeal for the Calvinistical doctrine from Geneva, and pulled down all those abbies and priories, and every thing that savoured of superstition, and establish'd a church government of provincial assemblies which, being divided into presbyteries, is the present government of the Church of Scotland. There are fifteen provincial assemblies; each of which consists of six or eight presbyteries; and the presbyteries also consist of so many parishes.

King James and King Charles the First, with much ado, establish'd episcopacy again in Scotland, and it continued all the reign of King Charles the Second; but at the Revolution presbytery took place again.[16] There are twenty-two commissary courts belonging to these presbyteries. Church censures are said to be very severe here, but I perceiv'd the poor only suffered by them. For a piece of money will save a man here from the stool of repentance, as much as in England. Most of those I saw expos'd in the churches, were for lying together before marriage, which the Minister of Dunfermline said was become an universal custom. And indeed he was severer upon the poor man and his wife, than upon one that stood at the same time for notorious adultery.

Altho' presbytery is the established religion of the country, yet the gentry are not generally of the principal, especially on the north of the River Tay. And at Edinburgh there are more episcopal meetings than churches, the gentry of this nation having more extended notions of religion than to be confined within the narrow bounds of presbytery. However, the clergy are better respected than the inferior clergy in England, even in those counties where the gentry don't go to hear them.

The Herald's-Office is kept with a great deal of regularity at Edinburgh. There is an exact register where every gentleman may go to be informed of his family and arms; and according to the ancient rules of chivalry, no gentleman's person can be seized even for debt, but by an officer from this office. The King at Arms for Scotland is Lyon, as Garter is for England, and is called Lord Lyon, and weareth the Arms of Scotland on a medal hung to a chain as the badge of his office. Under him are heralds [and] pursuivants, by whom all public proclamations are made, and messengers who execute all warrrants for debt. The heralds' designations are: Ross, Albany, Rothsay, Islay, Snowdon, Marchmont; and those of the pursuivants are: Dingwall, Unicorn, Carrick, Bute, Ormond, Kintyre.[17]

There is no nation where the title of lord is so much prostituted as in Scotland. In England a peer's title as well as person is sacred; even the judges there are but justices, and are call'd Mr. Justice, by surname; but here every person that sits upon a bench is called My Lord. The senators of the College of Justice, or Lords of Session, are not only lords upon the bench, but are called so in all deeds and society, not by their names, but their titles, as a peer is. I met a gentleman in the street of Edinburgh that I had known abroad by the name of Calderwood; and asking if that was not Mr. Calderwood, they said no, it was my Lord Polton. I asked how he came to be a peer. They said he was a Lord of the Sessions, who are all designed by their mansion-houses.[18] Every provost, or mayor of a borough, is also My Lord Provost, during his mayoralty, which I take to be dishonour to the peerage.

I know you will be surprised if I should leave Edinburgh, and give you no account of the regalia; but I must tell you, that the crown, sceptre, and sword of state of Scotland are not to be seen, as the regalia of England are in the Tower of London. These are kept in a vaulted room in the castle of Edinburgh, into which even bombs cannot penetrate, under six locks and keys, kept by the High Constable, the High-Marischal, and the other officers of the Crown. But as these are dispers'd, and some of them with the Pretender, there is no coming at the sight of these regalia; and it's a pity, considering that the kingdoms of Scotland and England are now indented into that of Great Britain, that such ensigns of grandeur and antiquity should lie buried in a vault, and not make a part of that noble solemnity, the coronation of the kings of Great Britain.[19] However, since I could not see them, I will give you their description, as I had it from the Herald's Office, and from some persons of worth, who, during the sitting of the Scots parliaments, had them under their care. For you must know, that since the kings of Scotland came to the throne of England, although the king could not be personally present in the Scottish parliament, the regalia were always brought thither, and lay upon a crimson velvet cushion on the table, where the Lord Register and other clerks sat; and every Act of Parliament, before it went into a law, was touched by the royal sceptre.

The first crown they had in Scotland, was a circle of gold, given by the pope to King Caractacus, for his zeal for the Christian religion, in imitation of the circle bore by the ancient Roman emperors.[20] Charles le Mayne added another with flower-de-luces to King Achaius, as a token that France would always support the Scotch nation.[21] But it was not till the reign of that fine prince, King James the Fifth, that in imitation of France and England, it was closed with a globe, and a cross a-top. As it now is, take the following description.

The imperial crown of Scotland is of pure gold, enriched with many precious stones, diamonds, pearls, and curious enamellings. The form of it is thus: first, it is composed of a large broad circle, or fillet (which goes round the head), adorn'd with twenty-two large precious stones, *viz.* topazes, amethysts, garnets, emeralds, rubies, hyacinths, in collets of gold of various forms, with curious enamellings; and betwixt each of these collets and stones, are placed great oriental pearls, one of which is wanting. Secondly, above the great circle there is another small one form'd with twenty points, adorn'd with the like number of diamonds and sapphires[o] alternately, and on each point there is a great pearl. Thirdly, the upper circle is heightned with ten crosses floree, each being adorn'd in the centre with a great diamond, betwixt four large pearls put crosswise, but some of the pearls are wanting;

and the number extant upon the upper part of the crown, besides what are in the under circle, and in the cross-patee, are fifty-one; and those crosses-floree are interchanged with ten high flower-de-luces alternately betwixt the great pearls below, on the points of the second circle.

This is said to have been the form of the crown of Scotland, since the league made betwixt Achaius of Scotland and Francis the Great of France. It differs from other imperial crowns, in that it is heighten'd with crosses-floree, alternately with flower-de-luces, whereas the crown of France is heighten'd only with flower-de-luces, and that of England with crosses-patee, alternatively with flower-de-luces. The Scotch crown, since King James the Sixth went to England, has been ignorantly represented by herald-painters, engravers, and others, after the form of the crown of England, with crosses-patee; whereas there is not one cross-patee, save that on the top of the globe, for all the rest are crosses-floree, such as we see on our old coins and churches. Those crowns were not anciently arched or close. Charles the Eighth is said to be the first king of France who wore a close crown; as appears by his medals coined in the year 1495, wherein he is called *Imperator Orientis*. Edward the Fifth of England, in the year 1483, is observed by Selden to have carried a close crown.[22]

Fourthly, the Scotch crown is thus closed: from the upper circle proceed four arches, adorn'd with enamelled figures, which meet and close at the top, surmounted with a celestial globe of gold, enamelled with blue semee, or powder'd with stars, cross'd and enamell'd with a large cross-patee on the top, adorned in the extremities with great pearls (such a cross tops the church of Holyrood House), and canton'd with other four in the angles. In the centre of the cross-patee, on the fore-part of the crown, there is a square amethyst, and on the other side of the cross there is a great pearl, and below it on the foot of the polar part of the cross are these letters, J.R.V., by which it would appear that King James the Fifth was the first that closed the crown with arches, and topp'd it with a globe and cross-patee. Yet it is evident that the money and medals coin'd in the reigns of King James the Third and Fourth, have a close crown. And it is no less clear that the arches of the crown were not put there from the beginning, or at the making of the crown, because first they are joined with tacks of gold to the ancient crown; and secondly, the workmanship of the arch is not so good. And there is a small distinction in the fineness betwixt the first and last, the latter being superfine gold, and the other not so exactly to that standard; whereof trial has been made.

Fifthly, the tiara, or bonnet of the crown, was of purple velvet; but in the year 1685, there was put in a cap of crimson velvet, adorn'd, as before, with four plates of gold, richly wrought and enamell'd, and on each of them a great pearl, half an inch in diameter, which appears between the four arches, and the cap is faced with ermine. Upon the lowest circle of the crown, immediately above the ermine, there are eight small holes, two and two together, in the four quarters of the crown, in the middle space betwixt the arches, to which there are tied two diamonds and precious stones. The crown is nine inches diameter, being twenty-seven inches about; and in height from the under circle to the top of the cross-patee, six inches and a half. It always stands on a square cushion of crimson velvet, adorn'd with fringes, and four tassels[p] of gold thread hanging down at each corner.

The Sceptre

The stem or stalk of the sceptre being silver double overgilt, is two foot long, of a hexagon form, with three buttons or nobs of the same. Betwixt the first button and second is the handle of a hexagon form, furling on the middle and plain; betwixt the second button and third there are three sides engraven. Upon that under the Virgin Mary (one of the statues on the top of the stem), there's the letter J, upon the second side under St. James, the letter R, and on the third under St. Andrew, the figure five. On the side betwixt the J and the R there are engraven fourteen flower-de-luces; and on the side betwixt the figure 5 and letter J there are ten thistles continued from one stem, from the third button to the capital. The three sides under the statues are plain, and on the other three there are antique engravings, *viz.* sacramental cups, antique Medusa's heads, and rullion foliages. Upon the top of the stem there is an antique capital of leaves emboss'd upon the abacus of which there arise round the stem three statues: first, that of the Blessed Virgin, crowned with an open crown, holding in her right arm our Blessed Saviour, and in her left hand a globe with a cross; next to her on her right hand stand the statue of St. Andrew, in an apostolical garment, and on his head a Scotch bonnet, holding in his right hand a cross, or saltire (part of which is broke off) and in his left hand raised up, there's an open book. On the Blessed Virgin's left hand, and St. Andrew's right, there's another statue, which seems to represent St. James with the like apostolical garment, with a hanging neck superadded, and upon his head a little hat like the Roman *pilium*; in his right hand, half extended, a book open, and in his left a pastoral staff (the head broke off); and above each statue being two inches and a half (except the Virgin Mary's, which is a little less), the finishing of a gothic niche.[q] Betwixt each statue arise a rullion, in form of a dolphin, very distinct, in length four inches, with foliage along the body, their heads upwards, and fronted inwards; and the turning of their tail ending in a rose, or cinquefoil outward. Above these rullions and statues stand another hexagon, button or nob, with oak-leaves under every corner; and above it a crystal globe of two inches and a fourth part of an inch diameter, within three bars, jointed above, where it is surmounted with six rullions, and here again with an oval globe, topp'd with an oriental pearl, of half an inch diameter. The whole sceptre, in length, is thirty-four inches.

The Sword

The sword is five foot long; the handle and pummel are of silver gilt, in length fifteen inches. The pummel is round, and somewhat flat on the two sides; on the middle of each, there is a garland of embossed work, and in the centre there have been two enamelled plates, which are broke off. The traverse, or cross, of the sword is silver gilt, seventeen and a half Inches long. The form of it is like two dolphins, their heads joining, and their tails ending in acorns. The shell hangs down towards the point of the sword, form'd like an escallop flourish'd (or rather like a green oak-leaf); on the blade of the sword there's indented with gold, Julius II. P. The scabbard is of crimson velvet, covered with silver gilt, and wrought in filagree[r] work into branches of oak, with leaves and acorns. On the scabbard there are four round plates of silver gilt; two of them, near the chape, are enamell'd blue; and thereon in golden characters, *Julius II. Pon. MAX. N.*[23] At the mouth of the scabbard, opposite to the hook, there's a large square plate of silver, enamell'd purple, in a cartouch azure, an oak-tree eradicate and fructivate or. and above the cartouch the papal ensign; *viz.* two keys in saltire argent[s] (three bowls form'd like roses, or cinquefoils) tied with trappings, and hanging down at each side of the cartouch. Above the keys is the papal tiara, environed with three crowns, and two labels turn'd up with crosses.

There is no nation where a man hath fairer play for his liberty, than in Scotland. Here are no sheriff's officers and marshal's men that will whip you off the street at London, and run you into a spunging-house at once; but here if you owe money, you are summon'd to show cause why you don't pay it, which if you don't do, you have six days allow'd you before a caption comes out against your person; which is executed by these messengers only, who are all put in by the Lord Lyon, and wear a greyhound on a green ribbon, as a badge, when they are in the execution of their office.[24]

The ladies dress as in England, with this difference, that when they go abroad, from the highest to the lowest, they wear a plaid, which covers half of the face, and all their body. In Spain, Flanders, and Holland, you know the women go all to church and market with a black mantle over their heads and body; but these in Scotland are all strip'd with green, scarlet, and other colours, and most of them lin'd with silk; which in the middle of church, on a Sunday, looks like a *parterre de fleurs*.

I have been at several concerts of music, and must say that I never saw in any nation an assembly of greater beauties than those I have seen at Edinburgh. The ladies are particular in a stately firm way of walking, with their joints extended and their toes out. But I cannot say that the common people are near so clean or handsome as the English. The young ladies are all bred good housewives; and the servant-maids are always kept at some work here. The spinning-wheels, both for woollen and linen, are always going in most houses; and a gentleman of a good estate is not asham'd to wear a suit of clothes[t] of his lady's and servant's spinning. They make a great deal of linen all over the kingdom, not only for their own use, but export it to England and to the plantations. In short, the women are all kept employ'd, from the highest to the lowest of them.

But the men here are not so usefully employ'd as in England. There the production of every county is improv'd by joint stocks amongst the inhabitants of the several counties. Iron-works, lead-works, manufactories, and every thing else that may conduce to the common welfare of the nation, are set on foot, and carry'd on. But here, altho' their rivers plentifully abound with salmon for exportation, their coasts with white fish and herrings, more than any other in Europe; yet the gentry, or landed men, never concern themselves about it as a thing below them; and leave those improvements to burghers of towns, who, for want of a sufficient stock, are not able to carry it on. Indeed, the nobility have of late run into parking, planting, and gardening, which are great improvements of their estates; but what is this to the bulk of a nation which (if encourag'd) hath as many natural commodities for exportation as any whatsoever, and more than South-Britain? But a finer education than what is necessary for trade hath been, in imitation of the French, the misfortune of this kingdom; but perhaps the Union with England may open their eyes to their own interest.[25]

The language of the low countries of Scotland is the same with that which is spoken all over England; only an Englishman will understand a Scotchman better by his writing than speaking; for the difference in the pronunciation of the vowels, which are the same in writing, make a great alteration in speaking. The Scots pronounce the five vowels, a, e, i, o, u, just as the French, Germans, and Italians do; and the English, according to that pronunciation, make them ae, i y, o, u. This difference of sound in the vowels makes a great one in the pronunciation.

The highlanders have a language of their own, which the Irish own to be the purest of that Irish which they spoke[u] in the province of Ulster in Ireland; which is also spoken in the greatest purity in the Western Islands that lie between Scotland and Ireland. They being an unmix'd people have preserv'd that language and the dress better than the Irish have done, who have been over-run with Danes, English, &c.

Letter XII

GLASGOW

Sir,

In my progress to the west, I would not go the direct road because I had taken Linlithgow and a great part of it in my return from Stirling. I therefore went by the skirts of that wild country, call'd Crawford-Moor, where I saw the ancient castle of Crawford, which gives the title of earl to the noble family of Lindsay;[a] though their residence hath been at the Struthers in Fife for many centuries; and where, and in Angus and Perthshire, are many eminent branches of this family living, particularly at Eulik.[1]

The first was Sir James Lindsay, son by a daughter of Walter, great Steward of Scotland who was created Earl of Crawford by his uncle Robert, the first Stuart king of Scotland; and they have been great men in all reigns since. One of them was hostage for King James the First; others Master of the Household and Lord-Chamberlain to King James the Second and Third; kill'd at the Battle of Flodden with K. James the Fourth; zealous for the Reformation; Lord High Treasurer at the Restoration of K. Charles the Second; President to the Convention of Estates, and President of the Council at the Revolution.[2]

Near these parts lie also the seats of the Lords Somerville and Carnwath, the former an ancient Norman family, who have been long considerable in Scotland, for William de Somerville is a witness to a grant of King David the First to the monks of Melrose. The Lord Carnwath's estate was forfeited in the late Rebellion.[3] And on the banks of the River Douglas is a pretty spot, call'd Douglas Dale, where stands the ancient paternal seat of the old family of Douglas, Dukes of Douglas. This family is certainly the most renown'd of any subject's family in Europe; where there is not a kingdom but their name is known, and some of their great actions recorded.[4] They have often marry'd the daughters of their kings; and were sometimes too great for subjects, by the vast number of their vassals, and often suffer'd for it. Yet the kings had that regard for the family that it was never extinguish'd. They have enjoy'd this country of Douglasdale without interruption, ever since the year 770. Sir James Douglas was the constant companion of K. Robert Bruce in all his atchievements. And that king having made a vow to visit the Holy Land, but death seizing him, he engaged his friend, the Lord Douglas, to carry his heart to Jerusalem, which accordingly he did. And his servant who carried the box was called Lock-heart; a good family in this country to this day, who give for their arms a heart within a padlock, as does the Duke of Douglas, a heart with an imperial crown.[5]

To give you the particular history of this noble family would be too long for a letter; but there is a folio history of this family, written by Mr. Hume of Godscraft, to which I refer you. I will only add, that about the reign of King David the Second, there were six earls of the name of Douglas, *viz.* Douglas, Angus, Ormond, Wigtown, Moray, and Morton; and there are now the Duke of Douglas, Duke of Queensberry, the Earls of Morton, Dumbarton, and March, and Lords Mordington; the worthy unhappy Earl of Forfar, the second branch of the family, being kill'd at the Battle of Sheriffmuir who, if he had liv'd, had equal'd any of his great progenitors.

This gentleman you knew in Flanders, lieutenant-colonel to the Black Scotch regiment of dragoons, and afterwards colonel to an old regiment of foot, in the reign of Queen Anne. He was declared envoy-extraordinary to the king of Prussia by King George; when the Rebellion breaking out in his native country, he desired leave to go down and serve there, although his regiment was in England; and commanding as brigadier, at the head of Morrison's[b] regiment, the colonel being absent, he was, after being taken prisoner, stabb'd by the highlanders in nineteen several places, because he was a Douglas; for the family, although they have often suffer'd by the Stuarts, never suffer'd for them.[6] He carried in his crest a hand holding a scymiter with this motto, *manus haec inimica tyrannis*; and it's remarkable, that in all the numerous family of Douglas, never one was engaged in all the plots for the Pretender. The present duke appears very hearty on all occasions for the

Protestant interest, and was a volunteer at the Battle of Sheriffmuir, but hath too great a spirit to court ministries.[7]

The castle of Douglas being built many hundred years ago, and having receiv'd frequent additions, cannot be suppos'd to be very regular; but as it is, is a very august noble pile, with its large park and gardens. Yet I think the house of Dudhope near Dundee, of which I gave you an account from thence, is a much finer situation, and belongs to his grace.[8] A little way from this is the town of Lanark,[c] the capital of the shire of Clydesdale, which being an inland town, is of no great signification; and in eight miles further I arriv'd at Hamilton.

The palace of Hamilton lieth in a fertile fine plain, between a great park of six or seven miles in circumference, walled round, and a lesser park behind the gardens, both well wooded and water'd, the great park having a river running through its middle and extremely well stock'd with deer. The great courtyard before the house is spacious, and to be ballustraded with iron, between pillars of stone, as that of Dalkeith is; and behind is a noble parterre, adorned with statues; and lower, spacious bounds for a canal and fish-ponds, with large gardens on each side, and at the bottom a fine park. The palace is designed to be a Roman H, but the two wings to the front are only finish'd; those to the garden are left till the duke is of age. The body of the front is very handsome, being adorned with pillars and pilasters of the Corinthian order, but it is not near eighty foot broad, while the wings are one hundred and fifty long. This I thought very preposterous, and makes it look like Greenwich hospital; but when the other part of the house is finished it will not appear so. It is built of the whitest freestone I ever saw; it looks like marble. The royal apartments in this palace, consisting of a dining-room, drawing-room, bed-chamber, dressing-room, and closet, are extremely well finished, with marble chimney-pieces and carv'd-work.[9] In the drawing-room are the pictures of Duke William Hamilton and his Duchess, with their six sons; *viz.* the late Earl of Arran, the Earl of Selkirk, the Earl of Orkney, the Earl of Ruglen, Lord Basil, and Lord Archibald Hamilton, in half lengths, done by Sir Godfrey Kneller; and in the closet are a vast quantity of very good pictures of the court of K. Charles the First.[10]

On the great stair-case joining to this apartment is a long and spacious gallery, finely lined with oak, and filled with an incomparable collection of pictures: Daniel in the Lion's Den, by Van Dyck is a masterly piece, and takes up one end of the room; the Marriage of Canaa, by Tintoretto,[d] which contains more figures than that celebrated one of Paul Veronese, in St George's at Venice, is also a masterly piece. There is a fine whole length of Fielding, Earl of Denbigh, going a shooting, with a blackamore boy showing him his game, done by Van Dyck; as also a whole length of Duke James Hamilton, that was beheaded; and of the Marquis of Hamilton, who was steward of the household, by the same hand as it is at Hampton Court. There are a great many other good pictures, and not one bad one.[11]

The offices of this palace join the town, which is the neatest and best pav'd I have seen, the houses being built of freestone, supported by pillars, and is larger than most of your boroughs-royal. Joining to the great park is a very romantick garden, call'd Baroncleuth,[e] which consists of seven hanging terrace-walks, down to a river side, with a wild wood full of birds on the opposite side of the river. In some of those walks are banquetting-houses, with walks and grottos, and all of them fill'd with large evergreens, in the shapes of beasts and birds.[12]

This noble family, though the first in the kingdom for rank, hath not been in Scotland above four hundred years; when an English gentleman of the name of Hamilton fled to King Robert Bruce, who bestow'd on him the lands of Cadzow,[f] in this county. In 1445, this family was nobilitated by the title of Lord Hamilton, and married to King James the Third's sister; by which they came to be declar'd in parliament, on the death of James the Fifth, that in case of the death of Mary, Queen of Scots, they should be next heir to the crown, and are regarded as a branch of the royal family ever since. They were created Duke of Chatelherault in France on the carrying Mary, Queen of Scots thither; were made Dukes of Hamilton in Scotland, by King Charles the First; and Duke of Brandon in England, by Queen Anne.[13] I cannot forbear doing the honour to this family, of giving you a speech of the Lord Hamilton, Governor of Scotland during the minority of Queen Mary, after the famous Battle of Pinkie, at a time when it was in his power to have married the princess to his own son, and so have secured the succession of the crown to his own family.[14]

I doubt not but that many of you, my lords, and more of the vulgar (whose forward preposterous understandings seldom judge of things, but by the various events they are liable to), may be apt to disapprove a war, that has been attended with consequences so fatal to most of us. I own that I advis'd you to undertake it. And as then, so I am still of opinion that 'tis one of those evils, the glory and liberty of the nation do not allow us to avoid. I know not but you may have other sentiments at this time; and have therefore called you together to congratulate your magnanimity if you remain unshaken, as I am, in your resolution to repulse the encroachments made upon us; and if you are other ways disposed, as I hope you are not, to upbraid your fear, the inglorious enemy of reason and courage. When I took the command of our armies upon me, you unanimously preferr'd an honourable war, to a peace you thought equally unsafe and disgraceful; and shall we be so mean as to yield to the signal injustice of fortune? No, I am persuaded, that, as grating as our misfortunes at Pinkie must needs be to you all, you'll nevertheless choose to pursue a noble revenge, rather than sit down with the affront, or submit to the threaten'd slavery. Come on it what will, I am fix'd in my first opinion. And I had rather preserve the monarchy at any rate, I mean, though at the expence of such of the subjects' fortunes and bloods, as have been, or may yet chance to be wasted, than to spare the estates and lives of private men, though never so great and deserving, with the loss of our common country. Let us labour by all means to save the ship that saves all. And to this effect, let us not grudge to cut down the mast, nor to see our own shares of the loading cut down and thrown over-board. If the foundation of an edifice stands firm, it is no great matter if the ceiling and the furniture be down. Our private losses are so many sacrifices that are due to the public. They weaken the state; I own it. But the ruin of the state itself, must needs involve us all in universal irretrievable miseries. Consider, my lords, with what an enemy we have to do, and on what terms we may purchase a peace. Our enemy, is he not the same old inveterate one, whose avarice has, by unjust laws, so often attempted to devour our existence? And is not this present war alone, sufficient to make us tremble at the very thoughts of falling under the power of tyrants, so unconscionably implacable? We cannot descend to the terms they propose, without stooping under the imperious yoke of a people that thirst for our blood, and whose insolence is whetted with fury. Cast your eyes on the other hand, on your ancient unalterable allies, the French; they never yet failed us in our greatest exigencies; and will not in the present juncture of our affairs. Neither do we want friends in Italy. Nay, there are few potentates in Europe that will unconcernedly look on, and behold our destruction. Resolve, in fine, whether we had best defend our liberties, or give them up; whether 'tis most expedient to die, if it must be so, free and independent, or to live eternal slaves to our greatest foes. 'Tis true, they offer us fair things; our laws and rights are by the treaty to remain untouched. But pray who is guarantee for this? And if the English shall, in an after-game, either break, or encroach upon the articles agreed to, who will redress our grievances? To what tribunal shall we appeal? 'Tis a jest to offer to set up for either liberty or property, when in effect we shall have given them away. We must begin by surrendring our mistress to a husband, that is, to a master; which done, I don't see why he may not, as such, subject her crown to his own; or rather unite and confound them in one. And thus Scotland must inevitably become a county or province in England. 'Tis impossible to reflect on the ambitious project without horror and detestation; and how can we choose but to have the meanest sentiments of, and greatest contempt imaginable for, such of our countrymen as shall show themselves villains enough to comply? The uncertain events and length of the war may perhaps intimidate some of us. But is it the first time that Scotland has seen herself expos'd to dangers of that kind? When reduc'd to the like extremities, did ever our ancestors hesitate to prefer their honour to life? And are we so far degenerated, as to render our selves and their offspring unworthy of the inestimable treasure they purchas'd with so much valour, and transmitted to us with so much glory? Had the malign influence of our birth involv'd us in slavery, how far we had been oblig'd to endeavour the recovery of that freedom we had never enjoy'd, I shall not determine. But since we are born free, 'tis plain that our posterity can never pardon our cowardice, if we become willing to resign the independency, our own birth, and forefathers' courage, have entitled[g] us to. If but a part of our estates and honours were invaded, we might plead some pretence of excuse for dispensing with it. But the body of the nation is attack'd; our country, nothing less than our country, is at stake; its ancient laws and fundamental constitution are on the point of being subverted. I cannot disown, but that it's hard to tell what success it shall please the Almighty to give to our arms. It's not only in these our days that the Scotch nation, equal to the Romans in this point, have stood firm in the midst of danger, and have conquered their hard fate by the steadiness[k] of their courage. Let us not affront the memory of those heroes that gave us a being. The more vigor we show, the more we shall encourage our friends abroad. One thing we are sure of, that our firmness will gain us praises from posterity, whereas tamely submitting will render us infamous.

This speech had its design'd effect; for, to prevent the English from getting possession of their queen by force, they sent her to France, which put an end to that war.

Buchanan and some other Scotch authors make this family of Hamilton original dependers on the family of Douglas, and that they became great by betraying that family to K. James the Second, who murder'd the Earl of Douglas with his own hands in Stirling Castle, altho' he had a safeguard; and that Hamilton married afterwards the Princess Mary, that king's daughter; whose brother K. James the Third, forc'd her to abandon her husband, Boyd, Earl of Arran, and to marry the Lord Hamilton. But I am apt to believe this to be invidious in Buchanan, to please his patron the Earl of Moray, a great enemy to the Hamiltons. For I have now before me the history of Scotland of Hector Boethius,[h] translated into English by Mr. John Bellenden,[i] Archdeacon of Moray and Canon of Ross, printed in 1536; who in his twelfth book, chapter the 5th, saith, the first daughter of K. James the Second was married to the Lord Boyd, of whom was begotten a son, was slain by the Lord Montgomery; and a daughter married to the Earl of Cassilis;[j] and after the death of the Lord Boyd, this daughter of K. James the Second was married to the Lord Hamilton; and that way the house of Hamilton is decorated[k] in the king's blood.[15]

This Mr. Bellenden being contemporary with the lady, and in being when the match was made, I think may be believ'd better than Mr. Buchanan, who did not write till a century after. And as for their dependance on the house of Douglas, Mr. Hamilton of Wishaw, in his account of the family of Hamilton, explodes that; but he being a cadet of the family, may be supposed to be a party-writer by the other side. However, Mr. Rymer, in his *Foedera Angliae* (*ad an.* 1423), shows they were so considerable barons then, as to be one of the hostages for the ransom of K. James the First.[16]

I have dwelt the longer on this story, because most foreigners who have writ of the affairs of Scotland, found the greatness of the Hamilton family on ingratitude and adultery. My Lord Clarendon and Bishop Burnet have told you so much of the two brothers, Duke James and Duke William, during the civil war, that I need only tell you that James was beheaded at London, and Duke William kill'd at the Battle of Worcester. But he that has most aggrandized this family was the Lord William Douglas, Earl of Selkirk who, marrying the daughter and heiress of Duke James, hath by her added to the family four hereditary peers, their sons, and mix'd the blood and arms of the Douglases with the Hamiltons.[17] There are of the peerage in this family, Duke Hamilton, the Earls of Abercorn, Haddington, Selkirk, Orkney, Ruglen; and the Lords Belhaven and Bergenny; and many considerable branches in Ireland.

From the palace of Hamilton, there runs a spacious avenue a full mile long, well pav'd and ditch'd on each side, with triple and quadruple rows of trees, in a direct line to Bothwell Bridge; where I pass'd the River Clyde, and where, in K. Charles the Second's reign, there was a rebellion, which the Duke of Monmouth was sent down into Scotland to suppress. It's a very advantageous pass, but they had neither artillery, nor officers to defend it, and so were soon reduced.[18] Near this bridge stands the ancient castle of Bothwell, often the residence and burial-place of the Earls of Douglas. It's a prodigious great pile, out of part of which the good Lord Forfar built a pretty neat box at a little distance, and is there interr'd. This castle hath often given the title of earl, but never lasted long in a family; and hath been generally unfortunate, so that no one now enjoys that title.[19] In six miles more, thro' a fine country, I arriv'd at this famous city of Glasgow, of which I shall now give you the description.

Glasgow is the beautifullest little city I have seen in Britain; it stands deliciously on the banks of the River Clyde, over which there is a fair stone bridge of eight arches. The city consists of four principal streets in the form of a cross, with the Town-House and market-place in the middle where, as you walk, you see the whole town at once. The houses are of freestone, of an equal height, and supported with pillars; and the streets being spacious and well pav'd, add to the beauty of the place. Here is also an university, founded by Bishop Turnbull in the year 1454. The college consists of two spacious courts of freestone; and the scholars wear scarlet gowns, as at St Andrews. Here are professors in all sciences, as there, and at Edinburgh; and the Duke of Montrose (who, as I told you from Stirling, hath a great power in the adjacent counties) is their chancellor.[20] The cathedral, which stands on an eminence at the end of one of the streets, is now divided into three churches; and there are five other very good ones in this city. Near this cathedral, stands the palace of the Duke of Montrose which, when finish'd according to the disposition of the offices already built, will be very noble, having a commanding prospect of the whole city and adjacent country; and, on the declension of the hill to the river-side, room enough for what gardens he pleases.[21]

The ancient and noble family of Graham, Dukes of Montrose, hath been considerable ever since Graham govern'd Scotland, in the minority of Eugene the Second. And we find William de Graham, one of the witnesses to the foundation of the abbey of Holyrood House, by K. David the First, in the year 1125. And under the great seal of Alexander the Third, we find three Sir David Grahams successively ratify'd in their lands, and high-sheriffs of the county of Stirling, under the same king, in 1284.

Sir David Graham was one of those barons, who, in 1300, sign'd that famous letter to the pope, asserting the independency of Scotland, and extolling King Robert Bruce, as the preserver of the liberties of the people; and Sir John Graham, the famous companion of William Wallace, so much celebrated by the ancient Scotch bards. We find Sir Patrick de Graham one of the hostages for King David, when he was taken prisoner at the Battle of Durham, in the year 1346. We find also the Lord Graham governor of the kingdom in the minority of K. James the Second, a great favourite of K. James the Third, and created Earl of Montrose by K. James the Fourth, with whom he was slain at Flodden.[22]

In the reign of K. James the Sixth they were Lord High Treasurer, Lord High Chancellor, and Viceroy of the kingdom. And in the reign of King Charles the First the behaviour of James, Marquis of Montrose is so well known that I need not repeat it. And indeed, saying any thing of him, without giving you his whole history, would be doing injustice to his memory; and to do that would be too long for a letter. Both parties own he was one of the greatest men of his time. My Lord Clarendon says of him, that he was in his nature fearless of danger, and never declin'd any enterprize for the difficulty of going thro' with it, but exceedingly affected those which seem'd desperate to others; and did believe somewhat to be in himself above other men, which made him live easier with those inferior to him, than with his superiors or equals. He was not without vanity, but his virtues were much superior, and well deserve to have his memory preserv'd and celebrated amongst the most illustrious persons of the age he liv'd in. His son, after the Restoration, led a private life; but his grandson, James, Marquis of Montrose, was, while very young, made captain of the horse guards and President of the Privy Council; and would have been the greatest man in Scotland of his age, but he was snatch'd away in 1684, leaving behind him a son, the present duke; who inherits the honour and virtue of his family, and is one of the gems that adorn the British crown.[23]

This city of Glasgow is a place of the greatest trade in the kingdom, especially to the plantations; from whence they have twenty or thirty sail of ships every year, laden with tobacco and sugar, an advantage this kingdom never enjoy'd till the Union. They are purchasing a harbour on the Firth near Alloway, to which they have but twelve miles by land; and then they can re-ship their sugars and tobacco for Holland, Germany, and the Baltic Sea, without being at the trouble of sailing round England or Scotland. Ships of burden do not come up to the city, but lie at Port Glasgow, where the custom house is kept, and from whence they bring their goods in lighters to the city.[24]

This city is strictly Presbyterian, and the best affected to this government of any in Scotland.

Letter XIII

GREENOCK

Sir,

From Glasgow I took a boat down the River Clyde, leaving the mountainous country of Lennox on the north, and the Barony of Renfrew[a] to the south; and in few hours arriv'd at the ancient town of Dumbarton, situated on the point where the River Leven runs into Clyde; and is one of the great strengths and passes between the low country and the highlands, and the gate of the Western Highlands. Its castle stands on a rock, as those of Edinburgh and Stirling do. It's environed by the River Leven to the west, by the Clyde to the south, by marshes that are overflow'd by the sea every tide to the east, and to the north the rock is perpendicular. The Britons kept this castle for three hundred years after the Romans left the island; and Bede says it was the best fortified city of the Britons in his days. Since the Scotch held it, it hath done them many great services at a pinch. It held out long against Edward the First of England, and when David the Second was beat, he fled for refuge to Sir Malcolm Fleming, Governor of Dumbarton Castle, who conveyed him safe to France. It was also from this castle that Mary, Queen of Scots was shipped off for France, when the English army came as far as Edinburgh to demand her for their Edward the Sixth.[1]

This country of Lennox gave the title of earl and duke to a branch of the family of Stuart, before they came to the crown of Scotland. The first was Alan,[b] second son to Walter, the Stuart or Seneschal of Scotland, who in some charters is also called *Dapifer Scotiae*, and was uncle to him, who, by marrying King Robert Bruce's daughter, came to be king. From this office of High Steward they took the surname of Stuart, which is now branched out into many families, who all give the arms the family bore before they were kings, which is a blue and white chequer. This family continued in great honour and splendour for many generations. The Lord Darnley,[c] a son of the family, married Mary, Queen of Scots, and was father to James the Sixth of Scotland, and First of England. In the year 1672 the last duke of the family died ambassador to Denmark, without issue. King Charles the Second being his next heir, bestowed the title on one of his natural sons by the Duchess of Portsmouth; but the lands, regalities, and superiority, belong to the Duke of Montrose, who is also hereditary sheriff of the shire.[2]

A little beyond Dumbarton is the famous lake Loch Lomond,[d] twenty miles long and eight broad, with some islands in it; of which the poet Necham:[e]

With rivers Scotland is enrich'd,
And Lomond there a lake,
So cold of nature is, that sticks
It quickly stones doth make.[3]

This town gave title of earl to a son of the house of Douglas; the present earl hath a command in the army.[4]

Behind Loch Lomond, to the northwest and west, lies the great county of Argyllshire which, with the countries of Lorn, Kintyre, and Breadalbane, adjoining, is inhabited by the clan of the Campbells, the only balancing power to the Macdonalds in the Highlands; and the whole under the power and jurisdiction of the Duke of Argyll, who is not only hereditary sheriff, but hereditary justice-general, and superior of these countries and the adjacent islands. I gave you an account of this noble family from Stirling; and as for the country, it's very mountainous, full of black cattle and deer, as the other parts of the Highlands.[5] Lorne is something better and affords corn; as does also Kintyre, which is a limb that runs out into the Irish Sea, thirty miles long, as the Land's-End does in England, and from whence you see Ireland very plainly. Breadalbane, or the heart of the Highlands, is amongst the Grampian[f] Hills, and is the highest part of the kingdom. The inhabitants all wear the highland dress, and speak Irish, and are as wild as they can be represented. The Duke of Argyll hath a noble seat at Inverary the capital of the shire, and another at Campbeltown.[6] A branch of this noble family of Campbell is also Earl of Breadalbane. Besides this large country of Argyll, the duke hath also the superiority and jurisdiction over the adjacent isles of Islay,[g] Tiree,[h] Jura, Uist,[i] Coll, Lismore and Mull;[j] which last island was the inheritance of the clan of Maclean,[k] where they still inhabit, but under the power and jurisdiction of the Duke of Argyll.

From Dumbarton I took [a] boat down the River Clyde, and in six miles rowing got to Greenock at the mouth of the river, where it empties itself into the Firth of Clyde which, like that of the Firth of Forth, extends itself for forty miles till it falls into the Irish Sea; and at its mouth, as the other, hath a mountain in the sea called Ailsa,[l] where the solan geese inhabit, as in the Bass. This firth hath Kintyre on one side, and the coasts of Cunningham, Kyle,[m] and Carrick[n] on the other, and is several miles broad. About the middle of this firth lieth the island of Arran, belonging to the Duke of Hamilton, and gives the title of earl to his eldest son.[7] It is about a dozen miles in circumference, is very mountainous and boggy, but hath a good harbour for ships in distress, called Lamlash. Nearer to the bottom of this firth, joining to the barony of Renfrew, is another large island, called Bute, a part of the patrimony of the family of Stuarts, before they were kings of Scotland; and which Robert, the second king of the family, gave to his brother John, as appears by the following charter, which I have seen.

> *Robertus Dei Gratia Rex Scotorum, Sciatis nos dedisse, & hoc presenti charta nostra confirmasse dilecto fratri nostro Johanni Senescallo de Bute, officium Vicecomitatus de Bute & Arran; datum 11 Novembr. 1400.*

This John Stuart of Bute must have been born before his father was king, for he carrieth the plain coat of the Stuarts, in a tressure of flower-de-luces, without the royal escutcheon.[8] They were Gentlemen of the Bedchamber to most of the succeeding kings; and Queen Anne called always Stuart of Bute cousin, when she spoke to him, and created him Earl of Bute. The present earl is Lord of the Bedchamber to King George, and one of the sixteen peers to the Parliament of Great Britain.[8]

In this island is also the castle of Rothsay, which gives title of duke to the Prince of Wales, and is always the title of the king's eldest son. In the church of Rothsay is this memorable epitaph, upon the monument of the last earl of Bute:

Per multos proavos regali stemmate cretus,
Qui fuerant fidi regibus usque suis;
Pulchra fuit cui mens habitans in corpore pulchro,
Cuique genus geniusque ingeniique vigor.
Ornarunt animum, virtusque scientia juris,
Et regum, & patriae, & religionis amor;
Illa & apostolico clero, tot fluctibus acto,
Vivens & moriens grande levamen erat.[9]

This town of Greenock is much embellish'd by its proprietor, Sir John Shaw, one of the richest commoners in Scotland, with a very fine harbour; and is in the shire of Renfrew, the ancient inheritance of the Stuarts, before they were kings.[10] They were barons of Renfrew, but Robert coming to be king, made it a shire; however, Baron of Renfrew is still one of the royal titles, and the first Roberts generally kept their court here. What the Stuarts were originally no historian can tell: but that when they were Barons of Renfrew, they were also treasurers to the king's household, and stewards of the kingdom, from which office the clan took the surname, all agree. The best account of them is given by Sir James Dalrymple, from undoubted authorities, which is as follows:

> Their barony was the shires of Renfrew and Bute, and the Stewartry of Kyle. The first of that family I find mention'd in charters and records, is Walter, the son of Alan, *Dapifer Regis*, founder of the monastery of Paisley,[o] who in the register book of charters of the Abbacy of Paisley, now in the custody of the Earl of Dundonald, proprietor of these lands, and where he hath his chief residence, is mentioned as the founder, and son of Alan; and particularly in a discharge granted by himself to the monks, of two chaldrons of meal, payable out of the mill, he is designed Walter, the son of Alan; and in confirmation by Pope Alexander, of the Abbacy of Paisley, to Alexander Stuart of Scotland, he is designed heir by progress to Walter the founder. There are also charters extant, granted by this Walter, designing himself

the son of Alan, and *Dapifer Regis*. The chronicles of Melrose and Fordun do design him Walter the son of Alan, *Dapifer Regis Scotiae, qui fundavit Pasletum*; and that he died in the year 1177 by the former, and 1178 by the latter, which was in the twelfth or thirteenth year of the reign of King William. And frequently in King William's charters in the said register of Paisley, Alan Dapifer is mentioned, and also in the foresaid confirmation by the pope, he is designed Alan the son of Walter the founder; he died in the year 1204. To him succeeded Walter, his son, designed *Senescallus Scotiae*. Fordun relates, that King Alexander the Second, at the feast on his birthday, in the year 1231, made Walter, the son of Alan, Steward of Scotland, Justiciar of Scotland. A manuscript of *Andreas Wintonius*, prior of the Inch in Loch Leven, who wrote in the time of the government of Robert, First Duke of Albany, and uncle to King James the First, dedicated to Sir John Weems, predecessor to the Earl of Weems, agrees with Fordun, that at St. Andrews, King Alexander made Walter (Alan's son) Steward of Scotland, the King's Justiciary. The manuscript contains many things useful to the history, and is in the hands of the Reverend Mr. James Kirktoun, one of the ministers of Edinburgh, a person well known in Scotish antiquities. This Walter is an ordinary witness in King Alexander the Second's charters, under the designation of *Senescallus & Justitiarius Scotiae*. And, as the same Wynton mentions, Walter (Steward and Justiciary of Scotland) was, in the year 1238, sent over to France, to bring Mary, daughter to Ingram de Coucy, to be Queen to King Alexander. *Anno 1241, obiit Walterus, Filius Allani junio*ris.

To Walter succeeded his son Alexander, Steward of Scotland, frequently so designed in his own and other charters, recorded in the register of Paisley. Fordun mentions him to be kill'd in the Battle of the Largs[p] in Cunningham, which he places in the year 1263, (*Chron. de Melrose*, 1262.) where the Norwegians were defeated, and ever since banish'd from any possession of the Isles. He is designed Alexander Stuart of Dundonald, great grandchild to the first Walter Stuart, and grandfather of the noble

Walter who married King Robert Bruce's daughter. Beside the records of Paisley, many of his charters are extant; and I have seen one by this Alexander, confirming the donation which Walter the father gave to the Church of St. Andrew's of Bromholm, of twenty shillings yearly, to be taken out of the burgh of Renfrew, with the seal entire; himself on horseback on the one side, and the chequer on the other for his arms, which the surname of Stuart do still bear.

To him succeeded James, Great Steward of Scotland, his son, who was one of the Wardens of Scotland after the death of Alexander the Third, and one of those who treated with K. Edward the First of England, in relation to the marriage betwixt the Maid of Norway and King Edward's son, and in the competition concerning the crown, betwixt Bruce, Balliol, and others. As also, after Balliol was defeated, and resign'd the crown, he is amongst those whom Prynne's History bears to have given allegiance to Edward Longshanks, and designed James *Seneschall de Scoce saluz*, &c. A little after, *15 die Maij apud Rokesburgh, venit Dominus Joannes quondam Seneschallus, praedicti Domini Jacobi Germanus, Miles.* And I have a charter of James Stuart of Scotland, designing himself son to Alexander Stuart of Scotland, and confirming the charter formerly mention'd, granted by Alexander Stuart of Scotland, his father, and Walter his grandfather; his seal appended is also entire. He died in the year 1309.

At the Battle of Falkirk, 1298, Sir John Stuart, designed of Bute, who contended with John Comyn[q] for leading the vanguard of the army, was kill'd. It seems he was the same person who (in the year 1296) in Prynne's History is call'd *Frater Germanus Domini Jacobi*; and, in the absence or restraint of his elder brother, the Steward of Scotland, acted as Steward for him. This probably hath been the mistake, why our historians omitted James Stuart of Scotland, predecessor and godfather to all the King James's, and insert John Stuart to be father to Walter Stuart of Scotland, who is well known to have been husband to Margery Bruce, the king's daughter; and, by her, father to Robert Stuart, who (in the absence of King David Bruce his uncle, and in defence of his title against Edward Balliol) did many brave actions, from the year 1335 to the year 1338, when he was chosen governor of the kingdom; which he freed from the English and Balliol's claim, and restored it to King David Bruce at his return from France. This king being afterward taken prisoner at the Battle of Durham (commonly placed in the year 1348), was again governor till the king return'd from England (in the year 1359) by the help of his two eldest sons, John (then Lord Kyle, designed *Seneschallus de Kyle*, afterward king) and Robert (designed *Seneschallus de Monteith*) afterward Duke of Albany.

Maurice Murray, Lord of Bothwell and Clyddesdale, and Earl of Strathearn, being kill'd in the Battle of Durham, Robert Stuart of Scotland was created Earl of Strathearn. At the same battle, John Ranulph (Earl of Moray) being kill'd, the Steward of Scotland married his relict, Eupham Ross, daughter to Hugh, Earl of Ross; as appears by a charter granted by Robert, Steward of Scotland, Earl of Strathearn, and Eupham his spouse, Countess of Moray, to John Maxwell, predecessor to Sir John Maxwell of Netherpollock, of certain lands within the earldom of Strathearn, which have of a long time belong'd to the lairds of Gleneagles.[r] John Haldane[s] (now of Gleneagles) hath the charter and lands, an ancient baron, nobly descended. There is a charter to the same person of the same lands; but then designed Sir John Maxwell by David, Earl of Strathearn, who was eldest son of the second marriage by the said Countess Eupham, and who got from his father (the said Robert) when he became king of Scotland, the earldom of Strathearn; it being then usual to renew the investiture or infeoffment upon the change of the superior, as well as upon the change of the vassal. The charter is dated at Edinburgh, May 10, 1372. *Coram his testibus, nobilibus viris & potentibus, Domino Joanne, Domini nostri, &c. Regis Scotiae primogenito, Comite de Carrick, & Seneschallo Scotiae, Roberto Comite de Fyfe & Monteith, fratribus nostris charissimis.*

King Robert confirm'd, on the 25th of April, in the third year of his reign, the said charter, by his son, David, Earl of Strathearn, whom he designed *dilectus filius*. And amongst the witnesses to the charter is *Joannes, Comes de Carrick primogenitus, & Robertus Comes de Fyfe & Monteith, filius noster dilectus.* This is a clear acknowledgment, both by the king, the father, and by the Earl of Strathearn himself (the eldest son of Eupham Ross), that the earls of Carrick and Monteith were his elder brethren. But of this, Sir George Mackenzie hath already said very much, and more proofs do daily occur, to rectify this universal mistake of our historians; which, together with the description of that ancient family, and the family of Darnley and Lennox, and other great branches descended thereof, deserve a particular treatise.[11]

I shall only repeat, that Fordun, in his Chronicle, *lib. xiv. pag. 73,* inserts a charter of confirmation of the pope's bull, granted by King David Bruce to the bishops, with the consent of Robert, Earl of Strathearn, his nephew, giving power to bishops to dispose in testament upon their own moveables; in which charter, the witnesses are: *Robertus Seneschallus Comes de Strathearn, nepos noster; Joannes Seneschaullus Comes de Carrick, filius suus primogenitus & haeres,* &c. before all the other earls, which is an attestation of the grand uncle, King David, owning the Earl of Carrick to be his father's eldest son, in this matter of importance. And there are two declarations in parliament concerning the succession of the crown (whereof one of them is extant with the seals of the nobility) by Robert, Earl of Strathearn, after he was king; the one in the first, and the other in the third year of his reign, asserting the Earl of Carrick to be his eldest son, and to succeed him in the kingdom.[12] For proving that this Robert Stuart (the first king) was grandchild to James Stuart of Scotland, there is a charter recorded in the public register of charters, by the same King Robert, in the first year of his reign, to Sir Adam Fullertoun, of the lands of Fullertoun and others, confirming the charters granted by himself, when Steward of Scotland, and by his grandfather James, Steward of Scotland, to Sir Adam Fullertoun. This Sir Adam Fullertoun was predecessor to William Fullertoun, now of that ilk in Kyle-Stuart, of these lands.[13]

Letter XIV

WIGTOWN

Sir,

This Barony of Renfrew, altho' small, hath many noblemen's seats in it. The castle of Dundonald, the ancient seat of the Stuarts before they were kings, gives now title of earl to the family of Cochrane.[a] And the celebrated abbey of Paisley was, at the Reformation, turn'd into a lordship in favour of the Lord Claud Hamilton, a younger son of the Duke of Chatelherault, who was created Earl of Abercorn and Lord Paisley. But that family afterwards settling in Ireland, the abbey and lands were purchas'd by the Earls of Dundonald, who now keep their residence there; which is so pleasant, that the Duchess of Beaufort, after the death of both her husbands, altho' an Englishwoman, chose it for her residence, and died there.[1]

Here is also the castle of Erskine, which gave name to the family of Mar, and of which they were long lords, before they came to be earls of Mar. The ancient family of the Lord Semple hath also their seat here. This family were bailiffs to the Stuarts for this barony, and remained so after the Stuarts came to the throne; but continuing (till of late) Roman Catholics, they have made no great figure since the Reformation.[2]

Here is also Halkhead, the ancient seat of the Lord Ross's family; who were originally Ross of Wark in Northumberland, but follow'd the fortune of K. Robert Bruce, and have been settled here ever since. The present lord was one of the sixteen peers in the last parliament; and his brother, General Ross, a leading man in the House of Commons.[3] Boyle of Kelburn, created Earl of Glasgow by Queen Anne, hath also his seat here; as hath likewise Cunningham, Earl of Glencairn, a very ancient and noble family, created earls by

King James the Second. They have been Chancellors of Scotland formerly; and the present earl is governor of Dumbarton Castle.[4]

From this county of Renfrew, I enter'd the beautiful country of Cunningham, all enclos'd as England, and extends for thirty miles along the banks of the Firth of Clyde, to the River of Ayr.[b] There are several branches of the name of Cunningham very considerable here. Sir James Dalrymple says that the first of this family was an English gentleman who, being concern'd in the murder of Thomas à Becket, fled hither; and gives for reason, that they carry a bishop's pall for their arms; I suppose, he means a crosier, or saltire. But, with submission, I believe it is a pitch-fork; for the Lord Glencairn's motto is, *over, fork, over*; and the name answers to husbandry; for in the High-Dutch and Saxon language, *Conigham* is a kingly situation, and the name, as well as arms, suit both the plenty and beauty of the country. This country was early inhabited by the Saxons, and never by the Highland Scots; yet the famous Sir William Wallace, that had so many exploits against the English, in K. Edward the First's reign, was a native of Cunningham, and his posterity are a considerable family in that country to this day.[5]

In a few miles riding in this beautiful country, I arriv'd at the castle of Eglinton, the capital seat of Montgomery, Earl of Eglintoun, a most ancient and noble family, who have been above three hundred years earls. He was a branch of this family, that Count de Montgomery, Captain of the Scotch Band in France, establish'd by Charles the Fifth for the defence of his own person and his posterity, who, in a tournament, kill'd King Henry the Second of France, by the splenting of his spear at a tilt, entring his helmet at the eye, and pierc'd his brain. This gentleman, being a son of Montgomery of Giffen, took part afterwards with the French Protestants in the time of the league and, being apprehended, was beheaded.[6] The family have been zealously Protestant since the Reformation; and the present earl was one of the sixteen peers in the last parliament of Queen Anne. He hath a great estate, and is a vast improver, but none of his seats come up to the dignity of his rank. They seem to be a French family originally, for they give the same coat of arms with the kings of France, in a double tressure; and Mr. John Montgomery of Giffen, a grandson of the family of Eglinton, is now one of the Gentlemen of the Bedchamber to the Prince of Wales.[7]

A little way from Eglinton lies Kilwinning, a pretty large village with some good seats in it, and of which that lord is bailiff. In two little miles more I got to Irvine, a tolerable seaport, consisting of two pretty good streets, and the houses well built; and upon the key, a good face of business, especially the coal-trade to Dublin.[8] This town also gives the title of viscount to an English family of the name of Ingram; yet altho' it's the best town in Cunningham, Kilmarnock (six miles further from the sea) is reckon'd the chief, and gives title of earl to the family of Boyd, a family that flourish'd in the reign of King James the Second, and was ruin'd by King James the Third. The Lord Boyd was so great a favourite, that the king gave him his daughter in marriage, created him Earl of Arran, and conferr'd all the great employments of the nation on his family. But that king's son, soon after he came to the throne, sent his lordship to Denmark to bring him a queen, and during his absence stripp'd the family of their all; some historians say, of his wife too; but others affirm that the Lord Hamilton did not marry her till the Lord Boyd's death. King Charles the Second (the best natur'd prince in the world) took pity of the family, and rais'd them again by the title of Earl of Kilmarnock. This town is famous for all kinds of cutlers' ware.[9]

On the rising grounds that separate Cunningham from Clydesdale stands the castle of Loudoun, a very noble seat with a commanding prospect over all this country, the ancient seat of a branch of the Campbells, and Earls of Loudoun. They are come of the Duke of Argyll's family, and give the same arms, but in different colours; what is sable and or in the duke's is argent and gules in this. An Earl of Loudoun was Chancellor of Scotland in all the difficult times of King Charles the First.[10] The Lord Clarendon and other historians of his time have said so much of him that I will not trouble you with the character of that very great man, which I am sure you have read there. His grandson, the present earl, was Secretary of State to Queen Anne, hath been one of the sixteen peers in the British Parliament ever since the Union, and is Knight Companion of the Most Noble Order of St. Andrew, or the Thistle. It was his brother, Colonel James Campbell, that you saw behave so well at the Battle of Malplaquet, at the head of the Grey Dragoons, of whom he is now colonel; and by marrying the only daughter of Sir John Shaw of Greennock, will add a new family to that illustrious and noble tribe.[11]

From Kilmarnock in eight miles I cross'd the River of Ayr, over a fair stone bridge to the town of Ayr, which looks like a fine beauty in decay. Here are the ruins of an ancient trading town; the market-place and two streets show what it hath been, but every thing is now out of order. It lies at the mouth of the river on the Firth of Clyde; but Irvine is by much a town of more business, altho' this was formerly the fifth town in Scotland. Here are the remains of a citadel built by Oliver Cromwell who, in imitation of King Edward the First, rode this country in a curb bit, and built citadels near all their great towns, which were generally demolish'd at the Restoration.[12]

A few miles above Ayr, on the river-side, is the ancient seat of the Lord Cathcart, a family that have been for many hundred years barons; but the glory of them is your acquaintance, Colonel Cathcart, whom you knew in Flanders Major to the Grey Dragoons. He had an old regiment of foot on King George's accession to the throne, is one of the Gentlemen of the Bedchamber to the Prince of Wales, and the eldest son of this noble family.[13]

This country is called Kyle: it's more mountainous but not near so beautiful as Cunningham. Here also is the old castle of Stair, the habitation of the family of the Dalrymples; a family that was never conspicuous till after the Restoration. Sir James Dalrymple of Stair, for his knowledge in the law, was appointed by King Charles the Second one of the Lords of Session, or Senators of the College of Justice, and in 1671 Lord President of the Session; in which post he continued till the Duke of York came to Scotland, when opposing the arbitrary measures then carrying on, and foreseeing the misery that must attend his country, on that prince's accession to the throne, he fled to Holland, where he led a private life till at the Revolution he came over with the Prince of Orange, was created Lord Viscount Stair, and restor'd to his post of President of the Session.[14] But his highest glory was to see four of his sons the greatest men in the nation, not by favour but by merit. The eldest son, John, was Secretary of State to King William, and created afterwards Earl of Stair. Hugh is now President of the College of Justice, or Session, the same place which his father had. Sir James, one of the finest gentlemen of his time, and a curious antiquary, was made Clerk of the Parliament and Session; and Sir David, whom you have so often heard in the English House of

Commons, Lord Advocate, or Attorney-General. The grandchild to this first noted Dalrymple, I mean the present Earl of Stair, I need say nothing of, since all Europe have been fill'd with his prudent and vigilant negotiations, when Ambassador in France. And he is now deservedly one of the Lords of the Bedchamber to the king, and Knight of the Most Noble Order of St. Andrew.[15]

I ought, when I was at Edinburgh, to have taken notice of the President Dalrymple's fine seat at North Berwick; but my going to the Bass diverted me from it. Sir David hath also left a very fine one between Edinburgh and Musselburgh; and the Lord Stair hath another called Newliston, a few miles from Edinburgh, where he is making a canal and several very grand improvements; but they being not far advanc'd, I did not trouble you with them from thence, altho' I think it not amiss to mention them here.[16]

Upon my mentioning this family to you, I cannot help making a remark which will hardly occur to you in the history of any other nation: that the same race should continue the capacity and learning in the family, as well as the honour and estate, for several generations. The Earls of Huntley were successively Lord Chancellors[c] for four generations, all great men in the beginning of the Stuarts; the Maitlands in the reigns of King James the Fifth, Queen Mary, and King James the Sixth. And what a prodigious favourite was Maitland, Duke of Lauderdale, to King Charles the Second? And yet all his predecessors up to Secretary Lethington, in Queen Mary's reign, were reckon'd greater men than he; as likewise his nephew who translated Virgil and died in France.[17] This family of the Dalrymples is a prodigy[d] of the like kind; and Colbert, a Scotchman in France, whose two sons, Monsieurs Colbert and Signally, and his grandson the present Marquis of Torcy, Secretary of State to Lewis the Fourteenth of France, are the same.[18] I can hardly give one instance in England of a family's[e] carrying the great capacity to the third generation, but the Finches, Earl of Nottingham, in which it's hard to distinguish whether the earl's father that was Lord Chancellor, the son the present Lord Finch, the earl himself, or his brother the Earl of Aylesford,[f] were the greater men. This I know, dear sir, is a digression from my subject, but I am sure you will pardon it, because you desired not a bare description of the country, but of the families so celebrated all over Europe for their antiquity.

In a few miles from Ayr I enter'd the country of Carrick, which, as Cunningham, lies along the banks of the Firth of Clyde; and the three, Kyle, Cunningham, and Carrick, compose on the parliament rolls the shire of Ayr, though they are three distinct jurisdictions, and have each their several bailiffs, who hold their courts independent. This country gave title of earl to Robert Bruce, before he was king of Scotland, by Martha the daughter of an Earl of Carrick in 1270, who falling in love with Robert Bruce, while her father was upon an expedition to the Holy Land, in which he died, married him, and was mother to that Robert that was afterwards king; the Stewart marrying his daughter got the estate which, with the title, belongs now to the Prince of Wales, who hath great superiorities, although no very great revenue from this country.[19]

The first good seat I met with in Carrick is Bargany, a good modern building, with pretty good gardens, which gives title of lord to a branch of the house of Hamilton. A few miles further is the castle of Cassilis, the ancient seat of the Kennedies, Earls of Cassilis, an Irish family; who being page to K. Robert the Third, got his daughter with child and married her. His son by that marriage was created Lord Kennedy, and in James the Second's reign, Earl of Cassilis.[20] There was a fine gentleman of the family Lord Chancellor of Scotland and Archbishop of St. Andrews, who, I told you from thence, founded St. Salvator's College there; and they carry their arms in a tessure, as a branch of the royal family.

Maybole,[g] the capital of this country, where all the courts are kept, is a very indifferent place and no seaport; and upon the River Girvan[h] is a beautiful little vale for some miles; and then I came to the town of Stranraer,[i] a royal borough on Loch Ryan,[j] but hardly a house two storeys high in the whole town, and a most miserable place. Don't take Loch Ryan, from its name, to be a lake of fresh water, as Loch Leven, or Loch Lomond; no, it's an arm of the sea that lies between two points that run out, the one called the Mull[k] of Galloway, and the other the point of Corsehill; and running deep into land makes a bay, where they have a good herring-fishing in the season. The country round this bay is called the Rhinns[l] of Galloway, where now I am returned. Near this I landed from the Isle of Man; and I cannot help saying that it's the coarsest[m] part of all the kingdom, hardly excepting Lochaber and Ross; but nature, you know, hath made the extremities of all countries mountainous:

the Alps, for example, between France and Italy, the Pyreneans between France and Spain; and the mountains of Tyrol[n] between Germany and Italy; and yet the people here live in as great plenty as there, and in Galloway there is a numerous gentry.

From Stranraer in four miles of very bad road I got to Portpatrick, a miserable place, where the pacquet-boats pass between Scotland and Ireland, and make but a short passage, having a full view of the coast of Ireland all the way; but the boats are not so good as those that pass the Firth of Forth from Leith to Fife. From Portpatrick I pass'd by the ancient monastery of Whithorn, having Ireland, England, and Isle of Man in full view, and arrived here.[21] This is a pretty good seaport town, but the harbour not near so good as Kirkcudbright; it lies upon the same sea, very commodious for the plantation trade. It is also a royal borough, and gives title of earl to Fleming, Earl of Wigton, a family that came from Flanders, and have made a very good figure in Scotland for above four hundred years. There is another branch in Ireland of an older standing, but whether this family came from thence I could not learn. I saw his seat called Cumbernauld[o] at some distance, in my way from Stirling to Lithgow; and I am told it is a very large one.[22] Near Wigtown is the seat of Stuart, Earl of Galloway, a branch of the royal family, and very powerful in this country.[23]

Sir James Dalrymple, in his account of Galloway, saith that in former times it had princes and lords of its own; of whom on record is Fergus, in the reign of Henry the First of England who, after many troubles that he had stirred, was reduced by Malcolm, King of Scots, to quit his country, and enter himself canon in the Abbey of Holyrood House at Edinburgh. He had two sons, Acthred and Gilbert, who disputed for the succession; but the younger had the better of his elder brother in battle, took him prisoner, and pulled out his eyes and tongue. However, the elder brother had a son, Allan, Lord of Galloway, married to Margaret, eldest daughter to David, Earl of Huntington, by whom he had a daughter, Devorgilla, who founded Balliol College at Oxford, and was mother to John Balliol, King of Scots. He had another daughter, Helena, married to Roger Quincy, Earl of Winchester, by whom Ferrers of Groby[p] came to be Lord of Galloway; but they adhering to the English, the Scotch kings gave the inheritance to the Comyns, afterwards to the Douglases, and now the title is in the Stuarts; but the Earl Ferrers in England is the lineal descendant of the first princes.[24]

Here are the breed of little strong pads, called from the country, galloways, which are very strong and hardy. The country is said to take its name from the Gauls, the first inhabitants of this country; but be that as it will, they seem to be a different race of people from the highlanders.

In my way hither I passed through the foggy road, nigh the Nick of the Balloch;[q] a road so stony and uneven that I was obliged to alight, and with much ado led our horses to the Kingsford of Minnock, so called from Robert the Bruce, his passing this river at that ford. And it was here that Lord Basil Hamilton, brother to the Earl of Orkney, lost his life by endeavouring to save his servant, whose horse was carried down by the stream; and nigh it stands the mountain Merrick,[r] two miles high, at the top of which is a fresh water spring, which affords water enough to keep a mill a-going; and at the bottom is a small lake call'd Loch Knockewart,[s] plentifully stock'd with trouts; and at Loch Enoch, a mile further, are as fine trouts as at Loch Leven. There is one other mountain adjacent called Craignan, properly so called, for it is rather a craig than a mountain, having no grass upon it.[25]

There are several other mountains and lakes, well stor'd with fish, within the barony of Buchan[t] and the Forest belonging to Alexander Mackie of Palgown,[u] who hath a very commodious and romantic seat on the lake, Loch Trool, in a valley environ'd with mountains on the north and east of a mile high. He keeps at least ten thousand sheep on these mountains, besides an incredible number of black cattle, and wild horses called galloways, and is one of the greatest graziers[v] in Britain, and has vast parks and inclosures.[26]

Not far from this is the famous mountain of Cairnsmuir,[w] full of deer and wild cattle, on the south of which stands an ancient seat belonging to Hugh Mackguffog of Rusco;[x] and to the south-west a handsome seat call'd the Cally, belonging to Alexander Murray of Brouchton, with a large park which feeds one thousand bullocks that he sends once every year to the markets of England, who is now worthily the representative for the Stewartry of Galloway in the Parliament of Great Britain; and opposite to this, on the other side of the River Fleet, stands a handsome seat called Cardinnes, belonging to Lieutenant Colonel Maxwell, with parks and inclosures also for feeding of cattle.[27]

Now, sir, I have finish'd Scotland from corner to corner. I know that you will expect I should say something of those many islands that lie round it, which you may accept, as I received them from Mr. Martin a native of those islands. Mr. Martin, in his accurate account of the western and northern islands of Scotland, published about twenty years ago, tells you that the island of Jura, belonging to the Duke of Argyll, is twenty-four miles long and seven broad, hath good pasturage for cattle and deer, and abounds with rivers and good springs.[28]

Islay, which gives title of Earl to the Duke of Argyll's brother, is twenty-four miles long and twelve broad, and also feeds plenty of deer and cattle.

Gigha[y] is six miles long, and a mile and a half broad.

Oransay four miles in circumference.

Colonsay[z] is four miles long and a mile broad, all belonging to the Duke of Argyll.

The isle of Mull is twenty-four miles long and as much broad, the ancient habitation of the clan of Maclean, but now belongs to the Duke of Argyll. However, since the late Rebellion the government hath always kept a garrison[aa] in the castle of Duart, the ancient residence of the chief of the Macleans, to keep the inhabitants in awe.[29] Flesh, fowls, and fish, is very plentiful[bb] in this island; and it is a government very much courted by the English officers for its cheapness.

The island of St. Columba's [cc] is two miles long and above a mile broad.[30] It was here that this famous saint built his two monasteries, one for men, and another for women; also St. Mary's Cathedral in the form of a cross; the body of the church twenty yards long, and the choir twenty more, the two cross isles ten yards each, and the cupola twenty-one foot square; the altar-piece of very fine marble, and the gate and windows neatly carv'd. Here are the burial places, as by the inscriptions, of the kings of Scotland, the kings of Ireland, and the kings of Norway, who by reason of the sanctity of the place, order'd their bodies to be buried there. There lie[dd] forty kings of Scotland, four of Ireland, four of Norway, and several of the chiefs of the Macdonalds, of whom there remains still some good monuments, with their statues in armour as big as the life.

The island Tiree,[ee] another branch of the Macleans, is eight miles long and three broad, and now belongs to the Duke of Argyll.

The island of Coll is twelve miles long and six broad.

The island of Rum is sixteen miles long and six broad. Half a mile from Rum lies the island of Canna,[ff] two miles long and one broad.

The island of Muck[gg] is four miles in circumference.

The island of Egg is three miles long and a mile and a half broad.

In all these islands there are little lakes and rivers, which afford plenty of salmon, trouts, and eels; and round them the best cod and ling in the world.[hh] The inhabitants all speak the old Irish language in its purity, and wear the same dress with the highlanders, and are all under the subjection of the Duke of Argyll. Further north, towards the north Highlands, is the Isle of Skye, forty-two miles long and above twenty broad, and belongs to a tribe of the Macdonalds; there are three little Islands round this, about five miles each in circumference. About eighty miles west from Skye lie nine islands, some of them seven miles, and some of them more in circumference; in which there are very good harbours for ships of any burthen. Barra is call'd the chief, and is inhabited by the Macneils.[ii]

North of these islands lies North Uist,[jj] twenty-one miles long and three or four miles broad, and several other little islands, whose names would be too tedious. Here is the great herring-fishing of the Dutch, where sometimes they load four hundred ships at a time. Here is also the greatest plenty of cod and ling, and a prodigious variety of sea fowl; and in the month of October they will kill you three hundred seals at a time, of which they make a good trade of their skins to the trunk-makers.

The island of Lewis is one hundred miles long and fourteen broad, and belong'd to the Earls of Seaforth, but now to the government, when they think fit to take possession of it.[31] But I believe York Buildings would hardly give two years purchase for it, though the Dutch would give any money to have it for their herring-fishing. In the little islands round Lewis are also solan geese in the season; and a particular fowl, not found elsewhere, call'd colk, all cover'd with down of different colours, with a tuft[kk] on its head like that of a peacock, and a train longer than that of a house-cock. There is one harbour in this island call'd Scalpay,[ll] of a mile and a half long and a mile broad, which will contain ships of any burthen.

I must not pass by Mr. Martin's favourite island of St. Kilda, twenty leagues west from this; it's but two miles long and one broad. The inhabitants, he says, are about two hundred, well-proportion'd and comely; they are zealous Protestants as far as their knowledge extends, very regular and just in their conversation, and strangers to luxury and excess. They have a chapel where they meet every Lord's Day, to repeat the Lord's Prayer, the Belief, and the Ten Commandments; and neither work, nor allow any stranger to work on that day. They have an altar and crucifix in their chapel, on which they lay their hands when they take the marriage oath, or any other oath. Their houses are of one storey of stone, and cover'd with turf. They make their beds in the walls of the houses, and lie on straw, although they have plenty of down and feathers; and they live all together in a little corner to the east of the island. The people all speak Irish, and are of the same race with the highlanders on the continent.[32]

Besides these islands to the west there are the islands of Orkneys to the north, inhabited by an ancient race of Danes and Norwegians, and the common people still speak that language, although they have been for some ages under the dominion of the crown of Scotland.[33] Those islands are divided from the mainland of Scotland by Pentland Firth, twenty-four miles long and twelve miles broad; and by reason of its cross tides, is a very difficult passage to strangers. They are twenty-eight islands in number; the chief, Pomona,[mm] is twenty-four miles long, and from nine to six miles broad. In this island lies Kirkwall, the only town in Orkney, consisting of one street nigh a mile long, the houses of stone and cover'd with slate; and is govern'd by a provost, four bailiffs, and a common council, like the other towns in Scotland. Its cathedral call'd St. Magnus is built of freestone, its roof supported by fourteen pillars on each side, and the steeple by four large wings in the middle. There is also a public grammar school, with two great markets every week and an annual fair. Stuart, Earl of Orkney, in the year 1574, began a noble palace here, which was never finish'd, tho' several of the rooms were curiously painted. Those islands give title of earl to George, brother to the late Duke Hamilton, Lieutenant-General of the King's Armies, Governor of Edinburgh Castle, Colonel of the Royal Scotch Regiment, and Knight of the Most Noble Order of St. Andrew, or the Thistle.

From those islands eighty miles further north lie the islands of Shetland, in all about forty-six; the chiefest of which, called the Mainland, is sixty miles long, and in some places sixteen broad. But as those islands afford very little of curiosity, (except the fishing which the Dutch enjoy there) I will conclude, having now, according to your desire, finish'd the whole; and am,

Sir,

Your Humble Servant.

Explanatory Notes

Letter I

1 At the end of his *A Journey through England* (1722) Macky said he was about to sail to Scotland from Douglas in the Isle of Man. *stewartry*: lands under the jurisdiction of a steward, in the case of Kirkcudbright, the whole county.

2 Kirkcudbright, which stands on the River Dee in Galloway, was created a Royal Burgh in 1455 but settlement dated back to the Britons, and the Romans erected a fort there.

3 He describes the River Medway and the town of Chatham in *A Journey through England* vol. I, p. 82.

4 *Britannia*: Charles I's flagship was a 100-gun Royal Navy ship, built at Chatham Dockyard and launched in 1682, and later rebuilt and re-launched at Woolwich on 30 October, 1719.

5 The main threat in 1723 was from the Jacobites, particularly feared by Prime Minister Robert Walpole following Atterbury's defection in 1722. In 1719 two Spanish frigates had landed a party of Jacobites led by Lord Tullibardine and Earl Marischal with 300 Spanish soldiers at Loch Duich. They held Eilean Donan Castle until forced to surrender in June.

6 *Trent*: Trento, in the north of Italy. Grand Tourists coming to Italy via Austria would have come through Trento. This is the first of Macky's many allusions to Italy when describing places in Scotland.

7 English travellers in Scotland often complained about unclean accommodation and the poor quality of the food. While Macky says the room he occupied at the inn in Kirkcudbright was dirty, instead of criticizing the limited diet available to him on Sunday he pays tribute to the inhabitants' strict observation of the Sabbath in their abstention from meat that day.

8 Article 22 of the 1707 Treaty of Union had decreed that 16 peers and 45 commoners were to represent Scotland in the Parliament of Great Britain at Westminster. Before its dissolution, the last Scottish Parliament devised the procedures for electing the 16 representative peers through 'open election' rather than by ballot.

9 Defoe expressed similar criticisms of the inhabitants of Kirkcudbright, *Tour*, 3 p. 189.

10 *old towers of stone*: tower houses were stone structures built for both living and defensive purposes.
the kings of Scotland came to the crown of England: James VI of Scotland became James I of England in 1603.

11 In 1715, William Maxwell, 5th Earl of Nithsdale (1676-1744) joined the rising in favour of James Francis Edward Stuart, son of the deposed James VII and II, was taken prisoner at Preston and sent to the Tower of London to await execution. Disguised with his wife's aid, he escaped and they fled to France. Their final years were spent in great poverty in Rome, in attendance on the exiled king.
Macky had a particular interest in the Earl of Nithsdale as he had informed on his activities earlier in France, when he was a secret agent.

12 *the famous Devorgilla*: Devorgilla, Lady Galloway (1210-1290). There are a couple of historical errors in Macky's account. It was her son John Balliol who was king of Scotland (1292-1296), not her husband, John Balliol (1205-1268). (Macky gets this right in Letter XIV.) She was the grand-daughter, not the daughter, of David, Earl of Huntingdon (1144-1219). Her father was Alan of Galloway (1186-1234).
Macky describes the founding of Balliol College by Devorgilla in his *A Journey through England* vol. 2, pp. 59-60.

13 The quotation comes from *The Original Chronicle* by Andrew of Wyntoun (c.1350-c.1422), prior of St Serf's at Lochleven in Fife. Macky presumably had access to one of the nine surviving 15th and 16th century manuscripts, as the first printed edition did not appear until 1795. He modernizes much of the Older Scots language, and omits twelve lines (between 'Locket and bunden with silver bright' and 'She foundit into Galloway') but nevertheless remains faithful to Wyntoun's lines.
coffore (coffer): a wooden chest

14 *a fair stone bridge of thirteen large arches*: The bridge, known as Devorgilla Bridge (or Old Bridge), stills stands today. Built in 1432, possibly on the site of a wooden bridge built by Devorgilla in the 1260s, it was rebuilt after flooding in 1620. Defoe and others (including Francis Grose in 1747) say it had nine arches. No-one else says thirteen.

15 The hanging garden has plants cultivated above ground level, often on a terrace, and the roots of the trees are embedded in an upper terrace rather than in the earth.

16 *Exchange and Town-House*: The Exchange was the building in which the merchants of a town assembled to transact business. The Town-House was the municipal building containing the public offices, court-house, and town hall.

17 The noblemen Nithsdale, Carnwath and Kenmure were taken prisoner after the Jacobite defeat at Preston 9-14 November, 1715.

18 Caerlaverock Castle, situated close to the border with England, played an important role in the defence of the Scottish realm. It

dates from the 13th century, with important additions made in the late 14th/early 15th century. The Maxwells, under their chief, Sir Eustace Maxwell, made a vigorous defence that several times repelled Edward I's attacks.

19 *Mary of Lorraine*: generally known as Mary of Guise, queen of James V and afterwards Regent of Scotland, was the mother of Mary, Queen of Scots.

20 *Sir Ralph Sadler* (1507-1587), English diplomatist sent by Henry VIII to Scotland after the death of James V to arrange for the marriage of the young Princess Mary of Scotland with Prince Edward of England.
Robert Maxwell, 5th Lord Maxwell (1493-1545), introduced and secured a bill in the parliament of 1542 that gave the Scottish people the right to possess and read the Bible in the common tongue.

21 *Robert, Earl of Nithsdale:* Robert Maxwell, 1st Earl of Nithsdale (1586-1646), a Royalist in the Civil War.
and the earl: William Maxwell, 5th Earl of Nithsdale (1676-1744), a Jacobite. See note 11 above.

Letter II

1 *the famous wells of Moffat*: Moffat was one of Britain's most fashionable spa resorts in the 18th century.
Scarborough ... Bath and Tunbridge: Macky introduces his account of Scarborough with a reference to its famous wells in *A Journey Through England* vol. II, p. 215. The walks and other diversions of Bath are described in the same volume, pp. 127-130, and those of Tunbridge-Wells in volume I, pp. 92-95.
raffling: a game of dice. According to the OED the current sense dates from the mid-18th century.

2 Drumlanrig Castle was completed in 1691 by William Douglas, 1st Duke of Queensberry (1637-1695).

3 *Gusto Grande*: effect created by deviating from the rules of art or architecture. According to Joseph Addison: 'Those who have surveyed the noblest Pieces of Architecture and Statuary both ancient and modern, know very well that there are frequent Deviations from Art in the Works of the greatest Masters, which have produced a much nobler Effect than a more accurate and exact way of Proceeding could have done. This often arises from what the *Italians* call the *Gusto Grande* in these Arts' (*The Spectator* no. 592. Friday, September 10, 1714).

4 *Chatsworth*: this seat was rebuilt by the 1st Duke of Devonshire between 1699-1702. Macky pays tribute to the duke's vision in *A Journey Through England*, vol. II, pp.177-183.

5 The tomb of the 1st Duke of Queensberry (d. 1695) and his Duchess (d. 1700) is sometimes known as the 'Durisdeer Marbles'.

6 The Barony of Drumlanrig was originally a property of the Earl of Mar. In 1388, when James 2nd Earl of Douglas and Mar died at the Battle of Otterburn, the Barony of Drumlanrig passed to his son William Douglas, who became 1st Laird of Drumlanrig. Macky may have seen the charter of donation in the charter room of Drumlanrig, but it's quite possible that his source is actually David Hume of Godscroft's *History of the House and Race of Douglas and Angus* (Edinburgh, 1644) which includes a facsimile of the 'Charter by James, Earl of Douglas, to William of Douglas, his soil, of the barony of Drumlangryg, 1384-1388'. Macky cites this work as the major source for Douglas family history in Letter XII.

7 William Douglas was one of the ambassadors commissioned to negotiate with King Henry IV for the release of King James I, at the time a prisoner in England. Between 1412 and 1416, he repeatedly proceeded to the Court of England on this business. He obtained from King James I a letter, dated at Croydon, 30th November, 1412, confirming to him the lands of Drumlanrig, 'Hawyke,' and Selkirk.

8 *Battle of Agincourt:* this was in 1415, not 1427.

9 *the late duke*: James Douglas, 2nd Duke of Queensbury (1662-1711). Macky described him in his *Characters* as: 'a gentleman of good estate, a fin natural disposition, but apt to be influenced by people about him; hath a genteel address, much the manner of a man of quality, of easy access, thin, of a black complexion, turned forty-five years old.'

Charles Douglas (1698-1778) succeeded his father James as 3rd Duke of Queensberry in 1711. Appointed vice-admiral of Scotland in 1722, he lived mostly in England, returning to Scotland only periodically. A number of Scots, including James Boswell, sought his patronage in London.

10 Lead was mined in Leadhills from the twelfth century. By the 1660s the lead mines were owned by Sir John Hope.

11 William Douglas, 1st Duke of Queensberry, obtained the peerage of Earl of March for his second son, William (c.1665–1705), for whom he purchased Neidpath Castle in the 1680s.

12 Macky describes his view of the Downs of Sussex in *A Journey Through England* vol. I, p. 97.

13 James Douglas, 4th Earl of Morton, Regent of *Scotland* 1572-76 during the minority of James VI.

14 Traquair House was gradually transformed from a medieval tower house into a comfortable country residence during the sixteenth and early seventeenth centuries.

the great Earl of Traquair: John Stuart, 1st Earl of Traquair (c.1600–1659), was greatly favoured by Charles I and his chief ecclesiastical adviser, Archbishop Laud. Among the 'schemes' he helped promote in Scotland were the resumption of the grants of Church lands and regulation of the ecclesiastical dress of the clergy through the king's authority.

15 *The present earl*: Charles Stuart, 4th Earl of Traquair (1659–1741). The family were Jacobite sympathizers nonetheless. Charles's son, the 5th Earl, welcomed Prince Charles Edward Stuart to Traquair during the 1745 Jacobite uprising.

16 *the late Rebellion*: the first of many references Macky makes to the Jacobite Rising of 1715.

17 He died on 27th March 1659, in Edinburgh, in obscurity and poverty.

18 *The Chronicle of Melrose Abbey*, compiled by the monks in the twelfth and thirteenth centuries, is preserved in the British Library (MS Cotton Julius B. XIII as well as Cotton Faustina B. IX).

19 *the Black Douglas* was the name usually applied to Sir James Douglas (circa 1286-1330), Robert Bruce's companion-in-arms in the Scottish Wars of Independence.
The Douglas who was killed at the Battle of Otterburn, 5 August 1388, was Sir James Douglas, 2nd Earl of Douglas, whose father, William Douglas, 1st Earl of Douglas, was the nephew of the Black Douglas.

20 Anna Scott (d. 1732), daughter of the 1st Earl of Buccleuch, married Charles II's illegitimate son James, Duke of Monmouth in 1663 and was created Duchess of Buccleuch and Countess of Dalkeith. She rebuilt Dalkeith Palace, bought Melrose Abbey from the 6th Earl of Haddington and Hawick from the 1st Duke of Queensberry in 1674.

21 *Duke of Roxburghe*: John Ker, 5th Earl of Roxburghe, became the 1st Duke of Roxburghe in 1707 for his services in bringing about the Union.
Floors: In 1721 William Adam was commissioned by Ker to make additions to the eastern end of the existing tower house to create a plain, but symmetrical, country house, so Macky's observations are very contemporary.
Friars: the house that the earls of Roxburghe built in the 17th century on the site of the Greyfriars monastery at Kelso. Macky refers to the royal grant that enabled this later in the paragraph: *grant of the dissolv'd monastery of Kelso*.

22 *created Earl of Roxburghe, and Duke by Queen Anne*: this refers to two different creations. Sir Robert Ker of Cesford (d. 1650) was made 1st Earl of Roxburghe in 1616 by James VI and I; John Ker, 5th Earl, was created 1st Duke of Roxburghe in 1707, as noted above, by Queen Anne.

23 Sir William Kerr (d. 1741), brother of the 1st Duke of Roxburghe, was Colonel of the Dragoons. He had served under the Duke of Marlborough in several campaigns and was wounded at the Battle of Sheriffmuir, 1715.

24 Kelso Abbey was founded in the early 12th century by a community of Tironensian Cistercian monks (named after the location of the mother abbey, Tiron Abbey, near Chartres in France). Repeatedly razed during border warfare during the next three centuries, parts of the structure were restored to become the parish church from 1649.

Letter III

1 Berwick Bridge, a red sandstone bridge with fifteen arches, was built over the Tweed between 1611-24, replacing the old wooden structure. It is still in use.

2 The barracks Macky describes here were designed in 1719-21, probably by Nicholas Hawksmoor.

3 *court de guard* (French *corps de garde*): guard house.

4 John Churchill (1650-1722), created Lord Churchill of Eyemouth (1682) and Duke of Marlborough (1703), started his career as a page of honour to James, Duke of York (later James II and VII), and accompanied the then exiled duke to Scotland in 1679.

5 French troops supported the rule of Mary of Guise in Scotland.

6 Broxmouth Park has been associated with the Dukes of Roxburghe since the mid-17th century. It was originally built as a dower house for Margaret, widow of the 3rd Earl of Roxburghe (d.1683). The landscape, originally laid out in the late 17th century, was inspired by French baroque gardens. A *parterre* was a formal ornamental garden.

7 Statesman and poet, Thomas Haddington (1680-1735), 6th Earl of Haddington, transformed the grounds of Tyninghame House through extensive tree-planting from around 1700.

8 The first Earl of Haddington was Sir Thomas Hamilton (1563-1637). Educated at the High School, Edinburgh and the University of Paris, he was a practising advocate by 1587 and held the office of Secretary of State for Scotland 1612-1626, and that of Lord President of the Court of Session 1616-1626.
the present earl: Thomas Haddington, 6th Earl of Haddington.

9 *Bass ... I took a boat and went up to it.* Macky would have been quite at home on a boat, of course.

10 Macky's account of the Bass Rock is taken, almost *verbatim*, from Robert Sibbald's text as it appeared in John Slezer's *Theatrum Scotiae* in 1693.
kittie-waike (or *kitty-wake)*: according to the *Dictionary of the Scots Language*, the second element in the name is an imitation of the bird's cry.

11 The Bass fort was used as a prison for Covenanters between 1673 and 1687. Jacobites seized the garrison in 1691. It was demolished in 1701.

12 The Lauders were granted part of the Bass, along with other lands in East Lothian and Berwickshire, by Malcolm Canmore in 1057.

13 Yester House was commissioned by the 2nd Marquess of Tweeddale in 1697, and built 1699-1728 by architects James Smith and Alexander MacGill. So it was still a work in progress, and when Macky saw it the floors of the upper rooms had yet to be installed.

14 William de Haya was butler to King William 'the Lion' of Scots (1165-1214). Sir Gilbert de la Hay, Lord of Erroll, was a Bruce

supporter, fighting at Methven and Bannockburn in the Wars of Independence. He was also a signatory to the Declaration of Arbroath in 1320. Macky confuses some first names: Sir Thomas de la Haye, actually the son of Sir David de la Haye, 6th of Erroll, was a hostage in England for King David II's ransom in 1354. Sir William de la Hay was a Commissioner to treat for the ransom of King James I in 1423.

The Hays supported Mary, Queen of Scots and rejected the Reformation.

Sir John Hay, Lord Yester (1625-1654), was created Earl of Tweeddale by Charles I. The *present marquis* referred to by Macky was John, 4th Marquess of Tweeddale (1695-1762), who succeeded to the title in 1715 and held the office of Scots representative peer from 1722.

15 John Maitland (d. 1644) was created 1st Earl of Lauderdale in 1624. His son John Maitland (1616-1682), became the 1st (and last) Duke of Lauderdale in 1672.

16 Lethington, a 14th century L-plan tower house, was built as a Border fortification on lands purchased by Robert Maitland of Thirlstane in 1345/46. John Maitland, 1st Duke of Lauderdale, made various changes to Lethington in the 1670s, including enclosing the park.

17 *Talmash, his lady's son by a former marriage*: Thomas Tollemache or Talmash (c. 1651 – 1694) was a son of Elizabeth Maitland, Duchess of Lauderdale, from her previous marriage to Sir Lionel Tollemache.

18 Sir William Maitland of Lethington (1525-1573) became Secretary of State to Mary, Queen of Scots, in 1560 and in the difficult years of the 1560s he spent time as Scotland's ambassador to the court of Elizabeth I of England. Following Mary's forced abdication in 1567, he served in the government of the Regent, James Stewart, Earl of Moray until his assassination in 1570. In the final years of his life he supported attempts to return Mary to power. Because of Maitand's shifts of allegiance, George Buchanan, a tutor to the young queen and a zealous Protestant in the 1560s, satirised Maitland in his tract, *Chamaeleon*, which was first printed in 1711.

Lord Burleigh: William Cecil, Baron Burghley (or Burleigh) was one of Elizabeth I's chief ministers.

John Maitland, 1st Lord Maitland of Thirlestane (1537-1595), was appointed Lord Chancellor of Scotland by James VI in 1586.

John Maitland (1616-1682), created 1st Duke of Lauderdale by Charles II in 1672, and made Secretary of State, a position in which he exercised enormous power, was nicknamed the 'uncrowned King of Scotland'.

19 Macky refers to St Mary's 14th century parish church, Haddington which was restored in the 16th century after damage during Henry VIII's 'rough wooing' (see note 28). The 'Lauderdale Aisle' was built onto the north side of the choir with a small chapel for the Maitland

family and a burial vault beneath. The memorial Macky describes commemorates John Maitland, Lord Chancellor to James VI, and his son, John, the 1st Earl of Lauderdale (d. 1645).

20 The Cockburns of Clerkington, Ormiston and Langton were ancient vassals of the earls of March. Sir Richard Cockburn of Clerkington (d. 1627) was Secretary of State for Scotland 1591-1596, succeeding his uncle, Sir John Maitland.

21 Adam Cockburn of Ormiston, Lord Ormiston (1656-1735), appointed Lord Justice Clerk in 1692, was one of the commissioners appointed to inquire into the Massacre of Glencoe on 28 May, 1695. His son, John Cockburn of Ormiston (d.1758), was an MP until 1741, an agricultural improver, and at one point held the post of Lord of the Admiralty.

22 *Palace of Seton*: the original castle at Longniddry was a square tower built during the time of Seier de Seton sometime after 1066. It was rebuilt and expanded by the successive heads of the family, becoming a castle-complex after the time of William Seton, 1st Lord Seton, c.1348. It was George, 6th Lord Seton, under James V and Mary de Guise, who was responsible for the re-creation. His son, George 7th Lord Seton, a loyal supporter of Mary, Queen of Scots, completed the work, adorning the roof of the 40 foot high Samson's Hall with embossed armories of Scotland, France, Lorraine, and the noble families that were allied to his family.

23 Mary, Queen of Scots, returned to Scotland from France in August 1561, following the death of her first husband, Francis II. George, 5th (and last) Earl of Winton lost his titles and estates for participating in the 1715 Jacobite Rising. Winton was condemned to death but managed to escape the Tower of London, living the rest of his life as a member of the Chevalier's Cabinet in Rome where he died in 1749.

24 *Winton*: The stone tower at Winton, built around 1480 and burned to the ground by Henry VIII during his 'rough wooing', was the site of Winton House built on the ruins by Robert, 6th Lord Seton, 1st Earl of Winton, in 1600 and extended by the king's master mason, William Wallace, in 1619. George, 5th Earl of Winton was a Jacobite supporter and Winton House was forfeited after his capture at the Battle of Preston, 1715.

25 *Lord Seton:* identified (but without a forename) as armour-bearer to Macbeth in Shakespeare's play, attends Macbeth in Act 5, Scene 3, Dunsinane Castle.
Sir Christopher Seton (c.1278-1306) married Christina, sister of Robert the Bruce, in 1301. He is renowned for saving the king's life at the battle of Methven, 1306. He was succeeded by his son, Sir Alexander Seton, one of the signatories of the Declaration of Arbroath, April 6, 1320. It was in fact his son, Sir Christopher's grandson, Sir Alexander Seton who defended Berwick Castle against Edward III's siege in 1333 (not 1332).

26 George, 5th Lord Seton (1531-1585) was Provost of Edinburgh

and supported Queen Mary of Lorraine, also known as Mary of Guise, when she became regent after the death of her husband, James V of Scotland, in 1542. In 1557 George Seton was one of the commissioners appointed by parliament to be present at the marriage of Queen Mary Stuart with the Dauphin of France, and he was Master of the Household after Mary returned to Scotland. She often stayed at his Palace of Seton. George's eldest son, Robert, 6th Lord Seton, also a supporter of Mary, Queen of Scots, was created Earl of Winton in 1600. Robert's second son, George, 3rd Earl of Winton (1584-1650), entertained Charles I and all his retinue at Seton House en route from London to Edinburgh for his coronation.

27 *sold by the commissioners of enquiry but the other day*: The forfeited Winton estate (see note 24) was put up for sale by auction on 6th October, 1719 and was purchased by the agent of the York Buildings Company for the sum of £50,300.

28 The Battle of Pinkie or Musselburgh (10 September, 1547) was the consequence of the resumption by Edward Seymour, Duke of Somerset (Edward VI's uncle) of Henry VIII's campaign to obtain the marriage of his son, Edward VI, and Mary, Queen of Scots by force. The campaign, known as the 'rough wooing', saw English armies rampage throughout the border country in an attempt to intimidate Scotland into acquiescence.

29 Archibald Pitcairne (1652-1713) was an eminent Scottish physician. From the late 17th century Edinburgh gentry built villas in Inveresk as retreats from the smoky city. 'Montpelier' became the by-word for an elevated position and healthy climate, influenced by 18th century travellers' appreciation of the French town.

Letter IV

1 Pinkie House was built by Alexander Seton (1555–1622), James VI's chancellor, who was created 1st Earl of Dunfermline in 1605. The house passed to John Hay, 2nd Marquess of Tweeddale, in 1694.

2 Macky is probably referring to the family group portrait of George 7th Lord Seton, with his four sons and daughters, painted by Frans Pourbus the Elder (not Holbein) in 1572. It is now in the collection of the National Galleries of Scotland.
Alexander Henderson (1583-1646), Professor of Philosophy at St Andrews University 1611-1614, Minister of Leuchars, Fife 1615-1639, opposed Archbishop Laud's attempt to reform the *Scottish* kirk. He was one of the authors of the National Covenant, a document which pledged to maintain the 'true reformed religion' against the policies of Charles I. Anthony van Dyck's portrait of Henderson (1641) now hangs in the Portrait Gallery of the National Galleries of Scotland. As the court painter, van Dyck (1599-1641) painted many portraits of Charles I, including several full-length studies, and of the king

on horseback, as Macky mentions below. His portrait of Charles, 2nd Earl of Dunfermline (1615-1673), one of the leaders of the covenanting army which opposed Charles I, was painted around 1635.

3 The portrait of John Hay, 1st Marquess of Tweeddale (1628-97), and his family was painted by Sir John Baptiste de Medina, around 1695, probably to commemorate Hay's elevation to marquess the previous year. According to the caption in the portrait section of the National Galleries of Scotland, 'Medina worked from existing portraits to compile this dynastic statement. The Marquess's wife is shown holding a wreath of flowers; she had died in 1688'. (http://www.nationalgalleries.org/collection/artists-a-z/M/5808/artist_name/Sir%20John%20Baptiste%20de%20Medina/record_id/2850#.UHjwsa6Cf84)

4 I have not been able to discover any other references to a painting of the Earl of Strafford and the Duke Lauderdale.

5 Dalkeith Castle was the stronghold of the Douglas Earls of Morton. The 8th Earl of Morton sold the castle and estate to Charles I, as a hunting ground, and then these were resold in 1642 to Francis Scott, 2nd Earl of Buccleuch. His daughter Anne, Duchess of Buccleuch (1651-1732), built the palace at Dalkeith in 1701, modeled on William of Orange's palace at Loo in Holland.
jointure-house: secondary residence. Smeaton House was designed as the Duchess of Buccleuch's summer residence on the Buccleuch estate, probably by the architect of Dalkeith Palace, James Smith.

6 Wanstead House, Essex was commissioned in 1715 by Sir Richard Child (1680-1750), created Viscount Castlemain in 1718, from a design by Scottish architect Colen Campbell. It was completed in 1722.

7 James Douglas, 4th Earl of Morton (c.1516-1581) was elected Regent in 1572. He was convicted of complicity in the murder of Henry Darnley and beheaded at Edinburgh Cross by the 'maiden', the pre-guillotine machine he had supposedly introduced to Scotland from England. References to the use of the 'Halifax Gibbet' in West Yorkshire date back to the thirteenth century.

8 see note 5.

9 James Scott, Duke of Monmouth and Buccleuch (1649-1685), illegitimate son of Charles II, husband of Anne Scott, Duchess of Buccleuch. While Lely painted his portrait, the work Macky says he didn't manage to see, of the duke on horseback, was probably by Jan van Wyck (c.1675).

10 Walter Scott (1565-1611) was created 1st Lord Scott of Buccleuch in 1606. He had served in the Netherlands under Maurice, Prince of Orange during the Dutch Revolt against Philip II of Spain, 1604-1609. During the 1590s he had been a famous border reiver.
Thomas Rhymer published his multi-volume *Foedera* from 1704 until his death in 1713.
The Battle of Solway was fought on 24 November 1542.

11 Robert Ker, 4th Earl of Lothian (1636-1703), became 1st Marquess of Lothian in 1701. The seat of the Marquesses of Lothian, Newbattle Abbey, occupies the site of a Cistercian monastery founded by David I.

12 Macky may be referring to van Dyck's portrait of Charles I and family (c.1632) in which his son (the future Charles II) rests a hand on his father's knee. Also in the painting are Queen Henrietta Maria, holding Princess Mary, and a number of courtiers. See note 2.

13 Mary of Guise was Regent of Scotland during her daughter's infancy.

14 Mark Ker was Abbot of Newbattle in 1547. His son Mark (1553-1609) had the lands of Newbattle erected into a barony in 1587 and in 1606 he was created Earl of Lothian. Robert, 4th Earl, was raised to the Marquessate of Lothian in 1701.
Robert Ker of Cessford was created Lord Roxburghe in 1599 and Earl of Roxburghe in 1616. The disputes over precedence are detailed in *The Manuscripts of the Duke of Roxburghe*, Historical Manuscripts Commission Fourteenth Report, Appendix, Part III (London & Edinburgh, 1894).

15 Ramsays were Bruce supporters in the Wars of Independence. The title earl of Dalhousie was created in 1633 for Sir William Ramsay (d. 1672).

16 Sir William St Clair, 11th Baron of Rosslyn, 3rd Prince of Orkney, actually founded Rosslyn chapel in 1446, not 1440. He held many titles, including that of *Duke of Oldenburg* (in Denmark).
Much of Macky's text ('Alexander, Earl of Sutherland, great grandchild to King Robert de Bruce ... appears to be all on fire') has been lifted from Robert Sibbald's account of the chapel in John Slezer's *Theatrum Scotiae* (1693).
He mistakenly writes *Princess's Pillar* instead of Prince's Pillar, now known as the Prentice Pillar or Apprentice Pillar, from the legend that this ornate pillar was carved by an apprentice while his master was away studying in Italy. On his return, the Master was shocked to find everyone praising the pillar and so angry that a mere apprentice had created such a work of art that he killed him. The master was hanged for his crime, and his face can be seen carved high up in the chapel, forced to gaze down upon the apprentice's work for all time.

17 Of those Macky, following Sibbald, says are buried in Rosslyn Chapel, George St. Clair, Earl of Caithness died in 1583.
The Sinclairs, Barons of Roslin, later became the Earls of Orkney and the Earls of Caithness.
William, 5th Earl of Sutherland married Margaret, daughter of Robert the Bruce.

18 George Buchanan (1506-1582): his History of Scotland, *Rerum Scoticarum Historia*, completed shortly before his death (1579), was published in 1582. John Lesley (or Leslie), (1527-1596): his *History of Scotland* from 1436 to 1561, *origine, moribus, et rebus gestis Scotorum* (10 volumes) was presented to Mary, Queen of Scots, in 1571.

The Battle of Rosslyn took place on February 24th, 1303, and involved three successive victories over the English. Sir John Comyn (a leading contender for the vacant throne of Scotland) was the overall commander and Sir Simon Fraser was leader of the army.

Letter V

1 Holyrood Abbey was founded in 1128 by King David I of Scotland, for Augustinian Canon Regulars. A palace was erected as a royal residence by James IV, and added to by James V between 1528 and 1536. Further renovation was carried out in 1633 to mark the Scottish coronation of Charles I, while his son, Charles II, ordered a substantial rebuilding of the palace in the 1670s which was undertaken by the Scottish architect, Sir William Bruce. Neither he nor his brother and successor, James VII and II, saw the completed building.

2 The Dukes of Hamilton first became hereditary keepers of Holyrood in 1646.

3 Physic gardens supplied medical herbs for the instruction of medicinal, surgery and apothecary students. One was established in 1670 on an allotment in St Anne's Yards, adjacent to the palace, by Robert Sibbald, physician to Charles II, and Andrew Balfour, botanist, founders of the Royal College of Physicians of Edinburgh (1681). The sun dial Macky saw was made by John Mylne in 1633 for Charles I, although it was popularly attributed to Mary, Queen of Scots.

4 *presence:* the Presence Chamber was where a monarch received company or those entitled to come into his or her presence.

5 *the Revolution* i.e., the deposition of James VII by William and Mary in 1688, often referred to as the Glorious Revolution.

6 James Drummond (1648-1716), 4th Earl of Perth, became Lord High Chancellor of Scotland in 1684. The chapel at Holyrood, which he had newly redecorated, was ransacked during rioting in 1688.

7 The Abbey Church was transformed into a Catholic chapel, the Thistle chapel, in 1688 by James VII's order, but was destroyed the same year by rioters. An illustration showing the twelve stalls for the Knights of the Order by P. Mazell after John Wyck is included in Antti Matikkala, *The Orders of Knighthood and the Formation of the British Honours System* (Suffolk, UK: Boydell Press, 2008), p. 300.

8 The sanctuary was a defined area, five miles in circumference, taking in most of Holyrood Park. While the Baillie of the Abbey had long provided 'protection' to those in need, the policy of granting sanctuary to debtors appears to have been formalised after Charles I appointed the Duke of Hamilton and his heirs to be Keepers of the Palace in 1646. Crown debtors or fraudulent bankrupts were exempt from sanctuary. In sanctuaries in London, of which there were several, no-one could be arrested, except by an order from the Board

of Green Cloth, a body responsible for auditing the royal household accounts.

9 Macky employs 'palace' for all of the Canongate mansions he mentions here. The grandest was Moray House, built in 1628, with its first floor balcony and entrance gatepiers with pyramid filials.

10 James Ogilvy, 4th Earl of Findlater, and 1st of Seafield (1663-1730), Chancellor of Scotland, lived in Moray House and may have been educated at Heriot's Hospital, a charitable school, which had been founded in 1628.

11 The Setons, earls of Winton, were loyal to the Stuart cause. The Canongate mansion known as Lord Seton's Lodging was acquired by the York Buildings Company after the attainder of George, 5th Earl of Winton (c.1678-1749), who supported the 1715 Jacobite Rising. He died in exile in Rome.

12 The Edinburgh mansion of the dukes of Roxburghe was renowned for its fine gardens. Panmure House was the town residence of the earls of Panmure, until the fourth earl, James, Privy Councillor to James VII, lost his title and estates after the Battle of Sheriffmuir, and died an exile in Paris.

13 *the fine palace of the Earls of Moray*: see note 9.

14 It was fashionable for the aristocracy to have private bowling greens. The oldest public lawn bowling green in Scotland is at Haddington (1709).

15 *an old Roman wall*: although the Roman Antonine Wall extended from the Clyde to the Forth, near Edinburgh, it's more likely that the wall Macky saw in the early 18th century was a medieval one which was visible in the 17th century, and gradually demolished from around 1764.

16 The open crown, supported by eight flying buttresses, may be modelled on the slightly earlier St Nicholas church, Newcastle.

17 The Tron kirk, constructed between 1636 and 1647 to a T-plan design by John Mylne, royal master mason, was founded by King Charles I to house the congregation displaced from nearby St Giles when he made that church a cathedral.

18 The Collegiate Church, or Trinity College Kirk, was founded in 1460 by Mary of Gueldres in memory of her husband, King James II (1437-1460). Lady Yester's Kirk was built from a donation by Margaret Ker, Lady Yester (c.1572-1647). The *new church in the middle of the Canongate* was the Canongate Kirk, built in 1688 by King James VII and II from a bequest left by Thomas Moodie in 1649. William III (and IV) had displaced James by the time the church was completed in 1691. Greyfriars comprised Old Grefriars (1614) and new Greyfriars (1718).

19 Parliament House was completed in 1639, not 1636. The life-size equestrian lead statue of Charles II as Caesar supplied in 1685 by James Smith, Surveyor of the King's Works, was probably imported from Holland.

20 The Advocates Library was formally inaugurated in 1689. As well as collecting legal works, it was also a deposit library. In 1925 the non-legal books in the collection were gifted to the new National Library of Scotland.
The armorial arms of France (fleur-de-lis) and of Scotland (red lion rampant) represented the 'auld alliance' and appeared on coins from the reign of James I of Scotland (1406-37).

21 The Bank of Scotland was founded by an Act of the Scottish Parliament on 1 November, 1695.
Representatives of the royal boroughs met in a dedicated assembly room on the south side of Parliament Square.

22 While the exact date of its foundation is unknown, the Royal High School is considered to be one of the oldest schools in Europe. The original Grammar School, providing a Latin education, was attached to Holyrood Abbey. In 1505 the school became the first in Britain to be designated a high school.
In March 1703 a contract was won by John Valentine, Venetian 'by Countary' to 'finish and compleat workmanlyke the present little room in the new house belonging to the said Incorporation lying in the high schoole yards at Edinburgh designed for a bathing roome, within the new Royall Bagnio or bathing roome' (Royal College of Surgeons of Edinburgh website: http://www.library.rcsed.ac.uk/docs/Bagnio_OSH.pdf).
Sir John Medina and his apprentice William Aikman painted a series of nearly 40 paintings of contemporary surgeons around 1700 to 1710.

23 See note 3. Sibbald's catalogue of the natural history collection, *Auctarium musæi Balfouriani, e musæo Sibbaldiano, sive Enumeratio & descriptio rerum rariorum*, was published by Edinburgh University in 1697.

24 John Adamson (1576-c.1651), Professor of Philosophy and Principal of the University of Edinburgh (1623-1651), bequeathed the skull of George Buchanan to the university. It is housed in Edinburgh University's Anatomy Museum.
John Hus, a preacher of Prague, banished from the city for openly teaching the Wycliffite heresies, was condemned by the Council of Constance and burned at the stake in 1415. His friend and admirer Jerome (Hieronymus) of Prague suffered the same fate. Bohemian nobles violently protested against their execution in 1416. The 'Bohemian Protest' was bequeathed to the university by William Guild (1586-1657), and became one of the attractions which brought a series of visitors to the College Library as part of the standard tour of the city of Edinburgh.

25 The University of Edinburgh was founded in 1583 at the instigation of Edinburgh Town Council, but the college library dates from 1580 as Macky says. The first Principal was Robert Rollock, a graduate of Scotland's oldest university, St. Andrews (1413), and a disciple of George Buchanan.

26 Edinburgh had schools for girls by the end of the fifteenth century, sometimes described as "sewing schools", and probably taught by lay women or nuns. Macky is referring to the Merchant Maiden Hospital, co-founded by Mary Erskine (1629-1707) and the Company of Merchants of the City of Edinburgh on the 4th of June, 1694, to house and educate destitute daughters of decayed merchant burgesses of the city.

27 Greyfriars Kirk was used as a barracks from 1650 to 1653 during Oliver Cromwell's invasion of Scotland.
The mausoleum of Sir George Mackenzie of Rosehaugh (1636-1691), a Scottish Lord Advocate whose persecution of the Covenanters gained him the nickname of 'Bloody Mackenzie', was modelled on an Italian design. The tomb of George Foulis, of Ravilstoun (d.1633), son of James Foulis of Collington, and his wife, Jane Bannatyne (d.1631), was erected by their son. The Foulis estate at Ravelston is now the site of the Mary Erskine School. Among the other graves Macky would have seen in the kirkyard are those of Mary Erskine (1629-1707), the architect John Mylne (1611–1667), the historian George Buchanan (d.1582) and, depending on the year of his visit to the cemetery, that of physician Archibald Pitcairne (1652–1713).

28 *Basilikon Doron*. Greek for "royal gift", was written in 1599 by James VI of Scotland, soon to become James I of England, in the form of advice for his son on kingship.
Walter Balcanqual (c.1586-1645) doctor of divinity and chaplain of James VI, was successively dean of Rochester and dean of Durham. As one of the executors of George Heriot's will, Balcanqual was instrumental in selecting a field of eight and a half acres to the south of the castle and Grassmarket for the site of the building, and he is thought to have advised the master masons on the original design by Inigo Jones.

29 Heriot's work, or *wark* in Scots, refers to the building and its construction.

30 Sibbald wrote in the *Theatrum Scotiae* (1693): 'Ptolomy calls this Place Στρατοπεδον Πτερωτον [stratopedon pteroton = winged camp], Castrum alatum, the Winged Castle, which is not so called from that kind of Wings which the Greek Builders (as says Vitruvius) call Πτερωματα [pteromata = wings], (which are double Walls so rising to the Height, that they resemble Wings: For it is likely there was no regular building in that Place at that time)'.

31 Leith, the seaport of Edinburgh, stands at the mouth of the Water of Leith. While the pier Macky saw dated from the early 17th century, he seems to be aware of the stone pier constructed between 1720-30 which joined to the wooden pier, and the small dock created on the west side of the river's mouth.

32 The full title is: *The sett, and decreet arbitral of King James the VI, of Blessed memory: containing the fundamental principles of the government of the city of Edinburgh, and deciding all differences*

betwixt merchants and crafts-men therein, as it is registrat in the books of Council: together with two acts of Town Council relating to the same. (1683)

Letter VI

1 The other two are Inchmickery and Inchgarvie.
2 The town crest has above it the words "Portus Gratiae" (Safe Harbour). After being granted a royal charter in 1541 (confirmed 1586), Burntisland became second only to Leith as an important seaport on the Forth.
3 The monks of Dunfermline Abbey were given the shire of Kirkaladunt by Malcolm II in the late 11th century. A good harbour enabled the royal burgh to grow and prosper, and to engage in trade with the Baltic. Defoe praised Kirkcaldy, noting 'it has some considerable Merchants in it' (vol. 3, 233).
4 The decline of the royal burghs of Fife was also remarked by Defoe: 'As you must expect a great Deal of Antiquity in this Country of Fife, so you must expect to find all those antient Pieces mourning their own Decay, and drooping and sinking in Ashes' (vol. 3, p. 240). Many of the Fife villages became holiday resorts with the arrival of the railway in the 19th century.
5 Castle Weems, or Wemyss Castle, has been the seat of the clan Wemyss since the 12th century. Destroyed during the Wars of Independence, the castle was rebuilt in the 16th century. David, 3rd Earl of Wemyss (b. 1678) had died on 13 March, 1720, and was succeeded by his son, David (b. 1699). It is unclear which earl Macky refers to by *noble lord*. The third earl had been one of the commissioners for the Treaty of Union with England and became Vice Admiral of Scotland in 1707. A famous elegy lamented his death. The lack of reference may indicate that Macky is referring to the period before 1720. A stone harbour was provided by David, 2nd Earl of Wemyss in 1664 to export coal and salt.
6 John, Lord Elcho of Weems was created 1st Earl of Wemys in 1633 by Charles I at Dumfermline.
7 The North Sea was known as the *German Ocean* until the early 20th century.
8 In 1559, following a rousing sermon against idolatry by John Knox, the interior of the cathedral was sacked by a Protestant mob.
9 The University of St Andrews, founded by Bishop Henry Wardlaw in 1411, was sanctioned by a Papal Bull in 1413, granted on the petition of King James I, the bishop, and the other dignitaries of the church in the ecclesiastical metropolis.
10 Bishop James Kennedy (1408-1465) was the youngest son of Sir James Kennedy of Dunure and Princess Mary, second daughter of King Robert III of Scotland. He became Bishop of St Andrews in

1440, and was previously Bishop of Dunkeld. He served briefly as Chancellor of Scotland in 1444, and as Regent during the minority of James III. He founded St Salvator's College in 1450. He is buried in the chapel, in a tomb he had built for the purpose.
St Andrews declined in the 17th and 18th centuries.

11 *visitation*: 'The action, on the part of one in authority, or of a duly qualified or authorized person, of going to a particular place in order to make an inspection and satisfy himself that everything is in order' (OED). Robert Sibbald notes of St Salvator College: 'Mr. Skene Doctor of Divinity and Principal of the College, has of late repaired and augmented the Fabrick thereof, having made a Collection for that end'. (*Theatrum Scotiae*, 1693).

12 The University of St Andrews owns three maces dating from the medieval period. The one Macky describes is inscribed: 'Johne Maiel, govldsmche and verlete off chamer til ye Lord ye Dalfyne hes made yis masse in ye toune of Paris ye zer of our Lorde MCCCCLXI' (goldsmith and personal valet to the Lord Dauphin [Crown Prince of France], has made this mace in the town of Paris in the year 1461). A pendant attached to the mace records that it was made and donated by James Kennedy, the 'illustrious' Bishop of St Andrews and founder of the College of St Salvator.
Defoe writes: 'They tell you a Story here of nine maces found under the Archbishop's Tomb ... But to me the Story does not tell well at all'. (*Tour*, vol.3, p.251) There is historical evidence that three maces were removed from the college for safekeeping: first to St Andrews Castle during the Reformation when the Regents of St Salvator adhered to Catholicism and quitted their office; and during the Civil Wars to Dunottar Castle just before English troops occupied St Andrews Castle.

13 St Leonard's College was established in 1512 as a college for poor clerks of the Church of St Andrews, based on the older Hospital and Church of St Leonard within the Priory of St Andrews. The founder was John Hepburn. Robert, Earl of March and Lennox increased the number of bursars and Sir John Scott of Scots-Tarbet founded a chair of Humanities.

14 Following a fire in 1702, the north side of the court was rebuilt as student lodgings.
Francis Scott, 2nd Earl of Buccleuch, a former student, presented to St Leonard's College 113 books in, or around, 1645. They are now part of St Andrews Special Collections. The silver arrow prize for archery continued to be exhibited into the 19th century.

15 St Mary's College was founded in 1537-39 by Archbishop James Beaton. Since 1579 it has been the university's theological college. Francis Hutcheson (1694–1746) was an influential Scottish moral philosopher. *An Inquiry into the Original of our Ideas of Beauty and Virtue* (1725) was a seminal Enlightenment work. He also published a text book for students, *Philosophiae Moralis Institutio Compendiaria* (1745).

16 The observatory was set up by mathematician James Gregory in 1673 but he left St Andrews for Edinburgh the following year, citing prejudice. He wrote: 'the affairs of the Observatory of St Andrews were in such a bad condition, the reason of which was, a prejudice the masters of the University did take at the mathematics, because some of their scholars, finding their courses and dictats opposed by what they had studied in the mathematics, did mock at their masters, and deride some of them publicly'. The observatory was finally dismantled in 1736.

17 *Conge d'Eslire*, meaning 'permission to elect'. John Murray, 1st Duke of Atholl was Chancellor of St Andrews University 1697-1724.

18 James Brydges (1674-1744), 1st Duke of Chandos, Chancellor of the University of St. Andrews 1724-1744, donated £1,000 to the University which was used to establish the Chandos Chair of Medicine and Anatomy.

19 The town church to which Macky refers is the parish church of the Holy Trinity in St Andrews. Above the ornate tomb of Archbishop James Sharp (1618-1697), murdered at Magus Muir en route to St Andrews by Covenanters, is a life size figure of Sharp kneeling, with crook and mitre, to receive the crown of martyrdom.

20 After Covenanters revolted in 1679 against Charles II's severe controls on non-conformity, a government army of about 5000 was sent north under the command of James, Duke of Monmouth to engage the rebels at Bothwell Bridge, on 22 June 1679.

21 David Hackston of Fife was one of the armed supporters of Richard Cameron, an extreme Covenanter. He fought at the Battle of Bothwell Bridge and was arrested and executed for the murder of Sharp shortly afterwards.

22 St Andrews Castle was the main residence of the bishops and archbishops of St Andrews from the 13th century. Cardinal David Beaton (1494-1546), the last Archbishop of St. Andrews before the Reformation, was murdered by Norman Leslie, Master of Rothes, and two accomplices on 29 May, 1546, following a property dispute.

23 *legate a latere*: the highest ranking papal legate. As one of the Regents following James V's death, he supported Mary of Guise and the alliance with France, and blocked Henry VIII's plans to marry his son to the young Mary, Queen of Scots. His brutal persecution of Protestants made him unpopular in Scotland.

24 Patrick Hepburn (1487-1573) succeeded his uncle John Hepburn as Prior of St Andrews in 1526. John was the one who established St Leonards College and funded the reconstruction of the town walls of St Andrews around 1520. The precinct walls remain the most complete in Scotland.

25 *links:* usually flat common ground covered with turf, often found near the sea-shore.

26 According to legend, the relics of St. Andrew were brought to Fife by a bishop, St. Rule, from Patras in Achaea. Among the cathedral ruins, St Rule's Tower (early 12th century) still stands today.

27 Leuchars castle, dating from mid-13th century, built on a mote-hill, was occupied at least as late as 1565, and part was still standing at the close of the 18th century. James, 5th Earl of Southesk, was atteinted for his role in the 1715 Rising.

28 Ferries plied the Tay from the 1100s and by the 1700s a regular ferry made the crossing of the Tay from Dundee to Woodhaven. A new pier and inn were built in 1715. The ferry service operated until the opening of the Tay road bridge in 1966.

Letter VII

1 *freshes*: the OED defines *fresh* as 'a flood of fresh water flowing into the sea; *esp*. an ebb tide, whose force is increased by heavy rains. Freq. in *pl. slike:* according to the OED this is a (now rare) Scots and northern word meaning mud, slime, sludge.

2 David, Earl of Huntingdon built St Mary's Church in 1192, after returning from the Third Crusade. During the Wars of Independence the church was sacked and rebuilt several times. The Steeple Tower, 156 ft high with a crown on it, was erected in 1495, and is still standing. In 1588, following the Reformation, the 'Collegiate' system was adopted – St. Mary's being the First Charge, while the south transept was rebuilt and named South Church (Second Charge). The Third Charge was established in 1609. In 1651, General Monck sacked Dundee for Cromwell and stabled his horses in the ruins of the South Church.

3 The hospital was originally founded in 1392 as an academy by James, Earl of Crawford and Lindsay (d.1397), who bequeathed certain lands and buildings for the maintenance of the poor citizens of Dundee.

4 Sir William Davison or Davidson of Corriehill (c.1640-1683), was a Royalist and Resident Agent/Ambassador of Charles II in Amsterdam.

5 James Francis Edward Stuart made a state entry into Dundee in December 1715, and proclaimed his forthcoming coronation at Scone. He briefly held court at Scone.

6 Dudhope Castle, seat of the Scrimgeours, was originally a 13th century tower house and in the 17th century became the property for a short time of John Graham of Claverhouse (Bonnie Dundee), himself a Scrimgeour 'on the distaff side'. The earldom of Dundee was created in 1660 for John Scrimgeour, 3rd Viscount Dudhope. Graham of Claverhouse was the Jacobite commander of the forces at the Battle of Killiecrankie on the 27th July, 1689.

7 *Te moriente novas accepit Scotia leges, /Accepitque novos te moriente Deos; / Illa tibi superesse nequit, nec tu potes illae, / Ergo, Caledonia, nomen inane, vale -/ Tuque vale, gentis quondam fortissime ductor, vale. / Ultime Scotorum, atque ultime Graeme.*

8 William III granted James Douglas, Marquess of Douglas and Earl of Angus (1646-1700), Dudhope Castle and the forfeited estates of Claverhouse in March 1694. Macky describes Douglas Castle in Letter XII.

9 Panmure House was built 1666-1670 by John Milne, Master Stonemason to the King's Majesty, for George Maule, 2nd Earl of Panmure (1619–1671). James, 4th Earl of Panmure, added the wings before forfeiting his title and estates after taking part in the Jacobite Rising of 1715. Panmure House then passed to the earls of Dalhousie, and was purchased by the York Buildings Company in 1719.

The house replaced Panmure Castle, an early 13th century residence, which was in ruins by the early 17th century. Panmure House, modified in the 19th century, was demolished in 1955.

the present countess: Margaret Hamilton, Countess of Panmure (d. 1731) married to the attainted James Maule, 4th Earl of Panmure (d. 1723). On 23 April, 1724 the York Buildings Company granted the countess a ninety-nine years lease of Panmure House and gardens at a rent of £100. Since Macky knew of this arrangement, the countess must have been allowed use even before the formal tack was granted.

10 *the inhabitants are more courteous, familiar and affable, than in the southern parts of Scotland*: Defoe, in contrast, finds the locals unfriendly and attributes this to their Anglophobia, on account of the Union: 'We did not find so kind a Reception among the common People of *Angus*, and the other Shires on this Side of the Country, as the *Scots* usually give to Strangers: But we found it was because we were *English* Men' (vol. 3, 257). Macky goes on to say that the gentry of Angus are 'universal enemies to the Union with England'.

11 David Carnegie (1575–1658) was created 1st Earl of Southesk in 1633. His brother John Carnegie (1611-1667) was created 1st Earl of Ethie by Charles I in 1647, and changed it to 1st Earl of Northesk in 1666. James Carnegie, 5th Earl of Southesk (1662-1730) was attainted for his part in the 1715 Jacobite Rising. He had fought at Sherrifmuir and escaped to France, where he died. David, 4th Earl of Northesk (d. 1729) was a representative peer from 1708 to 1715 in the post-Union Parliament.

12 Dunnottar Castle was home to the powerful Earls Marischal, from the 14th century when Sir William Keith, the 1st Earl Marischal, built his tower house. Hervey de Keith first held the office of Marischal under Malcolm IV. His descendents were made Hereditary Great Marischal by Robert the Bruce in 1324, while the office of Earl Marischal was bestowed on the Keiths by James II about 1458.

Sir Robert Keith (d. 1346), one of the Scots commissioners at Westminster for the settlement of the government of Scotland in 1304, joined Robert Bruce and commanded the Scottish horse at Bannockburn in 1314, and was one of the signatories to the Declaration of Arbroath in 1320. Sir William Keith was one of the *hostages* for the ransom of King James I when he was a captive in England in 1424 and 1426. William, 4th Earl Marischal, was an adherent of the Reformation. Sir Ralph Sadler, English ambassador in Scotland, in a report to Henry VIII, dated 27th March 1543, described the Earl Marischal as well inclined to the project of the marriage of Queen Mary with Prince Edward. He also mentions him as one 'who hath ever borne a singular good affection' to Henry. George, 5th Earl (c.1553–1623), went on the embassy to Denmark in 1589 to settle the marriage of Anne of Denmark and James VI, later James I of England. He founded Marischal College, Aberdeen in 1593. His son William, 6th Earl, received Charles I on his entry into Edinburgh in 1633 and, together with his younger brother John, supported the King in the civil wars.

George Keith, 10th and last Earl Marischal (1693-1778), was convicted of treason for his part in the Jacobite Rising of 1715, and as a result his estates, including Dunnottar, were seized by the government.

13 Edmund Calamy, an English non-conformist minister, visited Aberdeen on his tour of Scotland in 1709 and praised Aberdeen as 'one of the politest towns in North Britain' for there he and his companions 'met with the utmost civility during the whole of our stay' (Edward Calamy, *An Historical Account of My Own Life,* ed. J. T. Rutt, 2 vols. (London, 1829), II, p. 198.

14 George Gordon (1637-1720), Lord High-Chancellor of Scotland, was created 1st Earl of Aberdeen in 1682. His ancestors were the Baronet Gordons of Haddo. Macky's information is up to date: William, 2nd Earl of Aberdeen, had only recently succeeded to the title, becoming one of the sixteen peers for Scotland in 1721.

15 The section 'Old Aberdeen ... University of King Charles' is taken almost verbatim from Sibbald's description of the city in *Theatrum Scotiae.* Macky makes a couple of alterations. Firstly, he changes the date, 1631, Sibbald gave for the collapse of the King's College chapel steeple to 1641. In fact, the chapel's crown steeple, built in honour of James VI, was blown down in a storm in 1633. Macky also adds to Sibbald's list of college faculty, presumably to reflect the changes he had discovered since the latter's late 17th century account.

16 According to tradition, during the Wars of Independence, the people of Aberdeen helped Robert the Bruce enter the English-occupied castle in 1306. The password on the night the castle was taken was *bon accord,* and subsequently became the city's motto.

The Bridge of Don, now better known now as the Brig o' Balgownie, dates from the early 14th century.

The Cathedral Church of St Machar's, founded around 1131, is dedicated to an Irish saint who accompanied St Columba to Scotland. The stone building Macky, following Sibbald, describes dates from the 14th century. This church, including the chancel and library, was sacked by zealous reformers around 1560.

17 King's College was founded in 1495 by William Elphinstone, Bishop of Aberdeen and Chancellor of Scotland, although it was 1500 before building actually started. Bishop Patrick Forbes (1564-1638) was the Bishop in office when repairs of the steeple were undertaken. A William Gordon was Mediciner at King's College from 1632-1640. The library of King's College was formed around the donations of Bishop Elphinstone and early principals and regents of the college. Bishop Patrick Scougall (c.1607-1682) and his son Henry (1650-1678), Professor of Divinity, donated more than one thousand books to the library.

18 King's College was modelled on the University of Paris where Bishop Elphinstone had once taught. Much of the nomenclature for offices derives from there, including *procuratores nationum,* Proctors of the Nations, or geographical clusters into which the students were divided.

19 King's and Marischal Colleges were officially united as King Charles' University for twenty years from 1641.

20 Bishop Elphinstone persuaded James IV to make the above application to Pope Alexander VI in 1494 and the pope issued a bull in response in February 1495.

21 St. Germain's House, East Lothian, was built in the late 12th century as a hospital of the Order of the Star of Bethlehem. In the 16th century it became the property of the Seton family who built a house on the ruins of the hospital.

22 The remainder of Macky's account of Aberdeen, with the exception of the final paragraph, is taken almost verbatim from Sibbald's description in the *Theatrum Scotiae.*

23 The Holy Trinity Monastery was said to have been founded in 1211 by King William I and Queen Ermegard in order for the Trinitarians to support poor pilgrims and to help ransom captives in the Holy Land.

24 A Royal Mint once stood in Exchequer Road. Coins and dies bearing the name of the city and covering the period from the reign of Alexander II (1214-49) to that of James IV (1488-1513) are in existence.

25 Dr. William Barclay published a treatise extolling the virtues of the Well of Spa and commending the use of its waters to invalids: *Callirhoe; commonly called the well of spa, or The nymph of Aberdene: Resuscitat by William Barclay, M. of Art, and doctor of Physicke. What diseases may be cured by drinking of the well of Spa at Abendene, and what is the true use thereof.* (Edinburgh, 1615).

26 The Franciscan friary, founded in 1469, consisted of cloister and church, with a new church built in 1518-32. In 1567 permission was granted for 'the place of the Friars Minor' to be converted into a hospital, but the church stood derelict until 1624, when it was restored. Elphinstone and Dunbar, Bishop of Aberdeen 1518-1532, are sometimes referred to as the 'building bishops'. Dunbar completed the work on the Bridge of Dee begun by Elphinstone.

27 See note 12, Letter VI and note 17 above.
28 Dr Patrick Dun (1642–1713), Principal of Marischal College, endowed Aberdeen grammar school, though the school is usually considered to date from the 13th century.
29 St Nicholas Church is first mentioned in a Papal Bull dated 1157. A large new burgh kirk was erected in the 15th century. Like St Machar's, St Nicholas Church provided poor relief in an adjacent almshouse and workhouse.
30 In 1629, Sir Alexander Irvine, laird of Drum, founded four bursaries of Philosophy, and two of Divinity, in the Marischal College of Aberdeen, and four bursaries in the Grammar School, Aberdeen, bequeathng £10,000 Scots for this purpose.

Letter VIII

1 Kildrummy Castle, dating from the 13th century was abandoned in 1716 when John Erskine, 6th Earl of Mar (1675-1732) escaped to France following his failed Jacobite uprising. Macky describes the Alloway residence in Letter X.
2 The Forbeses were raised to a barony in 1271 by Alexander III. In 1723 the Lord Forbes was William Forbes, 13th Lord Forbes (1689-1730), having succeeded to the title in 1716. In 1720 he lost over £20,000 in the South Seas bubble. The title Lord Forbes of Pitsligo was created in 1633 for Sir Alexander Forbes (d. 1636). Alexander, 4th Lord Pitsligo (1678-1762) opposed the Union and fought in the Jacobite Uprising in 1715. He later supported the Jacobite Uprising in 1745, and was attainted in 1746.
3 Sir John Keith (d.1714) was created Earl of Kintore in 1677. His seat was Keith-Hall.
the late Duke of Gordon: George Gordon, 4th Marquess of Huntly, 1st Duke of Gordon had died in 1716. The title, Earl of Aboyne, created in 1660, was held by John Gordon (d. 1732) at the time Macky was writing. The family seat is Aboyne Castle. Frendraught Castle was built in the 17th cnetury upon an older castle belonging to the Crichton family.
When Charles, 13th Earl of Erroll, died unmarried in 1717 the earldom then devolved on his eldest sister, Lady Mary, who became 14th Countess of Erroll. The principal seat of the Earls of Erroll was Slains Castle, but it was razed by James VI in 1594. Another Hay residence, the Tower of Bowness in Cruden Bay, was extended by various earls of Erroll between the 17th and 19th centuries. James Boswell and Samuel Johnson stayed at the refurbished residence, which came to be renamed Slains Castle in 1773 and described it in their published travel accounts: *A Journey to the Western Isles of Scotland* and *Journal of a Tour of the Hebrides*. Another famous visitor was Bram Stoker: In early transcripts Stoker had Dracula landing at Cruden

Bay after his voyage from Transylvania. This was later changed to the North Yorkshire town of Whitby for the final published work.

4 Charles Hay, 9th Earl of Erroll (d. 1717) voted against the Union. He was an active Jacobite and received the Order of the Thistle from the Old Pretender, James VIII.

5 The earldom of Buchan was created for James Stuart, younger brother of John, 1st Earl of Atholl in 1469. The *present earl* referred to by Macky was David Erskine, 9th Earl of Buchan (1672-1745), who sat as one of the Scottish representative peers in the House of Lords between 1715 and 1734.

6 Statutory regulation of salmon fishing dates back to 1424, in the reign of David II.

7 *Stangs Castle*: Slains Castle. William Camden, also citing George Buchanan, refers to the cave near 'Stany's Castle'.

8 James *Ogilvy*, 4th *Earl of Findlater* and 1st Earl of Seafield (1663-1730) had a seat at Cullen House, Moray. John George Ogilvy (1717-1738) was the 5th Lord Banff; the family seat was Inchdrewer, destroyed by fire in 1713. Alexander Fraser (1710–1751), 14th Lord Saltoun, descended from Frasers of Philorth, the senior line. The family seat is in Sauchen.
Castle Gordon: the original seat of the Dukes of Gordon was built by George Gordon, 2nd Earl of Huntly in the 1470's.

9 Sir Adam de Gordon, Lord of Gordon, was granted the lands and lordship of Strathbogie as a reward for loyal service to Robert Bruce, and named them Huntly after the nearby village. Alexander, Lord of Gordon and Huntly (d.1470), was created Earl of Huntly in 1449. George, the 6th earl, was created Marquess of Huntly by King James, in 1599 (not 1549 as Macky says) and George, 4th Marquess (1649-1716) was made Duke of Gordon in 1684. James VII and II appointed him Captain of Edinburgh Castle shortly after his accession. The castle was surrendered to William's forces after a siege on 13th June, 1689.
the present duke: Alexander, 2nd Duke of Gordon (1678-1728).

10 In 1702, George Gordon, 15th Earl (1633-1703), broke with the Gordons of Huntly, dropped the Gordon surname and resumed the name of Sutherland. John Gordon, 16th Earl of Sutherland (1661–1733), a commissioner for the Union of England and Scotland, supported the Crown in the 1715 Rebellion and in 1719 his men took part in the Battle of Glen Shiel, which effectively ended another Jacobite rising.

11 See notes V, 10 and VIII, 8 above.

12 *Prentices Isle*: Macky is referring to the 'Prentice Aisle which was supposedly built by an apprentice in the absence of his master. A similar legend is associated with Rosslyn.

13 He describes the Leslie family and their seat at Rothes Castle in Letter IX.

14 Alexander Duff of Braco (1652-1705), a writer to the Signet in Edinburgh, used his knowledge of feudal law to acquire Balvenie estate, Banffshire, formerly owned and occupied by Comyns, Douglases and Atholls. The estate was inherited by his nephew who was raised to the peerage with an Irish title as Baron Braco of Kilbryde in 1735.
Robert Gordon (1580-1646) was created first baronet Gordon of Gordonstoun in 1642. At the time Macky was travelling, his descendant, Sir Robert Gordon, 4th Baronet (1696-1772), MP for Caithness, held the title.
Dunbars were hereditary sheriffs of Moray from the fourteenth century.

15 An English garrison was established at Inverness during the occupation of Scotland by Cromwell's army from 1652-1657. Defoe observes that when the English troops were disbanded, many soldiers chose to settle in Inverness and this explains the English accent and manners that were still notable in Macky's day. (Defoe, vol. 3, 266-267).

16 His account of Dumbarton is in Letter XIII.

17 *West Ocean* is better known now as the Atlantic Ocean while the *East of German Ocean* is the North Sea.
The Mackenzie clan has been associated with Ross and Cromarty since their rapid rise to power in the 15th century. Macky's belief that they were descendants of the Fitzgeralds, and had originally come from Ireland, may have been influenced by *The Genealogie of The Mackenzies Preceeding ye Year* 1661, written in 1669 and attributed to George Mackenzie, 1st Earl of Cromartie.
The charter which supposedly granted lands in Kintail and the castle of Eilean Donan to Colin Fitzgerald does not now exist and some historians believe it never existed.

18 King Philip V of Spain declared war on Britain in 1718 and took an opportunity to invade Britain by supporting the Jacobite cause. Spanish troops landed at Loch Alsh on April 13, 1719 and joined forces with the Jacobite army, assembled by the Earl of Seaforth, Cameron of Lochiel and Lord George Murray. The combined force marched to Glen Shiel where they were defeated by the Hanoverian troops on the 10th of June. The second planned attack on south-west England or Wales led by James Butler, Duke of Ormonde, was aborted when a severe storm at sea prevented him from landing.

19 To check the highland clans, General Monck, Cromwell's emissary, built the Fort of Inverlochy, a timber palisade, for 250 troops in 1654. When the fort was strengthened with 20ft high stone walls, fifteen guns and barracks for a thousand men in 1690, it was renamed Fort William after the king.

20 English troops saw action in Westphalia during the Third Anglo-Dutch War 1672-1674, but as Macky seems to suggest he and his correspondent were there at the time, he may be referring to either the War of the Spanish Succession (1701-1713) or the War of the French Succession (1713-1722).

21 *A second edition of Camden's description of Scotland* by Sir James Dalrymple (1650-1719) was published in Edinburgh in 1695.

22 *porte*: the Grand Signor's court.

23 Sir Alexander Fraser (1284-1332), High Chamberlain of Scotland, married Lady Mary Bruce in 1316. At the time, she was the widow of Sir Neil Campbell of Lochow (not Sir Nicholas).

24 According to tradition, Dunrobin was founded in 1098 or 1275 by Robert, Thane or Earl of Sutherland, after whom it received its name.

25 According to Jamieson's *An etymological dictionary of the Scottish language*, although the title 'earl' occurs in Scottish history before the reign of Malcolm Canmore, he has been long credited with introducing this Anglo-Saxon title to Scotland.

26 William, 5th Earl of Sutherland married the king's sister, Margaret Bruce, in 1342. He was taken prisoner after the Battle of Neville's Cross in 1346, and later spent ten years in England as a hostage for payment of David II's ransom of 100,000 merks. William and Margaret's son, John, was also a hostage, and died in England, at Lincoln, in 1361 while still a minor.

27 John Gordon, 13th Earl of Sutherland (1576-1615), had been accused of papistry and spent much of the last years of his life in prison on account of this. He was succeeded by his son John (1609-1663), 14th Earl of Sutherland who, in 1637, joined the supplicants against the service book introduced to the Church of Scotland by Charles I. He signed the Covenant in 1638. He was appointed Keeper of the Privy Seal of Scotland in 1649. The following year, he accompanied General David Leslie when he was sent by the parliament against the royalists in the north. His son, George, 15th Earl, (1633-1703) was appointed Keeper of the Privy Seal of Scotland in 1656.
his son John, the present earl: John Gordon, 16th Earl of Sutherland (1661-1733), was an early supporter of the Hanoverians. He was a privy councilor to Queen Anne, and in 1705 was named one of the commissioners for the treaty of union, which he steadily supported in parliament. He was one of the sixteen representatives of the Scots peerage chosen in the last Scots parliament in 1707, and subsequently re-elected three times. He raised a force in the north to act against the Jacobite insurgents in 1715.

28 Donald Mackey, or Mackay (1590-1649), was a staunch supporter of Charles I, and ardent supporter of the Protestant cause. Mackay's Regiment of Sutherland men became famous for a number of exploits, including the defence of the Pass of Oldenberg during the Thirty Years war in 1627. For this he was raised to the Scottish peerage and took his title as the first Lord Rea in 1628 from the Reay forest, part of the Forbes estate in Caithness which he had purchased.
General Hugh Mackey, or Mackay, of Scourie, Sutherland (1640-1692), served in France and Italy, and was part of the French army which invaded the Netherlands in 1672. After he married a Dutch

woman, he changed sides and joined the Scots Brigade, which supported the Dutch. Mackay was made Commander-in-Chief of the army in Scotland in 1689 after he assisted William of Orange to take the British crown, and went on to establish Fort William as a military base. He designed the ring-bayonet which allowed a rifle to be fired with the bayonet in place, saving valuable time in the heat of battle.

Mackay served with distinction in the Battle of Aughrim in Ireland (1691). He then returned to the Continent, fighting for William of Orange against the French, and was killed at the Battle of Steenkirk (1692).

29 Through this explanation of the changed spelling of Macky to Mackay, John Macky reveals his interest in establishing his own relationship to these illustrious forebears. Legal documents of the time confirm that the name was spelled Macky, and sometimes McKy. *The Book of Mackay* by Angus Mackay (Edinburgh, 1906), pp. 442-448.

30 Brig. Gen. Hon. Aeneas Mackay, Col-Proprietor of the Mackay Scottish Regiment in the service of the Netherlands (d. 1697), and Col. Hon. Robert Mackay, severely wounded at the Battle of Killiecrankie, served in Ireland and on the Continent (d. 1696). They were younger sons of John, 2nd Lord Rea.

31 See Letter IV, note 17.

32 Originally constructed during the thirteenth century, Brechin castle was reconstructed in the early 1700's as a simple three storied L shaped house. In 1643 Patrick Maule, 1st Earl of Panmure (1585-1661), bought the property from the Earl of Mar, and his descendant, James Maule of Ballumbie, the 4th and last Earl of Panmure (1658-1723), rebuilt the castle as Macky describes it and as it is today. The family lost the property when the estates were forfeited after Maule took part in the 1715 Rising. He died in exile in France. His wife obtained a long lease of Brechin Castle from the purchasers, the York Buildings Company, and the family later recovered it. Brechin Castle has been the home of the earls of Dalhousie since 1852.

33 Glamis Castle, the ancestral home of of the Lyon family, Earls of Strathmore, since the 14th century, stands on the site of a 12th century royal hunting lodge. The barony of Glamis was granted by Robert II to Sir John Lyon, Thane of Glamis in 1372. The castle was rebuilt as an L-plan tower house about 1435. The west wing was added, as well as a small north-east wing containing the chapel, in the 17th century. Much of the fortifications were swept away and replaced by the baroque setting of courts, statues and vistas described by Macky.

fire-rooms: rooms containing a fire-place.

34 The paintings in the chapel at Glamis Castle were commissioned from the Dutch artist Jacob de Wet in 1688 by Patrick, 1st Earl of

Strathmore. De Wet came to Scotland in 1673 under commission to carry out extensive work at the Royal Palace of Holyroodhouse.

35 *Sir Peter Lely* (1618-1680), a Dutch-born English baroque era artist, was appointed to the post of Principal Painter to Charles II in 1660. He is most famous for his portrait paintings. As well as those of the Lyon family, Macky singles out Lely's portrait of John Graham of Claverhouse, Viscount Dundee, a great friend of the Lord Strathmore of the time.

36 Before fleeing the country after the failed 1715 uprising James VIII/III, or 'The Old Pretender', stayed at Glamis Castle with 88 of his supporters. John, 5th Earl of Strathmore, a Stuart supporter, was killed at the Battle of Sherrifmuir, 13th November 1715.

37 The title Earl of Kinghorn was created in the Peerage of Scotland in 1606 for Patrick Lyon (1575-1615). In 1677, the designation of the earldom changed to 'Strathmore and Lyon'.

38 The Grays of Gray have long been connected to the Gowrie district. Gray House was one of three residences they built in the carse. They were descendants of a Norman family who settled in Chillingham in Northumberland and first came to Scotland as followers of Prince David, later crowned King David I in 1124. The family received a grant of land at Browfeld in Roxburghshire where Andrew Gray, second son of Baron Gray of Chillingham, settled in 1214. His grandson, also called Andrew, fought for Robert the Bruce in the War of Independence 1306-14 and was rewarded by Bruce in 1315 with the Barony of Longforgan and associated lands.
Andrew Gray (c.1390–1469) became 1st Lord Gray of Fowlis, and his son, also Andrew, succeeding to the title and lands in 1470, distinguished himself in affairs of state. In 1488 he became a Lord of the Privy Council; in 1489 he was appointed Justice General of Scotland North of the Forth; and in 1506 he became Justice General of Scotland.

39 Castle Lyon, better known as Castle Huntly, was built around 1452 by Baron Gray of Fowlis under licence from James II of Scotland. The castle changed hands in 1614 when it was acquired by the then Earl of Strathmore who changed its name to Castle Lyon.
Built from local sandstone on a precipitous site it is an imposing stronghold with a lofty tower and jamb style of the 15th century. Extensive renovations in the 17th century included an ornamental pond and six gates.
jointure-house: a house settled upon a wife as a jointure, that is, as her sole estate upon the death of her husband and limited to her for the rest of her life.

40 Drimmie House, about halfway between Perth and Dundee, was the family seat of the Lord Kinnaird. King William the Lion bestowed the barony of Kinnaird, in Gowrie, on the family by charter in 1170. Sir George Kinnaird of Inchture (d. 1689) was raised to the peerage of Scotland in 1682. His descendant, Patrick, 3rd Lord Kinnaird, opposed the Union, and died in March 1715.

Kinnaird castle, the seat of the Earl of Southesk, dates back to the 12th century. It was rebuilt in the 16th century. In the winter of 1715 the Old Pretender lodged at the castle; and, as a result of this and of the Earl's adherence to the Stuart cause during the 1715 Rising, his title and estate were forfeited.

Letter IX

1 John Erskine, 6th Earl of Mar (1675-1732), after proclaiming the Old Pretender King of Great Britain at Braemar on September 6, 1715, proceeded to seize Perth as headquarters for his rebellion. According to Daniel Szechi, by mid-October there were 2,666 foot and 917 horse quartered in the town. *1715: the Great Jacobite Rebellion* (New Haven: Yale University Press, 2006), p. 120.
After defeat by the Duke of Argyll's forces at Sheriffmuir on 13 November, 1715, Mar led his army back to Perth. Argyll, reinforced shortly after by 6,000 Dutch troops, advanced to Perth with the object of taking it and annihilating the Jacobite supporters. By the time he arrived, Mar's army had evacuated, so Argyll took possession. The guild hall was erected in Perth in 1722, so Macky's information is right up to date.

2 The palace of Ruthven, or Ruthven Castle, built in the 15th century, was the family seat of the Ruthvens, later Earls of Gowrie. As Macky says, the estate was confiscated by the king, James VI, after a number of plots against him by members of the Ruthven family. The Ruthven name was proscribed and the castle was renamed Huntingtower. The castle became the property of the Murrays of Tullibardine and through that line came into the possession of John Murray, 1st Duke of Atholl (1660-1724), as Macky notes a little later in this letter.
Patrick Ruthven (c.1520-1566), 3rd Lord Ruthven, was a Protestant privy councillor to Mary, Queen of Scots. He led the conspiracy to murder David Rizzio, her Italian secretary, in 1582. His son, William Ruthven, 1st Earl of Gowrie (c. 1543-1584), also one of the assassins, masterminded the conspiracy to kidnap the young James VI, for which he was attainted and executed in May, 1584.
The castle and lands were restored to the Ruthven family in 1586, the title passing to William's son, James Ruthven (d. 1588), and then to John Ruthven (1577-1600), who became the 3rd Earl of Gowrie, and Provost of Perth in 1592. John and his younger brother, Alexander (1581-1600), were killed by James VI's attendants who alleged they had attempted to murder the king. While the brothers may have been motivated by revenge for their father's execution, the facts of the mysterious 'Gowry conspiracy' have long been disputed.

3 The mother of the two brothers killed by the king's attendants was Dorothea Stuart, Countess of Gowrie (1543-1626), who had married William Ruthven in 1560. She was actually the daughter of Henry

Stuart, 1st Lord Methven (*c*.1495–1553/4), by his third wife, Janet Stuart, although Henry Stuart had previously been married to Queen Dowager, Margaret Tudor (1489-1541), widow of James IV, elder daughter of Henry VII of England and Elizabeth of York, and the elder sister of Henry VIII. She was also, as Macky notes, Elizabeth I's 'Aunt Margaret'.

4 Macky alludes to *An historical account of the conspiracies by the earls of Gowry, and Robert Logan of Restalrig, against King James VI of glorious memory* published by George Mackenzie, 1st Earl of Cromarty, in 1713.
William Murray (1574-1628), 2nd Earl of Tullibardine, rescued James VI at Perth after the alleged assassination attempt by the Gowries.
Thomas Erskine, later 1st Earl of Kellie (1566-1639), was with the king on the occasion of the Gowrie Conspiracy in 1600, and was wounded by Alexander Ruthven. He was afterwards awarded a third of the confiscated land of the Ruthvens. He travelled with the king to England when James ascended the English throne in 1603 and was made Captain of the Guard (1603-1617). He was given the barony of Kellie by the king and created Earl of Kellie in March 1619.
John Ramsay, later 1st Earl of Holderness (c. 1580-1626), became a favourite of James VI following the Gowrie conspiracy and received various titles in the Scottish peerage. When James moved his court to London in 1603, Ramsay was appointed Gentleman of the Bedchamber in the royal household. In 1621 he was created Earl of Holderness in the English peerage.

5 George Crawford, or Crawfurd (c.1695-1748), a Scottish genealogist and historian, was the author of a *Genealogical History of the Royal and Illustrious Family of the Stewarts from the year 1034 to the year 1710* (Edinburgh, 1710). Despite Macky's dismissal of Crawfurd's argument, it was possible for Margaret Tudor's second and third husbands to survive her. She divorced her second husband, Archibald Douglas, 6th Earl of Angus, in 1527 and married her third, Henry Stuart, the following year. Angus went on to marry Margaret, daughter of Robert Maxwell, 5th Lord Maxwell, in 1543.

6 In 1604 Scone Palace became the family seat of the Lords of Scone, a branch of the Murrays of Tullibardine, as Macky observes a little further on in his account. The palace was built on the site of Scone Abbey, a major Augustinian abbey, where the Kings of the Scots were crowned on the Stone of Scone, or the Stone of Destiny. Edward I of England carried off the Stone of Scone to Westminster Abbey in 1296, and placed it under a specially designed Coronation Chair. Elizabeth II was the last monarch to be crowned on the Stone of Scone, before it was returned to Scotland and deposited in Edinburgh Castle in 1996 along with the Scottish regalia.

7 The 17th century house Macky refers to was built by Sir David Murray who was granted forfeited Ruthven lands for his loyalty to James VI and I. The palace was later rebuilt in 1802 by the 3rd Earl Mansfield.

The 'Old Pretender' came to Scone during the Jacobite uprising in 1715 in the hope of being crowned King of Scotland, but had to flee on hearing of government troops in the area.
The 'housekeeper' at the time Macky wrote was David Murray, 5th Viscount of Stormont (1665-1731), who, like his son, James Murray, Earl of Dunbar (c.1690–1770), was a Jacobite.

8 Henry Mordaunt, 2nd Earl of Peterborough (1621-1697), was proxy for the Duke of York, later James VII and II, at his marriage to the Italian princess, Mary of Modena (1658-1718), on 30 September, 1673, in Modena. He then escorted the princess to England. As court painter to James and Mary, the Bolognese artist Benedetto Gennari the Younger (1633-1715) painted several portraits of the royal family between 1688 and 1692, going into exile with James's court to St. Germains-en-Laye.

9 Painted ceilings were a feature of Scottish Renaissance castles and palaces. A ceiling depicting King James and a hunt was removed from Scone Palace during renovations in the 19th century. Huntington castle still has its original painted ceiling.
setting: game-hunting sport that used a setter dog.

10 Macky's source for the details of the offices held by David Murray, 1st Viscount of Stormont, is probably George Crawfurd's *The peerage of Scotland: containing an historical and genealogical account of the nobility of that Kingdom* (Edinburgh, 1716). Crawfurd describes Murray's tomb with 'the noble Monument erected by himself of various colour'd Marble, with his Statue as big as the Life" (p. 464).

11 The Board of Green Cloth was the committee that audited the Royal accounts. The Old Pretender's court was itinerant, and Scone became his temporary counting house.

12 Dunkeld House was the winter seat of the dukes of Atholl. The family's principal seat was Blair Castle, dating from 1269 and extensively rebuilt in 1530 by the 3rd Earl of Atholl. According to the Murray Clan Society, the motto 'Furth Fortune and Fill the Fetters' means 'go onward with fortune and fill the shackles', and is engraved on the keystone over the main entrance of Blair Castle (http://clanmurray.org/tartans.html).
The original Earls of Atholl seem to have died out in the early 1300s, but the title was later revived. Sir John Murray of Tullibardine became the 1st Murray Earl of Atholl in 1629. The family were Royalists during the Civil War and were rewarded when Charles II promoted the 2nd Earl of Atholl to become the 1st Marquess of Atholl in 1676. His son, Sir John Murray, 2nd Marquess of Atholl (1660-1724), was appointed as one of the commissioners to the inquiry into the Massacre of Glencoe in 1693, Secretary of State, and Lord High Commissioner to the Parliament of Scotland. He was promoted by Queen Anne in 1703 to become the 1st Duke of Atholl and became Keeper of the Privy Seal of Scotland. This is the duke Macky refers to here.

13 Dupplin Castle, dating back to the 13th century, was razed and rebuilt several times in the following centuries. The unfinished building Macky describes here was only completed in 1725, and was destroyed by fire in 1827. The architect was James Smith (c.1645-1731) who had been overseer of His Majesty's works for King James II, responsible for renovations at Edinburgh Castle and Holyrood House, including fitting out the Chapel Royal. His extensive architectural works included designing or refurbishing Drumlanrig Castle and Queensberry House (with his father-in-law, Robert Mylne), Dalkeith Palace, Traquair House, and Yester House. He has been credited with the introduction of the Palladian style to Scotland.

14 The double portrait of Charles I (1600-49) and James Duke of York (1633-1701) is by Sir Peter Lely.
As a young man, van Dyck joined Rubens' workshop around 1616-1617. While a portrait of van Dyck was long attributed to Rubens (1577-1640), this has now been re-attributed to van Dyck himself. Van Dyck's most famous painting of his teacher is of the older Flemish artist mourning his wife.
Prince Rupert of the Rhine (1619-1682) was the nephew of King Charles I of England, who created him Duke of Cumberland and Earl of Holderness. He had a long career as a soldier and colonial administrator. Sir Peter Lely painted his portrait several times, both full-lengths and bust portraits.
James Douglas, 4th Earl of Morton was Regent of Scotland 1572-76 during the minority of James VI. Although I have not been able to identify the portrait of Morton Macky mentions here, Antonio or Anthonis Moro (1519-1576), a Dutch artist, was sent to England to paint a portrait of Mary Tudor, who became Queen of England in July 1554. In 1554, Mary married Philip of Spain, who appointed Moro as court painter.

15 The portrait of the Earl of Kinnoull is probably that of the second earl painted by van Dyck.
Cromwell was in Scotland 1650-1651. There is a painting of *Cromwell and his cavalry at Dunbar* 1650 by A. C. Gow but Macky refers specifically to a half-length portrait. He may be referring to a portrait by van Dyck, or one of many by Robert Walker, the chief painter of the parliamentary party. The portrait of General Monck could be by an artist from the studio of Sir Peter Lely.

16 Anthony van Dyck painted a number of double portraits, including those of other artists (Frans Snyders Rubens) and their wives, but I haven't been able to find one of himself and his wife. Defoe also mentions the bronze equestrian statue of Charles II, but doesn't refer to the double portrait.

17 The title, Earl of Kinnoull, was first conferred in 1633 on Sir George Hay (1572-1634), Viscount of Dupplin and Baron Hay of Kinfauns (1627), and Lord Chancellor of Scotland from 1622 to 1634. His cousin was James Hay (c.1580-1636), one of the favourites of James VI and I, a Gentleman of the Bedchamber, who was also raised to the

peerage, as Earl of Carlisle in 1622. Sir George Hay was one of those who attended James VI to Perth on 5th August, 1600, when the Earl of Gowrie and his brother Alexander were killed; and he received the lands of Netherliff or Nethercliff out of the forfeited Gowrie estate.

18 Sir George Hay (c.1595-1644), 2nd Earl of Kinnoull, was captain of the yeomen of the guard from 1632-1635, and a Privy Counsellor to King Charles I, to whom he remained loyal at the breaking out of the civil wars. In 1643 he refused to sign the Solemn League and Covenant.

Macky refers to Sir Thomas Hay, Viscount of Dupplin, 7th Earl of Kinnoull (d. 1719), who was one of the commissioners for the Union, and supported that treaty in the Scottish parliament. He was afterwards a representative peer from 1710-1714. In 1715, on his way north to organize the rebellion, the Earl of Mar visited his brother-in-law's seat at Dupplin. The youngest of Kinoull's three sons, the Hon. Colonel John Hay of Cromlix, accompanied Mar to the north of Scotland. Sent with a detachment of 200 horse to take possession of Perth, he entered that town on the 14th September, 1715, and there proclaimed for the Chevalier. He was forfeited by act of parliament, and joined the exiled court in France.

The earl of Kinnoull at the time Macky was writing was his son, George, 8th Earl of Kinnoull (d. 1758), who from 1710 was M.P. for Fowey in Cornwall. In the following year he was appointed one of the tellers of the Exchequer and created a peer of Great Britain, by the title of Baron Hay of Pedwardine. He succeeded to the title of 8th Viscount of Dupplin in 1718/19.

19 Balhousie was acquired by Francis Hay (1658-1675) who built an L-plan tower house in 1631 for the Hay family.

Macky gives his description of Stirling in the next letter (Letter X).

20 The Grahams of Montrose were descendants of the Grahams of Dalkeith and Eskdale who had received lands from David I. Sir David de Graham married the Earl of Strathearn's daughter, receiving the lands in Kincardine (Strathearn) as a dowry. He was awarded Montrose by Robert Bruce for his loyal support during the Wars of Independence and began building Kincardine Castle.

James Graham, 1st Marquess of Montrose (1612-50), obtained a commission as Lieutenant-General in Scotland from Charles I, and in the Scottish civil war led the main Royalist force on behalf of the king to victory at Tippermuir, on September 1, 1644, Inverlochy, on February 2, 1645, and Kilsyth, on August 15, 1645. A Parliamentary army under David Leslie, 1st Lord Newark (c. 1600–1682), laid siege to Kincardine Castle and destroyed it around 1647.

21 Drummond Castle was built in 1491 by the Drummonds of Drummond. They were created Earls of Perth by James VI and I in 1605, and during the following decades additions were made to the castle by James Mylne, Master Mason to Charles I. One of the main towers was ruined in a siege by Cromwell in 1653, but the castle was

restored after the English troops left. Strangely, Macky does not mention the mansion house built to the east of the castle in the 1690s by James Drummond, the 4th Earl of Perth. This earl supported the Jacobite cause, joined James VII in France, and was made Duke of Perth by the Chevalier. His son, the second duke, commanded the Jacobite cavalry at the Battle of Sheriffmuir in 1715, was attainted, and died in 1720 in France, as Macky says later in this paragraph. Margaret Drummond, sister of John Drummond of Stobhall, married David II but they had no children. In 1367, John's daughter, Annabella Drummond, married John Stewart, Earl of Carrick (1337-1406), future High Steward of Scotland and King Robert III of Scotland.

22 The 4th Earl of Perth accompanied the Earl of Nottingham on his mission to Spain to witness the ratification of the peace treaty between England and Spain. Philip III ratified it on 30 May, 1605, not 1603.

23 Sir Thomas Moncrieff, 14th chief of the Clan Moncrieff, was made a baronet by King James VII. A new seat built for the chief at Moncrieff in 1679 was the first major country house completed by architect Sir William Bruce of Kinross (1630-1710).

24 The Melvilles, originally a Norman family - de Mallevilles - came to Scotland with David I when he returned in 1124 after 30 years spent at the English court. The king granted the family lands in Midlothian, outside Edinburgh.
George Melville, 4th Lord Melville (1636-1707), a staunch Protestant, supported an unsuccessful rebellion by James, Duke of Monmouth, the illegitimate son of King Charles II. As Macky observes in the next paragraph, he had to flee to Holland but returned with Queen Mary and William of Orange and became Secretary of State for Scotland and the 1st Earl of Melville. His son, David Melville, 2nd Earl of Melville and 3rd Earl of Leven (1660-1728), sat in the new parliament at Westminster as a representative peer of Scotland from 1707-1710. Melville Castle, the original family home, was a tower house. It was inherited through marriage by Henry Dundas (1742-1811), who took the title 'Viscount Melville' although he was not connected with the Melville line. Dundas employed Henry Playfair, the famous Edinburgh architect, to design the building that stands today.

25 *the late earl*: George Melville, 1st Earl of Melville (d. 1707), was one of the Scottish aristocrats who persuaded Sir John de Medina (1659-1710) to move from London to Edinburgh in 1693 where he settled (and later died). Medina, born in Brussels, of Spanish extraction, became the leading portraitist of his time. His portraits of George Melville and his son David are now in the collection of the National Galleries of Scotland.

26 Sir John Melville of Raith was an early supporter of the Reformation. He was executed by Cardinal David Beaton's successor, Archbishop John Hamilton, on the grounds that he consorted with Beaton's assassins.

Robert Melville, 1st Lord Melville (1547–1621), was created a peer of parliament by the title Lord Melville of Monimaill in 1616, not 1611.

27 David Melville, 2nd Earl of Melville and 3rd Earl of Leven, was Commander in Chief of the forces in Scotland in 1706 and was appointed as one of the commissioners for the Union of England and Scotland. Previous offices included Privy Counsellor (1689) and Governor of the Bank of Scotland (1697-1728).

28 Falkland Palace, dating from the 12th century, was rebuilt by James IV and James V. James IV had work carried out between 1501 and 1541. James V added to the buildings, transforming the structure into a sophisticated Renaissance palace, with the help of architects from France. The palace became a favourite country residence and hunting lodge of the Stuarts. It was occupied by Oliver Cromwell's army during the second civil war and fell into ruin in 1654 after his troops burned it down and cut down the great oak Forest of Falkland to provide timber for a fort at Perth.
Nunc Seges est ubique Troja fuit: Now there are cornfields where Troy once stood... (Ovid, *Heroides* 1.1.53)
The Murrays of Atholl were the hereditary keepers of Falkland Palace. John Murray, 1st Duke of Atholl (1660-1724), was the keeper at the time Macky was writing.

29 James V married Madeleine of Valois, daughter of Francis I, in Notre Dame de Paris on 1 January, 1537. He went on to found the Order of the Knights of the Thistle, or of St Andrew, in 1540. He and twelve knights formed the membership, in emulation of the Order of Saint Michael of France, of which he was a member. According to tradition, the Order of the Thistle was a revival of an ancient Order of St Andrew.

30 James V (1512-1542) asserted law and order in the Borders and Highlands, then turned his attention to the Western Isles where he negotiated a peace agreement among warring chieftains in 1531. He established the College of Justice the following year and took an active part in dispensing criminal justice through the King's Court.
Lord of the Isles: The most powerful lord and greatest landowner after the kings of Scotland and England. Their Lordship included the Hebrides (Skye and Ross from 1438), Knoydart, Ardnamurchan, and the Kintyre peninsula. In 1493 James IV brought the Lordship of the Isles to an end, and last Lord of the Isles, John Macdonald II, forfeited his estates and titles to the Scottish king.
make the rush bush keep the cow is an old Scottish expression. According to the OED 'it was used originally with reference to the successful repression of cattle-stealing: to enable cattle to remain in their fields without a guard; (hence) to deter thieves or invaders; to uphold the law strictly or effectively'.

31 'Christis Kirk on the Green' and other poems were attributed to James V in the early 17th century, but this attribution is doubtful. Legends grew up about James V's love of travelling incognito around his realm.

James V died just a few weeks after defeat by Henry VIII's army at Solway Firth, 24 November, 1542. Two of his sons died in infancy.

32 Sir Robert *Carey* (c. 1560-1639), later created 1st Earl of Monmouth, rode from near London to Edinburgh in about sixty hours, to bring the news of Queen Elizabeth's death to James VI, in March 1603. It was his uncle, Henry Carey (1526-1596), who was created Viscount of Falkland by James VI and I in 1620.
Falkland Palace was a favourite residence of James VI. The chapel ceiling, dating from the time of James V, was re-decorated for the coronation visit of Charles I in 1633. Charles's insistence on an Anglican form of worship during his short visit was resisted by Scottish Presbyterians who viewed his efforts to impose a new prayer book as an attempt to revive 'popery' in Scotland.
Sir David Murray, 1st Viscount of Stormont (c.1621-1631), was brought up at court and, following his loyalty during the Gowrie conspiracy, was granted the stewardship of Fife, based at Falkland Palace. See note 7.

33 A borough or burgh is a town with a corporation and special privileges granted by royal charter. In Scotland a borough is a body corporate, consisting of the inhabitants of the district, erected by the sovereign, with a certain jurisdiction.

34 Balgonie Castle, originally built for Sir Thomas Sibbald of Balgonie around 1360, passed through marriage to the Lundins and finally the Leslies. The original tower house was greatly expanded in the course of the 17th century. From 1635 on Sir Alexander Leslie, 1st Earl of Leven, added a two-storey building at the south-east corner of the courtyard, and rebuilt the northern range, adding a storey. After claiming the title in the 1660s, John Leslie, 2nd Earl of Leven, built a grand stair, linking the original tower and north range, in the place of a wooden bridge. Then in 1681 David Melville, 7th Earl of Leven, inherited Balgonie and built a three storey range of buildings linking the north range with the south-east block.

35 Leslie House, Fife, seat of the Earl of Rothes, had been, like Panmure House, a project of the king's master mason, John Mylne. Sir William Bruce oversaw the works after Mylne's death, and probably made his own amendments. Built between 1660-1670 on the site of previous houses, the mansion originally known as 'the Palace of Leslie' was built in the style of Holyrood Palace. It was reckoned to be the largest house of its time with 80 bedrooms; the long gallery was said to be 3 feet longer than the one at Holyrood. Unfortunately, the house was seriously damaged by fire on Christmas Day 1763.
John Leslie (c.1630-1681), 7th Earl of Rothes, was created 1st Duke of Rothes by Charles II in 1680. He also held the offices of Lord High Treasurer of Scotland and Lord Chancellor of Scotland, among others.
James Stuart (1633-1701), Duke of York and Duke of Albany, was the younger son of Charles I and younger brother of Charles II. He succeeded his brother and became King James VII of Scots and King

James II of England and Ireland on 6 February 1685.
the present earl: this was John Hamilton-Leslie, 9th Earl of Rothes (d. 1722).

36 Sir Norman's son, Andrew, the 6th Lord Leslie, was one of the great barons of Scotland who in 1320 signed the Declaration of Arbroath. Leslie-Rothes, became the senior line with George Leslie who was created 1st Earl of Rothes around 1457 or 1458. He had already been created Lord Leslie in 1445.
John Leslie, 6th Earl of Rothes (1600-1641), as one of the main leaders of the Scottish Covenanters, opposed the proposed introduction of the Book of Common Prayer by Charles I in 1638. On the conclusion of what became known as the Second Bishops' War (1640), Rothes was one of the commissioners sent to London to conclude the peace negotiations. After signing the Treaty of Ripon, 26 October, 1640 he remained in England at the royal court. He died of consumption in August 1641, before Charles could deploy him as part of his plans to venture into Scotland.

37 *Lashly*: Here Macky appears to transliterate the local pronunciation of 'Leslie'.

38 Lochleven Castle dates from the 14th century, although the stone defensive wall is older and may have been built around 1300 during the Wars of Independence. The tower house held Robert, the High Stewart and future Robert II, prisoner in 1369. Mary, Queen of Scots, was imprisoned there in June 1567, under the instructions of her brother, Lord Moray, and was forced to abdicate in favour of her infant son, James VI. The castle was the property of Sir William Douglas, Moray's relative. His son, George Douglas, in love with Mary, devised various plans to help her escape from Lochleven, but it was his younger sibling, Willie, who played the key role in her escape. In May 1568, dressed as a servant girl, she escaped across the loch in a boat Willie had prepared for the purpose.
Sir William Bruce of Kinross (1630-1710), the celebrated architect, who designed Holyrood *Palace*, was described as 'the Christopher Wren of North Britain' by Daniel Defoe. He purchased the estate, including the island in Lochleven, from James Douglas (c.1632-1686), the 9th Earl of Morton, in 1675. Bruce, w*ho* had lived in Holland and travelled in France before the restoration of Charles II in 1660, had a detailed knowledge of Baroque gardens, a style he introduced to Scotland. He and his son John Bruce began work on the gardens in 1679 but did not start work on Kinross House itself until 1685. The house, in the Italian style of architecture, was built upon a finely-wooded promontory between the town of Kinross and the banks of Loch Leven, placed deliberately so it looks directly across the loch to the romantic ruin of Lochleven Castle. Financial constraints meant that work on the interior was not completed and Bruce had not moved into Kinross House at the time of his death in 1710.
Melville Palace is described in Letter IX.

40 Thomas Bruce, 2nd Earl of Ailesbury (1656-1741), was the son of Robert Bruce, 2nd Earl of Elgin (1626-1685), who had been created 1st Earl of Ailesbury by Charles II in 1664.

41 In 1589 James VI gave the lordship of Dunfermline, including the famous abbey, as a marriage gift to his Queen, Anne of Denmark, and three of their children were born there, as Macky notes. Anne ordered William Schaw to rebuild the existing Abbey Guest House as a Royal Palace intended to be the Queen's main residence. (The royal couple spent much of their time living apart.) Repairs to the Palace at Dunfermline were undertaken in advance of a visit by Charles I in 1633 and it was last used by Charles II, in 1651. It fell into disrepair and is now in ruins.

42 The first foundation was a Benedictine priory, introduced by Queen Margaret, wife of Malcom Canmore in 1070. Their son, David I, raised the priory to the status of an abbey in 1128. The abbey's domestic buildings were rebuilt by Robert the Bruce after the English troops destroyed them in 1303 during the Wars of Independence. Like Malcom and Margaret, and later Scottish monarchs, Bruce is buried there (though not his heart). During the Reformation the Abbey was sacked and the religious community there came to an end. William Schaw was also responsible for rebuilding the abbey after the Reformation.

43 Whether the 'barbarous' custom variously called *Jus Primae Noctis* and *Droit du Seigneur* in French ever existed has been much debated. In his *Hystory & Croniklis of Scotland*, which Macky cites elsewhere in his *Journey* (Letter XII), Hector Boece (1465-1536) recounts how the 'law' was introduced to Scotland by King Evenus III in the 1st century BCE and remained in effect until Malcolm Canmore abolished it in 1089 at the instigation of his devout wife, Margaret.
The custom of the grace drink, or grace cup, has been attributed to Queen Margaret who established as a rule at her table, that whosoever stayed till grace was said was rewarded with a bumper.

44 The office of heritable baillie of the lordship was given in 1593 by Queen Anne to Alexander Seton, who afterwards became Earl of Dunfermline; and was regranted by Charles I to the 2nd Earl of Dunfermline. In 1665 it passed to the Earl of Tweeddale, in lieu of a debt due to him by the Earl of Dunfermline; was confirmed or vested in 1669 to the Marquess of Tweeddale by royal charter; and, in common with the other heritable jurisdictions in Scotland, was abolished in 1748.

Letter X

1 The Douglas Earls of Morton held Aberdour from the 14th century and extended the original castle over the centuries. James Douglas,

4th Earl of Morton (c. 1516-1581), Regent from 1572-1578, was executed on 2 June 1581, beheaded by the 'Maiden' which he was said to have introduced from England. Morton undertook major extensions to the castle in the 1570s and, influenced by contemporary English gardens, such as Hampton Court, laid out the terraced gardens. Macky may have seen the renovated building developed by William, the 7th Earl of Morton (1582-1648), which included a Renaissance east wing and a walled garden, built in the 1630s.

2 Sir James Douglas, Lord Dalkeith and Aberdour (c.1356-1441), was married in 1387 to Elizabeth, fourth daughter of King Robert III. James, 4th Lord Dalkeith (d. 1504), succeeded to the joint barony of Dalkeith and Aberdour in 1456, and became Earl of Morton in 1458 on his marriage to Lady Joan Stewart, third daughter of James I. *The present earl*: Robert Douglas, 12th Earl of Morton (d. 1730), had succeeded his brother, James, to the title in 1715.

3 James Stuart, 1st Earl of Moray (c.1531-1570), was Regent from 1567-1570.
His seat at Donibristle Castle was destroyed by fire in 1592, and his heir, James Stuart, 2nd Earl of Moray, murdered that same night, is remembered in the ballad 'The Bonny Earl O' Moray'. Macky describes the new house, built and extended between 1700 and 1720 for Charles Stuart, 6th Earl of Moray (c.1660-1735), whom he refers to as *the present earl*.
old tapistry at Brussels: Macky resided in Brussels a number of times, the last time between 1723-1724.

4 Charles Stuart, 6th Earl of Moray, was the son of Alexander Stuart, 5th Earl of Moray (d. 1701), who held the office of Secretary of State in 1680 and that of Lord High Commissioner in 1686, but was deprived of various offices and imprisoned in 1690 as a suspected Jacobite. Charles acceded to his father's titles in 1701 and died, unmarried, in 1735. He was succeeded by his brother, Francis.

5 Culross Palace was built between 1597 and 1611 by George Bruce, a successful merchant with links to the Low Countries, using materials he imported. A model 17th century garden, complete with raised beds, a covered walkway and crushed shell paths, can still be seen by visitors today.
The earldom of Kincardine, commonly called Kincairn, was created in 1643. The title was held by descendants of the Bruces of Blairhall and Clackmannan, as Macky asserts. On the death of the 3rd Earl of Kincardine in November 1705, his titles devolved on his kinsman Alexander, who had married Christian, daughter of Robert Bruce of Blairhall.

6 The Cistercian Abbey of Culross was founded by Malcolm, 7th Earl of Fife, in 1215 for the monks of Kinloss, Moray. The choir of the abbey church was then taken over as the parish church, by an Act of Parliament in 1633.

7 John Erskine, Lord of Alloway, or Alloa, in Clackmannanshire was created Earl of Mar by James III in 1436.

Originally a tower house, Alloa Castle was remodelled by John Erskine, 6th Earl of Mar, supposedly inspired by the Palace of Versailles when he was an exile in France following the 1715 Jacobite Rebellion (see notes to Letter VIII, 1 and Letter IX, 1). The new structure, set in 42 acres of gardens running all the way down to the Forth, was destroyed by fire in 1800.

8 *one street that runs down to the harbour,... with rows of lime-trees*: This street, one of Alloa's oldest, is still named Lime Tree Walk.

9 *rope-walk*: this was an area of ground where ropes were made.

10 Henricus de Erskine possessed the barony of Erskine, Renfrewshire, during the reign of Alexander II (r.1214-1249). His grandson, Sir Robert Erskine of Erskine, was one of the commissioners who negotiated the release of David II, with his son Thomas given as a hostage for the ransom. He was rewarded for his services with lands and offices, including Keeper of Stirling Castle, Lord High Chamberlain of Scotland and Justiciar of the North. He paid homage to Robert II and assisted at his coronation at Scone in March 1371.

11 For several generations this family was charged with keeping, during their minority, the heirs apparent to the Scottish crown. Alexander, 2nd Lord Erskine, had the charge of James IV, and John, 5th Lord Erskine (and 16th Mar), had the keeping of James V during his minority. On his coming of age he was sent by James V in 1534 ambassador to France, to negotiate a marriage with a daughter of the French king; he accompanied James to France in 1537 for the betrothal of his master to Princess Magdalen. On the death of James, he became tutor and guardian to the infant queen Mary. His heir, Johm, became the guardian of Mary's son, the future James VI and I.

Robert, 4th Lord Erskine, was killed at the Battle of Flodden in 1513.

12 *concredid*: entrusted (now obsolete)

13 The bridge Macky describes dates from the late 15th or early 16th century.

14 Stirling Palace was commissioned by King James V in 1538 on the occasion of his second marriage, to Mary of Guise.

15 The 'clergyman' was Adam Erskine, abbot of Cambuskenneth, and nephew of John Erskine, Earl of Mar and Regent of Scotland. In 1562 the site passed into the hands of the latter. It is said that he quarried the stones from the ruins of Cambuskenneth Abbey to build his town house, Mar's Wark, in the 1570s, close to the castle. Mar lived in the building until the end of the 17th century. Following the failure of the 1715 rebellion, the house was converted into barracks. The shell of this once grand building still stands at the head of the Old Town.

16 Argyll's Lodging: originally a fine 17th century town residence built c.1630 by Sir William Alexander, founder of Nova Scotia, Secretary

of State for Scotland and created 1st Earl of Stirling in 1633. On his death in 1640 the mansion passed to the Argyll family and was extended by the 9th Earl in 1666. Charles II stayed here before being crowned at Scone in 1651, and the 2nd Duke of Argyll set up his headquarters here in 1715 before the Battle of Sheriffmuir.

17 According to Campbell family history, chiefs of the clan claim descent from Gillespie (Archibald) Campbell, who acquired the Lordship of Lochow on his marriage to Eva, daughter of Paul o Duibhne, Knight of Lochow, in the eleventh century. Duncan of Lochow, later Argyll, was their son (d. 1097). Duncan's descendant, Sir Colin Campbell, knighted by King Alexander III in 1280, was styled MacChaillan More in Gaelic (meaning great McCallum), a title inherited by the Chief of the Argyll family. In 1291 he was one of the nominees on the part of Robert Bruce in the contest for the throne of Scotland. Like him, his brother Sir Nial Campbell of Lochow swore fealty to Edward I in 1296 but afterwards joined in defending Robert Bruce's claim, fighting with him at Methven and Bannockburn. Sir Colin Campbell (c.1433-1493), 2nd Lord Campbell, was created Earl of Argyll in 1457.

18 Archibald Campbell (c.1607-1661), eldest son of the 7th Earl of Argyll and 1st Marquess of Argyll, chief of the Campbell clan from 1638 and leader of the Covenanters. He crowned Charles II King of Scots at Scone, but was beheaded when Charles regained the throne of England. His son, Colonel Archibald Campbell, 8th Earl of Argyll (1629-1685) was, like his father, beheaded on the 'Maiden'.

19 Archibald Campbell, 10th Earl of Argyll and 1st Duke of Argyll (1658-1703), was one of the Scottish leaders of the Glorious Revolution (1688-89). His son, John Campbell, 2nd Duke of Argyll,(1678-1743), took part in the Duke of Marlborough's campaigns in the Low Countries and later became a Major General. Argyll led the government army at the Battle of Sheriffmuir and defeated the Jacobites led by the Earl of Mar. In 1719 he was rewarded by being created Duke of Greenwich.

20 The Grahams, dukes of Montrose, descended from Sir David Graham of Kincardine, were granted the estate of Cardross by Robert I. James Graham, 4th Marquess of Montrose, was created 1st Duke of Montrose in 1707.

21 See note 15 above.

22 Crieff held the country's most important cattle market. Many of those sold were then driven south 800km to London's Smithfield.

23 The image of highlanders as robbers and thieves, and given to general lawlessness, was promoted by Camden's *Britannia* (1546), to which Macky refers several times elsewhere in his *Journey*.

24 The Callendar family had been associated with the area since the Middle Ages, with their principal seat at Callendar House. I have been unable to identify 'Crocsforth'.

25 *Goodman of Bal'lengeich:* The assumed name of James V of Scotland when he made his disguised visits through the country districts around Edinburgh and Stirling.

26 John Cowane (c.1570-1633) was a wealthy Stirling merchant and Town Councillor. He bequeathed 40,000 merks for the building of a hospital or almshouse, for sustaining a certain number of decayed guild brethern, and which came to be known as Cowane's Hospital.

27 The title *Earl of Stirling* was created in 1633 for poet and statesman William Alexander, 1st Viscount of Stirling (1576-1640), who founded and colonized the region of Nova Scotia in Canada.

28 Alva House, originally a tower house, was extended by Sir Charles Erskine, 1st Baronet, in 1636. His son, Sir John Erskine, 3rd Baronet of Alva (1672–1739), Clackmannanshire, joined Mar in the 1715 Rising. He was later able to make his peace with the Hanoverian regime and return to Scotland from France, by disclosing the large deposit of silver ore he had been mining secretly on his estate.

29 Charles Elphinstone, 9th Lord Elphinstone (1682-1757), served as a captain in the army in Flanders from 1706 and was wounded at the Battle of Agremont 1708.

Letter XI

1 Callendar House was a 14th century tower house, built by the Callendar Thanes of Callendar. In 1345 the Callendar lands were granted by David II to Sir William Livingston (d. 1346). Alexander, 5th Lord Livingston (c.1500–1553) was guardian of Mary, Queen of Scots, during her childhood. The marriage agreement between Mary and the French Dauphin was signed at Callendar House. The Livingstons were raised to the peerage as Earl of Linlithgow in 1600, and Earl of Callendar in 1641. The Callendar estates were forfeited and purchased by the York Buildings Company, after James Livingston, 5th Earl of Linlithgow and 4th Earl of Callendar, supported the Jacobite Rising of 1715, but the Company leased the house back to the earl's daughter, Lady Anne Livingston, from 1724.

2 A royal manor house stood at Linlithgow (or Lithgow) from the twelfth century and, fortified during the Wars of Independence, was used as a base and garrison by the English army at the time of the battle of Bannockburn in 1314. After it was destroyed by fire James I and successive Stuart monarchs set about transforming it into a grand royal residence in the fifteenth century. They brought masons and craftsmen from the continent to work on the palace's elegant stonework. New royal apartments were built for James IV and his Queen, Margaret Tudor, daughter of English King Henry VII, and a royal chapel was erected. James V, born in Linlithgow Palace in 1512, changed the entrance, added a gatehouse, and installed the splendid fountain in the palace courtyard in 1538. James VI added

further apartments and a long gallery, and the fine Renaissance facade, 1618-1624.

3 According to one tradition, the Order of the Thistle was instituted by Archaius, an early king of Scotland, who took for his device the thistle and rue, composed in a collar, with the motto *pour ma defence*. See Letter IX, note 29 for James V and the founding of the Order of St Andrew, and Letter V, note 7 for the role of James VII and II.

4 Oliver Cromwell had demolished Linlithgow's old Town House with its large campanile in 1650; the sophisticated replacement, including a six-stage balustraded tower to the rear, was built in 1668-1670.

5 Alexander, 7th Lord Livingston, was appointed by James VI guardian of his eldest daughter, the Princess Elizabeth, later briefly Queen of Bohemia, in 1596. He was keeper of Linlithgow Palace and was created earl in 1600.

6 Kinneil House, once a principal seat of the Hamilton family, was built on the site of a medieval tower house. In 1667, William and Anne, Duke and Duchess of Hamilton, were responsible for a major extension that united the tower house and palace. The village was cleared to allow a park to be established, the villagers mostly relocating to the rapidly growing town of Boroughstoneness, or Bo'ness, a short distance away, where the duke's extensive coal-mines and salt-pans were located.

7 Built in the 15th century by the powerful Crichton family, Blackness Castle became a royal castle in 1453, serving as a garrison fortress and state prison. Because of its resemblance, from the seaward side, to a great stone ship that has run aground, Blackness is often referred to as 'the ship that never sailed'. Between 1537 and 1543 James V fortified the castle and it withstood Henry VIII's 'rough wooing'. However, in 1650 Oliver Cromwell's heavy guns devastated the defences, forcing the garrison to surrender.
Many Covenanters were imprisoned here in the 1670s and 1680s, during the so-called 'Killing Time'.

8 Hopetoun House was built 1699-1707 for Charles Hope, 1st Earl of Hopetoun (1681-1742), on the occasion of his marriage to Lady Henrietta Johnstone, daughter of the Marquess of Annandale. His mother, Lady Margaret Hamilton, widow of Sir John Hope (1650-1682), commissioned architect Sir William Bruce, who had also designed Kinross House. (His father had drowned when the *Gloucester* went down in 1682, as Macky points out later.) The grand staircase Macky mentions was carved by local craftsman Alexander Eizat who had worked with Bruce during renovations at Holyrood Palace in Edinburgh. In 1721, the first earl (created 1703) asked architect William Adam to remodel and enlarge the house, and it is to this programme of work that Macky refers in his next paragraph. The alterations were not completed until 1767.

9 Giuseppe Chiari (1654-1727) is mostly famous for his Italian frescoes. I have found no reference to his painting of Noah and his family, however, his teacher, Carlo Maratti painted a series of paintings of Old Testament prophets, including Noah.
10 See note 8 above.
11 Craigiehall was also designed by Sir William Bruce and completed in 1699 for William Johnstone, 2nd Earl of Annandale and Hartfell, 1st Marquess of Annandale (1664-1721), who had acquired the Craigie estate through marriage. Johnstone opposed the Union, but later served as a representative peer from 1709-13.
11 William Johnstone, the 1st Marquess of Annandale died in 1721, having travelled in the Low Countries, Italy, France, Germany, and Switzerland between 1712 and 1714.
12 By 'the present marquess' Macky may mean Johnstone's eldest son, James, who succeeded his father as 2nd Marquess of Annandale in 1721. He spent most of his adult life travelling in Italy and died at Naples in 1730 while on his second grand tour.
13 Barnton House, dating from the 14th century, was acquired by the Crichtons and then sold, first to the Dundas family in 1460, then to Sir Robert Barton in 1507. Barton later became Lord High Treasurer of Scotland and took up residence in Barnbougle Castle after his marriage to the heiress, Barbara Mowbray. Renovated in the course of the 17th century, at the time Macky saw it, Barnbougle was the seat of Sir Archibald Primrose (1664-1723), created 1st Earl of Rosebery in 1703.
14 Macky's list of early Scottish kings derives from the *Scots Origynale* perpetuated by medieval historians, including Andrew Wyntoun, whose chronicle he cites elsewhere. Macky refers to portraits of the early Scottish kings at Holyrood Palace in Letter V.
15 This list is omitted here.
16 *the Revolution*: refers to the accession of William and Mary in 1688 and eviction of James II and VII.
17 The detailed list of 'The Blazoning of the Ensigns Armorial' and Coats of Arms of the Scottish Nobility is omitted here.
18 Sir William Calderwood (c. 1660-1733) was raised to the bench and became a Lord of Session under the title Lord Polton in 1711.
19 When he fled to France in 1689, James II and VII took various Stuart relics, including the Stuart Sapphire with him. These were inherited by his son and grandson.
20 *King Caractacus*: a first century British chieftain who led the initial British resistance against the Roman invasion. An 18th century tradition, popularised by the Welsh antiquarian and forger Iolo Morganwg, credits Caractacus (Caradog) with the introduction of Christianity to Britain.
21 According to tradition, Achaius was an 8th century king of Scotland who added to the arms of Scotland a double field sowed with lilies to commemorate an alliance reached with Charlemagne.
22 Charles VIII, King of France from 1483, died in 1498. Edward V (1470–1483) was briefly king of England from April to June 1483,

when he was deposed. He and his brother died in the Tower of London, presumed murdered at the instigation of their uncle who acceded to the throne as Richard III.
John Selden was a 17th century legal antiquary and historian.

23 Julius II (1443-1513) was crowned pope on 28 November, 1503.

24 Spunging houses were buildings where debtors were confined under house arrest. Messengers-at-Arms were appointed by the Lord Lyon King of Arms to execute warrants of the Court of the Lord Lyon. Their greyhound badge of office derived from that of the Linlithgow Pursuivant of Arms, a Scottish pursuivant of arms of the Court of the Lord Lyon.

25 Daniel Defoe made very similar observations in his *A Tour thro' The Whole Island of Great Britain* (1724-1727).

Letter XII

1 Crawford Castle, South Lanarkshire, was formerly known as Lindsay Tower. Struthers Castle, in Fife, dating from the 14th century became the chief family seat. The 16th century house underwent extensive alterations in the early 18th century. By *Eulik* I believe Macky means Edzell Castle in Angus, former seat of the Lindsays of Glenesk.

2 Robert II granted the title of Earl of Crawford to David Lindsay (c. 1360-1407) in 1398. A member of a younger branch of the family, Sir John Lindsay of the Byres (d. 1482) was one of the hostages for King James I's ransom in 1424. David Lindsay, 5th Earl of Crawford, 1st Duke of Montrose (1440-1495) was Master of the Royal Household and Great Chamberlain. His son, John Lindsay, 6th Earl of Crawford (c. 1483–1513), was killed at the Battle of Flodden, fighting for James IV.
Patrick, 6th Lord Lindsay of the Byres (d. 1589), was one of the first of the Scottish nobles to join the reformers. Patrick's great-grandson, John Lindsay, 17th Earl of Crawford, 1st Earl of Lindsay (c. 1598-1678), created Earl of Lindsay in 1633, was a leader of the Covenanters. In the same year he became Lord High Treasurer of Scotland.

3 The Somervilles were descended from Sir Gualter de Somerville of Normandy, whose son William de Somerville was created Lord of Carnwath by David I in the 12th century. Carnwath House, originally a fortified tower house, and nearby Couthalley Castle were seats of the Somervilles. Sir Robert Dalzell, 5th Earl of Carnwath (1687–1737), was attainted in 1716 for his active involvement in the 1715 Rising.

4 This powerful family's original seat was Douglas Castle in Lanarkshire, built in the 13th century. In 1703, Archibald Douglas, 3rd Marquess of Douglas (1694-1761), was created Duke of Douglas, with his principal seat at Douglas Castle. The castle was again rebuilt around this time, with an enclosed courtyard with a corner tower.

5 Sir Simon Lockard (Lockhart) of Lee accompanied Sir James Douglas on his expedition with the heart of Bruce to the Holy Land in 1330. Douglas was killed in a battle with the Moors, in Spain. The Lockharts, in consequence, have ever since carried a heart placed within a padlock as part of their armorial bearings, with the motto, *Corda serata pando,* 'I lay open locked hearts'.

6 Archibald Douglas, 2nd Earl of Forfar, 3rd Earl of Ormond (1692-1715), served as a brigadier-general in the Hanoverian army raised by the Duke of Argyll for quelling the Jacobite Rising in Scotland. Queen Anne appointed him envoy to Prussia in 1714, but I have found no evidence of his service, nor of the 'Scotch Black' regiment, in the Flanders campaign. He died of the many wounds he sustained at the Battle of Sheriffmuir, at the age of 23.

7 Archibald Douglas, 1st Duke of Douglas, was present at the Government victory at Sheriffmuir.
manus haec inimica tyrannis: this hand is hostile to tyrants.

8 Dudhope Castle, part of the forfeited estates of Graham of Claverhouse, was granted to James Douglas, Marquess of Douglas and Earl of Angus (1646-1700), in March 1694. See Letter VII.

9 Hamilton Palace, once considered the grandest seat in Scotland, was built in 1695 by architect James Smith for William, 3rd Duke of Hamilton (1634-1694) and his wife Anne (1632-1716), and then extensively modified. It included state-rooms, containing sumptuous stucco-work, later extended by William Adam in the 1740s.

10 *the late Earl of Arran:* James, Earl of Arran, had succeeded his father as 4th Duke of Hamilton in 1698 and was created Duke of Brandon in the peerage of Great Britain in 1711. He was killed in a duel in Hyde Park, London on 15 November 1712.
Sir Godfrey Kneller (1646-1723) was the leading court and society portraitist in Britain in the late 17th and early 18th centuries.

11 Macky may be referring to the 1615 painting of *Daniel in the Lion's Den* by Peter Paul Rubens, not Van Dyck. The landscape painting, 'The Marriage at Cana', was painted by Jacopo Tintoretto (Robusti) c.1561. Tintoretto appears as one of the figures in Paolo Veronese's 'The Wedding Feast at Cana', 1563.
William Feilding (c.1582-1643), created Earl of Denbigh in 1622, held positions at court under James I and Charles I. The painting by van Dyck Macky refers to was painted around 1633.
James, 1st Duke of Hamilton (1606-49), a Royalist, was convicted of treason and beheaded at Westminster on 9 March, 1649. His full length portrait was painted by the Dutch artist, Daniël Mijtens (c. 1590-1647/48), known in England as Daniel Mytens the Elder. I have been unable to source the portrait of his father, the Marquess of Hamilton.

12 When Lady Louisa Mary Knightley visited Barncleuth (formerly Baroncleuth) in 1870 she described it in her journal as 'a quaint old tiny house with a charming old-fashioned garden, terraced along

the glen, with clipped yews and sweet-scented flowers wandering at their own will a garden out of a story-book'. (*The journals of Lady Knightley of Fawsley 1856-1884* (1915).

13 Sir Walter fitz Gilbert (1274-c.1346) was rewarded by Bruce with the barony of Cadzow and Cadzow Castle. His descendants took the name of Hamilton.
James Hamilton, 6th Lord of Cadzow (c.1415-1479), married Mary Stewart, Countess of Arran, daughter of James II of Scotland and sister of James III of Scotland. He was created a Lord of Parliament and assumed the title 1st Lord Hamilton in 1445.
James Hamilton, 2nd Earl of Arran (c.1516-1575), was Regent for the infant Mary, Queen of Scots. He was created Duke of Chatelherault in 1548 when Mary went to live in the French court.

14 The Battle of Pinkie on 10th September 1547, near Prestonpans, was a major defeat for the Scottish army.

15 Mary Stewart (c.1452-1488) daughter of James II of Scotland and Mary of Guelders, married, firstly, Thomas Boyd, 1st Earl of Arran, before 26 April 1467; and secondly, James Hamilton, 1st Lord Hamilton, between February 1474 and April 1474. Her marriage to Boyd was annulled before 1468. Dispensation from the Pope was granted 25 April 1476, thereby legitimising the two children already born. The son, James Boyd, 2nd Lord Boyd of Kilmarnock, died in 1484, killed in a feud with Hugh Montgomery of Eglintoun. The daughter, Margaret Boyd (d. 1516), took David Kennedy, 1st Earl of Cassilis, as her second husband in 1509.

16 The sources cited by Macky are: George Buchanan's History of Scotland, *Rerum Scoticarum Historia* (1582). *Scotorum historiae a prima gentis origine /The History and Chronicles of Scotland (1526)* by Hector Boece (Latin Boethius), translated into Scots by John Bellenden c. 1531. *Account of the Shyres of Renfrew and Lanark* by the antiquary William Hamilton, 3rd of Wishaw, written either in 1696 or 1710. Macky must have seen the manusctript as this last work was not published until 1832. The manuscript is preserved in the National Library of Scotland, Edinburgh. The final source cited is Thomas Rhymer's multi-volume *Foedera* (1704-1713).

17 James Hamilton, 1st Duke of Hamilton (1606-1649), a Royalist military general in the English civil wars, was defeated by Oliver Cromwell at the Battle of Preston, August 1648, taken prisoner, tried, and executed on 9 March, 1649. He was succeeded by his younger bother, William, 2nd Duke of Hamilton (1616-1651), who died from wounds received at the Battle of Worcester in 1651. The careers of the brothers are described in Gilbert Burnet's *Memoires of the Lives of the Hamiltons* (1677) and *History of the Rebellion in England* (3 vols., 1704-1707) by Edward Hyde, Earl of Clarendon (1609-1674).
Lord William Douglas (1634-1694) 1st Earl of Selkirk, married Anne Hamilton, 3rd Duchess of Hamilton, legally changed his surname

to Douglas-Hamilton and received his wife's titles becoming the 3rd Duke of Hamilton.

18 The Covenanters rebelled against Charles II's suppression of non-conformity but were defeated on 22 June, 1679 at Bothwell Bridge by a government army of about 5000, sent north under the command of the Duke of Monmouth.

19 Bothwell Castle dates from around 1242. Originally owned by the Moray family, it was obtained by the Black Douglases before passing to the Crown in the 15th century. In 1669 it passed to the Earls of Forfar but by the end of that century they abandoned the castle in favour of Bothwell House, a large mansion built just to the east of the castle. Stones from the castle were apparently used for the purpose. An engraving by John Slezer (*Theatrum Scotiae*, 1693) shows the house as gabled, possibly L-shaped in the traditional Scottish style of the period.

20 Glasgow University was founded by William Turnbull, Bishop of Glasgow, in 1451, not 1454, which was the date of the bishop's death. James Graham, 1st Duke of Montrose (1682-1742), was appointed Chancellor of the University in 1714.

21 The first stone-built Glasgow Cathedral was dedicated in the presence of David I in 1136. Destroyed or severely damaged by fire, this cathedral was succeeded by a larger one consecrated in 1197, with major rebuilding in the 13th century adding the quire and the lower church, as well as the doorways of the sacristy and of the Lower Chapter House. After the Reformation a wall was put across the nave to allow the western portion of the nave to be used for worship by a congregation which became known as the Outer High. The Lower Church was used by another congregation, the Barony. The Duke of Montrose's Glasgow town house in Drygate, built in 1682, was known as the Duke's Lodging. In the 18th century it was extended with building work between 1703-1719, including a new coach-house. Only some of the proposed alterations and additions to the Duke's Lodging by architect Alexander McGill, drafted 1717-1718, were actually executed. By 1720 the cost of the project led the duke to postpone some of the work, although offices and stables were built.

22 Macky's source for Graham family history is *The peerage of Scotland: containing an historical and genealogical account of the nobility of that Kingdom* by George Crawfurd (1716), pp. 336-338. While Macky is selective in what he borrows from Crawfurd, he echoes his wording closely. He (or his printer) mistakenly gives the date 1300, instead of 1320, for the Declaration of Arbroath. He also transposed the chronological order of Sir John Graham's death at the Battle of Falkirk (1298) and Sir David Graham's signing of the Declaration of Arbroath.

23 The Earl of Clarendon's assessment of the character of James, 1st Marquess of Montrose (1612-1650), also comes from Crawfurd's *The Peerage of Scotland,* where it is quoted (p. 346). His son and heir, also James, died in 1669. His grandson James, 3rd Marquess

of Montrose (1657-1684), died at the age of 27. James, the 4th Marquess of Montrose, a supporter of the Act of Union, was elevated to a dukedom in 1707, and was appointed Keeper of the Great Seal of Scotland from 1716 to 1733.

24 Glasgow was well positioned to send shipping to the West Indies and America, and by the 18th century many Scottish merchants had acquired great wealth by importing sugar, rum and tobacco and selling these on into Holland, Germany, the Baltic and Russia.
In 1667, the town council of Glasgow purchased land for the construction of a harbour and breakwater. Port Glasgow (on some 18th century maps it is shown as *Newport Glasgow*) became Glasgow's first deep-water port.

Letter XIII

1 Built on a volcanic rock, the stronghold, later castle, of Dumbarton has long had strategic importance. The Romans left Britain in C.E. 367 and, according to a letter written by St Patrick, and other artifacts, there was a British settlement and fortress here led by the King of Strathclyde in about C.E. 450. Malcolm II incorporated the kingdom of Strathclyde in 1018.
Edward I captured Dumbarton Castle in March 1296 and installed his own governor there. David II sought refuge at Dumbarton in 1333 after the Scots lost the Battle of Halidon Hill on 19 July, and sailed from here to France, attended by Sir Malcolm Fleming. Mary, Queen of Scots sailed to France from here as a child in 1548.

2 Charles Stuart, 6th Duke of Lennox and 3rd Duke of Richmond (1640–1672), succeeded his cousin, Esmé Stuart, on 10 August, 1660. He died at Elsinore on 12 December, 1672, while on a diplomatic mission to Denmark. As he was childless, his titles reverted to the king, Charles II, who bestowed them on his natural son, Charles Lennox. The revenues of the estates were settled for life on the widow of the 6th Duke, the dowager duchess, and on her death in 1702 the Marquess of Montrose purchased most of the Scottish properties.

3 This is a translation of a Latin couplet by Alexander Necham (d. 1217) quoted by William Camden in the section on Lennox in his *Britannia* (1546). Macky was familiar with Dalrymple's translation. See Letter VIII, note 21.

4 Colonel George Douglas, 1st Earl of Dumbarton (1635-1692), created 1635. The present Earl (and the last Earl of Dumbarton) was his son, George Douglas, 2nd Earl of Dumbarton (1687-1749), also a military officer.

5 His account of the Campbells of Argyll is in Letter X.

6 Inveraray Castle, the principal seat of the Dukes of Argyll, was originally built in the 15th century by Colin Campbell, 1st Earl of

Argyll. Campbeltown was built on property acquired by the Duke of Argyll and erected into a royal burgh in 1700.

7 The family of the Duke of Hamilton was discussed in the previous letter.

8 In the 18th century the charter was held in the *Charta penes comitem de Bute,* according to George Crawfurd, *The peerage of Scotland: containing an historical and genealogical account of the nobility of that Kingdom* (p. 55). Macky could be using Crawfurd as his source here, as elsewhere.
Robert, the second king of the family: the second Stewart king had the title Robert III.
Although the exact date of birth of John Stewart of Bute, an illegitimate son of Robert II, is unknown, there's a consensus that it appears to have been c. 1360; his father ascended the throne in 1371. Sir James Stuart, Sheriff of Bute (d.1710), was created 1st Earl of Bute in 1703. His son James Stuart (d. 1723) became the 2nd Earl of Bute upon his father's death. He held the office of representative peer 1715-1723 and that of Lord of the Bedchamber 1721-1723.

9 Macky would have found this epitaph for Sir James Stuart, 1st Earl of Bute (d.1710), in Crawfurd's *The peerage*, p. 57.

10 Sir John Shaw, or Schaw, Baronet, of Greenock (d.1752), was MP for Renfrewshire, 1708-10, and for Clackmannanshire, 1722-27. He supported the Jacobites in the 1715 Rising. Seeing the advantages to developing trade with the Americas, he proposed to erect a harbour, the costs to be met by a tax on all malt ground at the mill of Greenock, by an annual sum of £15 to be raised by the feuars, and by the anchorage dues of all foreign vessels in the bay. The work was carried out between 1707 and 1710.

11 From *A second edition of Camden's description of Scotland* by Sir James Dalrymple ((1695).

12 Macky here points out the importance of David II's acknowledgment not only of Robert, Earl of Strathearn, later Robert II (r.1371-1390) as his successor, but the recognition of John, Earl of Carrick, Robert's eldest son (who succeeded his father as Robert III in 1390). The latter's illegitimate birth (1337) was only legitimised when his parents married in 1347.

13 The Fullartons (Fullertouns), possibly of Norman origin, settled in Ayrshire in the 12th century, having accompanied Walter, son of Alan, ancestor of the High Stewards, from Shropshire in England, about the beginning of that century. Adam de Fullertoun, received a charter from James, High Steward of Scotland, of the lands of Fullarton, between 1283 and 1309. In 1327 Robert I granted Walter de Fullertoun lands of Oulertoun in the sheriffdom of Forfar in Angus. William Fullarton of Fullarton (d. 1754) studied agricultural science and greatly improved his estate in Kyle Stewart.

Letter XIV

1 The High Stewards occupied Dundonald Castle from the mid 12th century. A fortified tower house was built for Robert II on his accession to the throne of Scotland in 1371 and it was used as a royal residence by the early Stewart kings. In the 17th century Dundonald was purchased by the Cochranes, who were created Earls of Dundonald in 1669.
After the Reformation, ownership of the Abbey passed to Lord Claud Hamilton, who became Lord Paisley, and his son, who became the first Lord Abercorn. Lord Claud transformed some of the monastery buildings into a grand mansion-house, known as the Place (or 'Palace') of Paisley. The Cochranes owned this house when they were raised to the peerage as Earls of Dundonald.

2 The Erskines, later Earls of Mar, and the Semples were loyal supporters of the Stuarts.

3 Macky's source is George Crawfurd's *A General Description of the Shire of Renfrew: Including an Account of the Noble and Ancient Families ... from the Year 1034 to the Year 1710* (Paisley, 1710).
Halkhead (Hawkhead) estate was originally owned by the Stewarts and acquired in 1367 from the future King Robert II, then Earl of Strathearn, by Sir John Ross for an annual payment of a pair of gloves, or two pennies of silver, to the king. The original tower house was extended considerably in 1634 when orchards, large gardens and terraces were developed.
Sir William Ross (c. 1652-1738) was one of the commissioners for the Union and was chosen one of the sixteen peers for Scotland in 1715. General Charles Ross (d. 1732), MP for Ross-shire from 1707, took an active part in the debates of the House of Commons, in support of the Tory administration. In 1712 he was promoted to the rank of general in the army with command of the Royal Irish Regiment of Dragoons.

4 The Boyles, originally an Anglo-Norman family, grew rich through shipping and shipbuilding during the 17th century. David Boyle, Lord Boyle of Kelburn (c.1666-1733), became Earl of Glasgow in 1703. He was one of the commissioners who supported the Act of Union in 1707. Kelburn Castle, claimed to be the oldest castle in Scotland continuously inhabited by the same family, dates back to the 13th century. The tower house is dated 1581 and extensions were made in 1700.
It was actually James III who created Alexander Cunningham, 1st Lord Kilmaurs, Earl of Glencairn, on 28 May, 1488. The earl died a fortnight later at the Battle of Sauchieburn. The principal seat at Kilmaurs was replaced by a mansion, Kilmaurs Place, designed but left unfinished by William Cunningham, 9th Earl of Glencairn (1610-1664), who was Lord Chancellor of Scotland during the last four years of his life.
Colonel William Cunningham, 12th Earl of Glencairn (c. 1676-1734), like his father, was Governor of Dumbarton Castle.

5 The device or ensign of the Cunningham coat of arms is a sable shakefork (pitchfork). Dalrymple's conjecture about the resemblance to a bishop's pall is discredited by Macky, and others.
Wallace's birthplace is now usually said to be Elderslie (formerly spelled Ellerslie) in Renfrewshire rather than Ellerslie in Cunninghame, Ayrshire.

6 Montgomery, an Anglo-Norman family, settled in Scotland in the 12th century. Hugh, 3rd Lord Montgomerie (1460-1545), was created Earl of Eglinton in 1508, having previously entered upon a feud with the Earl of Glencairn, which long continued between their descendants, and occasionally involved violence.
Gabriel, Count de Montgomery (1530-1574), a French nobleman, was a captain in Henry II's Scots Guards. He killed Henry II in a tournament on 29 June, 1559. He was executed for treason - fighting for the Huguenots in the wars of religion ravaging France.

7 Lieut. Colonel John Montgomery of Giffen, a grandson of Alexander Seton of Foulstruther, took the name Montgomery on becoming the 6th Earl of Eglinton (1612).

8 The Scottish coal trade to Ireland in the early 18th century centred principally on the port of Irvine. By the last quarter of the century Irvine had been overtaken by Ayr in the export trade.

9 Henry Ingram was created 1st Viscount Irvine in 1661 for his loyalty to Charles I during the civil wars. The Ingrams were a Yorkshire family, with no connection to Scotland.
On the Boyds, earls of Arran, see Letter XII, note 15. Sir William Cunningham, 10th Lord Boyd, was created Earl of Kilmarnock in 1661 by King Charles II.
The heyday of Kilmarnock's cutlery manufacturing was the 18th century.

10 The barony of Loudoun came into the Campbells' possession in the reign of Robert the Bruce through the marriage of Duncan, son of Donald Campbell, Lord of the Isles, to Susanne Crawford, heiress of Loudoun. The original late 12th or early 13th century tower was expanded in the 15th century, and in 1714 the architect Alex McGill carried out alterations for Hugh Campbell, 3rd Earl of Loudoun (d. 1731), and oversaw landscaping of the grounds in 1716.
The title was created in 1633 for John Campbell, 2nd Lord Campbell of Loudoun, who in 1641 was appointed Lord Chancellor of Scotland, an office which he held for 19 years.

11 *The present earl*: Hugh Campbell, 3rd Earl of Loudoun, Joint Secretary of State for Scotland 1705-07, was appointed a Knight of the Thistle in 1706. He was one of the commissioners for the Union and a representative peer for Scotland from 1707 until his death in 1731. His brother was Sir James Campbell of Lawers (1667–1745), a distinguished military officer. He became lieutenant-colonel of the 2nd dragoons or Scots Greys in 1708, led a successful charge at the battle of Malplaquet on 11 September, 1709, and rose to colonel of the Scots Greys in 1717.

12 Ayr's Auld Brig dates back to 1470 when it replaced the original timber bridge. Ayr was Scotland's main west coast port until Irvine developed the export coal-trade, and then Glasgow overtook both. Cromwell's forces demolished Ayr's medieval castle in 1654 to make room for a huge citadel from which they governed much of Scotland. *curb bit*: a horse's bit or bridle with an attached chain or strap to check the horse.

13 Macky must be referring to Auchincruive House, as Cathcart Castle, the hereditary seat of the Cathcart family, passed out of that family's possession in 1546. Originally a tower house, Auchincruive was replaced by a mansion in the 18th century. Sir Alan de Cathcart, grandson of the Alan de Cathcart who was a loyal Bruce supporter, was made Lord Cathcart in 1447, with which he obtained lands in Ayrshire, including the estate of Auchincruive.
Charles Cathcart, 8th Lord Cathcart (c.1686-1740), served in Flanders and was Major of the Scots Greys by 1709. He was appointed one of the Grooms of the Bedchamber on the accession of George I, and was present at the battle of Sheriffmuir, having joined the Duke of Argyll at Stirling.

14 Stair House, a tower house on the banks of the River Ayr, was built in 1450 by William de Dalrymple. His descendant, Sir James Dalrymple, 1st Viscount Stair (1619-1695), is regarded as one of Scotland's greatest jurists. In 1671 he became Lord President of the Session, but resigned this office ten years later after declining to take the Test, an oath required by statute, the effect of which was to assert royal supremacy over the church. In 1682 Dalrymple had to depart Scotland for Leiden in the Netherlands, and only returned to Scotland following the Glorious Revolution of 1689. The following year, 1690, he received the title of Viscount Stair.

15 The eminent sons of Sir James Dalrymple, cited by Macky, were: John Dalrymple, 2nd Viscount Stair (1648-1707), most remembered in Scotland for his part in the 1692 Massacre of Glencoe. He was created Earl of Stair in 1703, and played a key role in the 1707 Treaty of Union. His heir, John Dalrymple, 2nd Earl of Stair (1673-1747), served as a soldier in the Nine Years' War and the War of the Spanish Succession and as British Ambassador in Paris.
Sir James Dalrymple (1650-1719), the antiquary. See Letter VIII, note 21.
Sir Hew Dalrymple (1652-1737), created the first baronet of North Berwick by King William in 1697, was appointed President of the Court of Session on 7 June 1698.
Sir David Dalrymple (1665-1721), an eminent lawyer, the fifth and youngest son of the first viscount of Stair. He was created 1st Baronet of Hailes in 1700. In 1706 he was one of the commissioners for arranging the articles of Union, and was Lord Advocate of Scotland 1709-1720. His grandson was the celebrated historian and lawyer, Sir David Dalrymple, 3rd Baronet, Lord Hailes.

16 Leuchie House was purchased from the Marjoribanks family in 1701 by Sir Hew Dalrymple. This 'fine seat' was demolished by his son, who built a new mansion in 1779.
Newhailes (New Hailes) was the name given to the Palladian villa at Whitehill built by architect James Smith. Sir David Dalrymple bought it from Lord Bellenden in 1709 for 40,000 merks, and began landscaping the surrounding park. Work also began on a new south east wing, to house his large collection of books. The library was completed by his son, James, who also added the west wing.
Newliston House, was the favourite country residence of John Dalrymple, 2nd Earl of Stair, who designed extensive alterations between 1722-1744 to the 17th century house, in the style of Versailles. Landscaping, incorporating the canal, was carried out by a large workforce, including soldiers from the Scots Greys stationed there to serve as Stair's bodyguard.

17 John Maitland, 2nd Earl of Lauderdale (1616-82) established a lasting personal friendship with Charles II after accompanying the then Prince of Wales into exile in the Netherlands 1648-50.
Secretary Lethington was William Maitland of Lethington (1525-1573), Secretary of State to Mary, Queen of Scots.
Richard Maitland, 4th Earl of Lauderdale (1653-1695) was a Jacobite, and joined the exiled court of James II/VII in France. While there he translated the works of Virgil into English, published posthumously as *The Works of Virgil Translated into English Verse* (1709). He died in Paris.

18 Jean Baptiste Colbert (1619–83), a French statesman, claimed to be the descendant of a noble Scottish family, but the evidence for this is lacking. His eldest son was Jean-Baptiste Antoine Colbert, Marquis de Seignelay (1651-1690), also a politician. His nephew was Jean-Baptiste Colbert, Marquis de Torcy (1665-1746), French diplomat and Louis XIV's minister of foreign affairs.

19 Robert de Brus, 6th Lord of Annandale, became Earl of Carrick in right of his wife, Marjorie, Countess of Carrick (c. 1253-1292). Walter Stewart married Marjorie Bruce, daughter of King Robert Bruce.

20 John Hamilton, 1st Lord Bargany (d. 1658), was the natural son of the 1st Marquess of Hamilton. The title was created for him in 1641. It was his son, the 2nd Lord Bargany, who built Bargany House in 1681.
Cassilis House, with a tower dating from the 14th century, was re-modelled in the 17th century. James Kennedy, younger of Dunure, married Mary Stewart, daughter of Robert III. His descendant, David Kennedy (1463-1513), was created 1st Earl of Cassilis in 1509 and died at the battle of Flodden.

21 The monastery of Whithorn (white house - *candida casa*) was founded by St. Ninian in the 4th century, according to Bede. Archaeological evidence suggests there was a Christian settlement at Whithorn as early as the 5th century. From the 7th century pilgrims visited the shrine of St. Ninian in Whithorn. In the 8th century a

Latin poem, *Miracula Nynie Episcopi*, was written by a monk at the monastery at Whithorn.

22 The Flemings first came to Scotland before 1150. Malcolm Fleming (1300-1362) was created 1st Earl of Wigtown in 1342. The Flemings constructed Cumbernaud Castle in the late 14th century, as a strong stone tower. It was besieged by General Monck in 1651, but was not completely destroyed. It continued in part use while the new classical styled house, to designs by William Adam (1689–1748) for John Fleming, 6th Earl of Wigtown, was built nearby. Cumbernaud House was completed in 1731.

23 Alexander Stuart, 1st Lord Garlies (d. 1649), a favourite of James VI (James I of England), was created 1st Earl of Galloway in 1623. His branch of the Steuart family were distant relatives of the Stewart king of Scotland.
Cruggleton Castle, the residence of the earls of Galloway from the 12th century, passed to the Kennedies by the 17th century, and was in ruins by 1684.

24 Dalrymple's source for the blinding and murder of Acthred (Uchtred) by his brother Gilbert (Gille Brigte) was most likely the chronicle of John of Fordun. Acthred's grandson Alan (d. 1234) succeeded as Lord of Galloway in 1200. Devorgilla of Galloway was Alan's daughter by his second wife, Margaret of Huntingdon, daughter of David, Earl of Huntingdon. The Ferrers connection was through Helen of Galloway (d. 1245), Alan of Galloway's daughter from his first marriage. William Ferrers, 1st Baron Ferrers of Groby (c. 1240-1287) was Helen's grandson and the younger son of Roger and Margaret de Quincy, Earl and Countess of Winchester.

25 The Path is part of one of Scotland's oldest roads, running through Glentrool Forest west of the Water of Minnock to the Nick O' the Balloch and then to Maybole and Ayr. It was the pre-turnpike route from Whithorn to Ayr.
In August 1701, Lord Basil Hamilton (1671-1701), sixth son of the Duke of Hamilton, his brother the Earl of Selkirk and a servant were crossing the swollen Water of Minnock, when the servant become entangled in the river. Lord Basil attempted a rescue but unhappily both master and servant drowned.

26 Compare this description from the parish account, 1725:
'This Barony of the Forrest or Buchan has on the S. the Loch of Troul, where the said Palgown has a seat overlooked by a mountain on the north, betwixt which and the Lake the house is very pleasantly seated, the Lake appearing like a large pond under the house well stocked with pikes, there being a prodigious number of large oak trees, (all lying a cross one another M. D.) lying in its bottom that within the opposite mountains on the other side, one would be astonished (in a clear day M. D) to think where they came from. The house is surrounded with pretty groves of Scots Pines black cherries, and other kinds of planting, which make a fine umbello

to the house and from the front a walk down to the lake which enters upon a little mole prettely planted in devices with seats and a beautifull litle boat lodg'd ther under a shade for taking pleasure in a fine day upon the water.' *Geographical Collections relating to Scotland* ed. Walter MacFarlane, from Advocates Library MSS (Edinburgh: Scottish History Society, 1906).

27 Rusco Castle, or Rusko Castle, a 15th or early 16th century keep, to which a long and lower 17th century wing was added. Hugh Blair McGuffog (or Hugh McGuffog) acquired Rusco Castle following his marriage to Elizabeth McGuffog, heiress of Rusko in 1680.
Cally House, a country house, stands on the site of a 12th century motte, where a wooden castle once stood in a commanding, defensive position overlooking the Fleet Estuary. In 1658 Richard Murray who inherited the family estate of Broughton, Wigtownshire married Anna Lennox and acquired Cally. Their son, Alexander Murray II took over the estates of Broughton, Cally and Killibegs in 1690. The landscape and climate were well suited to breeding hardy polled (hornless) black cattle, generally known as galloways, for a growing English market.
Alexander Murray II (d. 1751) was the MP for the Stewartry between 1715 and 1727. He commissioned William Adam to design a new mansion and gardens at Cally, but the proposals for a 'Great House' were not fulfilled in Murray's lifetime.

28 As Macky says, Martin Martin's *A Description of the Western Isles of Scotland*, first published in 1696, is indeed his source for the final part of his account. He echoes Martin's wording, although he is highly selective in the few details he chooses to include in his *Journey*. In several places he gives the wrong area calculations of some of the islands (Islay, Tiree, Coll, Rum, Skye, and Lewis), presumably through careless copying of Martin's figures.

29 This is, of course, Macky's own addition.

30 i.e. Iona.

31 Colin Mackenzie, 1st Earl of Seaforth (1596/7-1633), inherited Lewis from his father, and the island remained in the possession of the Mackenzies of Kintail until their position as earls of Seaforth came to an end in 1716, following their support for the Jacobite cause.

32 *continent*: i.e. mainland.

33 Orkney was annexed as part of Scotland by James III in 1468 after its rents had been pledged as surety for the king's Norwegian bride Margaret, but the dowry was not paid.

Textual Notes

Letter I

a Kircudbright
b hather
c gains
d Macdweles, Mackys, Macqhys, Maclurgs
eDernagilla
f Baliol
g Bernard-Castle
h Carlavrock
i Lorrain

Letter II

a Cliddisdale
bQueensbury
c grotto's
d Desdier
e Hauyke
f publick
g Entrokin
h Penmanmawr
i Hopton
j Need-Path
k Moreton
l Stormond
m cloysters
n have
o Hadington
p Buccleugh
q Roxborough
r Friers
s visto's
t Tiviot

Letter III

a Aymouth
b Ailsey
c one at time
d Lothain
e Bleinheim-House
f visto
gThirlston
h was
i Ormeston
j figue
k Seaton
l cieling
m story
n Cockeny
o Long Nidry
p gardiner
q battel
r course
s Ask

Letter IV

a Pinkey
b Van Dyke
c Giffards
d Dutchess
e stories
f Hallifax
g Scot
h belongining
i holley
j busto's
k Of
l Frasier

Letter V
a meuse
b coaches-houses
c letts
d consorts
e chuse
f Knights Companions
g Cannongate
h Herriot
i Earl of Finlater
j Gile's
k Throne Church
l Gelder
m Sir Robert Sebald
n effigies
o nich
p Bristol, Paterrow
qNeals
r Caulton
s Fews
t *Arbiterale*

Letter VI
a Loudon
b Inch-Colme
c Inch-Kieth
d Kircaldy
e Dyzart
f Petenweem and Craile
g Salvadore
h Lenox
j Duke of Athol
k Chandois
l Archbishoprick
m bishopricks
n Cromwel
o Woolsey
p Habourn
q begun
r compleatest
s Barrack

Letter VII
a choak
b Diddup
c constablary
d Gillecranky
e Penmure
f Mauls, Earls of Penmure
g Marr
h Sheremore
i Arbroth
j Melross
k Montross
l inhabitanss
m Glascow
n Carneagy
o Kinard
p Mairnes
q Dinnoter
r marshal
s Faterassey
t Stonehive
u Dun
v Elphingstone
w vauletd
x Bamf
y Dune
z Bervy
aa Irwin

Letter VIII
a Kildremmy
b Forbes's
c Kintyre
d Friendright
e Arrol
f Salton
g sirname
h Esham
i Breco
j Cathness
k Cromatry
l Mackenzy
m Kildair
n voluntiers
o Larges
p Kincardin
q Forth
r lock
s Luthae
t plad
u Dalrimple

v Lovet
w Rochow
x Zetland
y Mackys
z Mule
aa Strahnaver
bb Dunbriton
cc Braid-Albin
dd Kerney
ee Glames
ff Lion
gg Dewitt
hh Leley
ii Kingorn
jj Gowry
kk Tiviotdale
ll Dremmy

Letter IX

a DUMFERLING
b linnen
c Goury's
d Ruthen
e Metheun
f Mr. Askin and Mr.Ramsey
g Tullibarn
h Celly
i Scoon
j Burley
k Strathern
l Duplin
m Balhousey
n Airne
o Sterling
p Moncreif
q Lanthorn
r Melvil
s of
t shew
u of
v cows
w Balgony
x terras
y vastibule
z even
aa Douglasses
bb other two
cc rhe

Letter X

a 1006
b Abendour
c Dinnibersell
d Innerkilthin
e Allaway
f Blair-Hall
g Clackmanan
h Erskin
i Elphingston
j bason
k Flowden
l Majecty's
m heighth
n Cumbethskennet
o Cambel, Lord of Lockow
p Mackcallan
q Sir Neal Campbell of Lockhow
r Criff
s ponyard
t Dumblain
u Ballingith
v Cowen
w Firth
y Pinparden

Letter XI

a Banockburn
b Callander
c Kinniel
d Boroughstouness
e Joseppo
f callonaded
g Frescati
h Bolognia
i Craggy-hall
j Haytrop
k Raglin
l Barnbugle
m council
n run
o saphires
p tossels
q nich
r filagreen

s saltyre addresse
t cloaths
u Spake

Letter XII

a Lindesay
b Morison's
c Lanerk
d Tentoret
e Baroncleuh
f Cadeow
g entituled
h Boetius
i Bellandine
j Cassills
k decorit

Letter XIII

a Renfreu
b Allen
c Darnly
d Lock-Lomond
e Nichmere
f Grampean
g Ila
h Tiry
i Wyst
j Mall
k Macklean
l Ilsay
m Keyl
n Carreck
o Pasley
p Largis
q Cummins
r Glenagies
s Hadden

Letter XIV

a Cochran
b Air
c Lords-Chancellors
d prodigee
e families
f Ailsford
g Minnibol
h Girvant
i Stranrawer
j Lockrian
k Mul
l Rinns
m coursest
n Tirol
o Cummernald
p Grooby
q Ballock
r Mairock
s Locktwachtoun
t Asbuchan
u Mackye, Palgoun
v grasiers
w Carnsmure
x Ruscoe
y Gigai
z Colonsa
aa garison
bb plenty
cc St. Columbus
dd lies
ee Tirey
ff Canney
gg Musk
hh Word
ii Mackneals
jj North-Vest
kk tuff
ll Scalpar
mm Polmona

Index

C

I

J

www.ingramcontent.com/pod-product-compliance
Ingram Content Group UK Ltd.
Pitfield, Milton Keynes, MK11 3LW, UK
UKHW041637190726
13854UKWH00006B/2534

9 781845 301460